PROFESSIONAL LIVES OF
COMMUNITY CORRECTIONS
OFFICERS

PROFESSIONAL LIVES OF COMMUNITY CORRECTIONS OFFICERS

The Invisible Side of Reentry

Faith E. Lutze
Washington State University

Los Angeles | London | New Delhi
Singapore | Washington DC

Los Angeles | London | New Delhi
Singapore | Washington DC

FOR INFORMATION:

SAGE Publications, Inc.
2455 Teller Road
Thousand Oaks, California 91320
E-mail: order@sagepub.com

SAGE Publications Ltd.
1 Oliver's Yard
55 City Road
London EC1Y 1SP
United Kingdom

SAGE Publications India Pvt. Ltd.
B 1/I 1 Mohan Cooperative Industrial Area
Mathura Road, New Delhi 110 044
India

SAGE Publications Asia-Pacific Pte. Ltd.
3 Church Street
#10-04 Samsung Hub
Singapore 049483

Printed in the United States of America

Library of Congress Cataloging-in-Publication Data

Lutze, Faith E.

Professional lives of community corrections officers : the invisible side of reentry / Faith E. Lutze, Washington State University.

pages cm
Includes bibliographical references and index.

ISBN 978-1-4522-4226-2 (pbk.) —
ISBN 978-1-4833-1161-6 (web pdf)

1. Parole officers—United States. 2. Community-based corrections—United States. I. Title.

HV9470.L87 2014
364.6'202473—dc23   2013031692

This book is printed on acid-free paper.

Acquisitions Editor: Jerry Westby
Editorial Assistant: MaryAnn Vail
Production Editor: Libby Larson
Copy Editor: Mark Bast
Typesetter: C&M Digitals (P) Ltd
Proofreader: Ellen Brink
Indexer: Maria Sosnowski
Cover Designer: Anupama Krishnan
Marketing Manager: Terra Schultz

MIX
Paper from responsible sources
FSC
www.fsc.org   FSC® C014174

13 14 15 16 17 10 9 8 7 6 5 4 3 2 1

BRIEF CONTENTS

DETAILED CONTENTS

PREFACE

Community Corrections Officers: The Invisible Side of Reentry

C ommunity corrections is a unique profession that possesses the coercive power of the criminal justice system to manage offenders' risk and garners the power of the helping professions to address offenders' needs. Parole officers, also known as community corrections officers (CCOs), reside at the nexus between prison and the community. Their work is multifaceted, involving offenders, the police, courts, prisons, social services, public health, education, labor, and the community. Their professional knowledge is extensive and is often used to bridge the gaps in offender management between the formal institutions tasked with managing offenders' behavior and the informal systems of control and support provided by the community. Community corrections officers have the expertise to create a continuum of care for offenders that provides continuity across systems to effectively manage risk, reduce recidivism, achieve long-term reintegration, and enhance public safety. Due to their position strategically located at the end of the criminal justice process and in the community, community corrections officers are fully poised to orchestrate the successful reintegration of ex-offenders into the community.

Unfortunately, community corrections is rarely highlighted as an important resource to proactively achieve public safety. It is continuously viewed in the shadow of prisons, seen as "less" than law enforcement, and maligned for being too much like social work. In spite of the fact that community corrections is responsible for supervising the release of approximately 750,000 inmates from prison each year in the United States, a population that has grown 3.6 times that experienced in the 1980s, it remains a profession easily blamed by policymakers for the failures that should be attributed to the entire criminal justice system as well as other public institutions.

It is clear that many of the traditional approaches to reentry in an era resulting in mass incarceration have not been very successful. The likelihood of those released from prison to fail has remained stubbornly consistent over time with approximately 65% being returned to prison within 3 years after release and at least a third of these failing within the first 6 months. To address this failure, policymakers often turn to more of the same by designing tougher laws and investing more in prisons, police, and courts. When attention is paid to community corrections it is often in reaction to a rare, heinous event committed by an offender on supervision. These events often result in reactionary policies that further restrict the discretion of officers or serve to increase their responsibilities by enhancing their coercive control and power over offenders through such strategies as intensive supervision, electronic monitoring, and other intermediate sanctions. Even when reentry initiatives encompass more holistic approaches, the focus is often on addressing offenders' needs or reorganizing systems to coordinate services across providers and not about directly investing in community corrections officers. Although providing for the needs of offenders and coordinating services are extremely worthy of investment, little consideration is given to whether community corrections officers have the support, resources, and expertise required to effectively manage the complex combination of risks and needs of offenders or the opportunity to collaborate with professionals in other agencies. Even when the need for systemic change is evident, either by managing risks or needs, CCOs are consistently asked to do more with less.

Regardless of what policymakers and correctional leaders do, CCOs have little choice but to deal with the reality of offenders' lives and the importance of safely reintegrating them into the community to prevent future harm. To be successful they cannot afford to work in isolation because the risks and needs of offenders are too great to ignore. Thus, CCOs work across the criminal justice system by using the police, courts, jails, and prison to manage risk, problem-solve threats to community safety, and coordinate successful outcomes. To address the multiple needs of offenders they must engender the expertise and resources available through social services, public health, education, and labor to arrange the services necessary to address serious issues such as homelessness, mental illness, substance abuse, educational and skill deficits, unemployment, and a multitude of other stressors due to living in poverty. Their position, located in the community, allows them to create opportunities for offenders through building relationships with community stakeholders essential to offenders' ability to develop prosocial relationships, become reunited with family and friends, obtain employment, establish a stable and safe place to live, and work toward long-term freedom from state control. It is clear that community corrections officers' jobs are important to achieving the goals not just of corrections but of the entire criminal justice system.

This book brings the important work of community corrections officers out of the shadows of the prison and into the light of informed policymaking based on the reality of community corrections officers' work and their importance to the success of the criminal justice system. I argue that community corrections officers are "street-level boundary spanners" who are in the best position to lead effective reentry initiatives built on interagency collaboration and a shared responsibility for reentry. In general, boundary spanners are people able to permeate the borders between diverse professions to create a mutual understanding of the other's role and through shared communication, work to fill gaps in service, build trust, remove service barriers, and create the conditions necessary to achieve mutually beneficial outcomes. The criminal justice system alone cannot be solely responsible for assuring public safety when the risks and needs of offenders returning to the community from prison are so great. Therefore, community corrections' power and utility are based in its ability to provide a fluid response to reentry inclusive of control, support, and treatment—a response led by community corrections officers.

I refer to those commonly called "parole officers" as community corrections officers. This distinction is important for several reasons. First, parole, or early release from prison, is what happens to offenders and refers to a mechanism of release. Using the term *parole officer* binds the concept of community supervision officers to the prison instead of to the community where they work and ex-offenders live. Second, tying community supervision to the prison inspires policies and strategies that become perceived as mere extensions of the prison, a place where offenders can be quickly and easily returned, instead of being based in the community where emphasis is placed on looking forward toward achieving long-term reintegration. Finally, the term *community corrections officer* captures the significance of two of the most important responsibilities community corrections is tasked with: (1) the use of coercive power to effectively manage ex-offenders' needs and the risk they pose to the community and (2) their responsibility to enhance public safety by working in collaboration with the community to achieve long-term reintegration. Community corrections is about engaging both people and places. Its success is interdependent and involves the well-being of the "community" to work with "corrections" to assist both CCOs and offenders to manage risks and address needs. Although this book focuses on reentry and therefore the work of "parole" officers, I believe the roles and responsibilities of probation and parole officers overlap, and many of the most serious issues (e.g., large caseloads, safety, offender attributes, professional orientation, community conditions) are shared across all of those who work in community corrections.

Therefore, it is my hope that this book is used to educate and inform students and professionals interested in both probation and parole specifically and community corrections generally.

As research on community corrections officers has grown into a large and varied endeavor, there are few, if any, holistic contemporary reviews of CCOs and how they actually go about their work. Reviews of probation and parole officers are generally relegated to a few chapters within books covering the entire system of probation and parole. Or they are studied in direct relationship to the outcomes of a specific supervision strategy or intervention designed to better manage offender outcomes. Unlike studies of other professional roles in the criminal justice system, there are few in-depth qualitative or participant observation studies exploring community corrections officers' professional culture, beliefs, philosophy, or satisfaction with their work. This book hopes to remedy the shortcomings of the existing literature on both accounts by bringing the research on community corrections officers together in one place and filling in the gaps in research with the findings of a qualitative case study based on interviews with 42 community corrections officers supervising active caseloads in Spokane, Washington. Given that Spokane is a midsized metropolitan area (City of Spokane: 208,000 people; Spokane County: 470,000 people; U.S. Census Bureau 2010) experiencing many of the same challenges as similarly situated cities throughout the United States, the experiences and perceptions of the Spokane CCOs will resonate with other community corrections officers across the country.[1]

The Spokane study[2] is used in this book in two primary ways. First, the interviews are used as real-life examples supporting the findings provided in survey research conducted across the country and, when relevant, internationally. In this way, the Spokane study becomes a conduit to highlighting how the findings from multiple studies may appear in real life for CCOs supervising offenders in the field. Second, the Spokane study is used to fill in the gaps in research where little is known about community corrections officers in the broader research literature. When I began this book, I thought the Spokane study interviews would only be used to illustrate the importance of the findings of other studies. When I further explored the existing research on community corrections officers I learned there were still many gaps in the research regarding CCOs and the contextual aspects of their work. For example, little has been published from CCOs' perspective about their beliefs concerning working with and building professional relationships with offenders, their beliefs about the communities where offenders live and whether they desire to work with community stakeholders, their concerns about the effectiveness of their own agencies to support their work, and finally their thoughts about collaboration and working with other agencies to manage offender risks and needs. Thus, I believe the Spokane study is important primarily because it brings to life what at times can be abstract, emotionless statistics, and it fills some important gaps in the literature about community corrections officers.

It is from an extensive review of the research dedicated to learning more about CCOs and from the Spokane interviews that it became clear that community corrections, in spite of its importance to the overall success of the system and offenders, remains an invisible profession. Its utility to enhance public safety is totally missed by many policymakers and, too often, corrections leaders. To envision how to effectively empower community corrections officers' position requires a holistic understanding of their professional roles, including their relationships with offenders, their work within the community, their place within their agencies, how and when they use evidence-based practices, and the extent of their collaboration with other institutions. It is only within this broader understanding that one can fully and effectively invest in community corrections and value its boundary-spanning capacity to effect positive change.

Therefore, Chapter 1 provides a brief review of the history, mission, and responsibilities of community corrections. The challenges confronting community corrections are extensive. The contemporary political and social movement to become more punitive has driven prison populations to a level of mass incarceration that has seriously burdened our communities at all levels to great financial and human costs. The responsibility for managing such a large prison and community corrections population has seriously stressed our institutions' effectiveness. In addition, the fact that poverty is the most common attribute shared by those in our criminal justice system, and especially corrections, it cannot be easily ignored. The effect of poverty poses serious challenges to CCOs, offenders, and communities to provide what is necessary to achieve successful reentry. It is important to understand the social, political, and economic context of community corrections in order to appreciate the setting in which CCOs are expected to function. Without understanding this broader context, one is likely to set unrealistic expectations for CCOs and offenders to be successful, fail to provide support where it is most needed, and narrowly define the role of CCOs in ways that professionally isolate them and oversimplify their relevance to the success of the criminal justice system.

Chapter 2 reviews how the professional lives of CCOs have been traditionally placed on a continuum with surveillance and crime control at one end and assistance and rehabilitation on the other. This bifurcated view of CCO roles is far too limiting, and a review of the research shows that a fluid approach to supervision is most effective. Those who are most successful in improving compliance to supervision and reducing recidivism balance both surveillance and assistance through a dynamic approach to supervision. CCOs clearly recognize the complexity of offenders' lives and the importance of addressing their risks and needs. They also value the professional relationships they build with offenders and expect a mutual exchange of trust and respect to guide their ongoing interactions. Unfortunately, many challenges confront CCOs in accomplishing their professional goals as they are at times challenged by their peers, court-ordered conditions that conflict with the reality of offenders' lives, departmental policies that at times limit their discretion or burden them with administrative tasks that impinge on their time with offenders, and the structural limitations caused by the responsibility of managing excessively large caseloads.

Chapter 3 considers how CCOs' relationships span beyond the individual needs of the offender to the needs of the community and how the community can enhance the likelihood of an offender's success. Although supervision outside of an institutional setting is labeled "community corrections," the focus tends to be on individual offender characteristics and CCOs' responsibilities, with little consideration for how corrections is also about "place." Very little is known about what CCOs think about the communities they serve, whether CCOs want to work more closely with citizens, and whether they view the places where offenders and their families live as assets or liabilities to their work. This chapter relies heavily on the Spokane interviews to explore how community corrections agencies attempt to become more visible and involved in the community by building partnerships with local groups and engaging offenders, their families, and stakeholders within the community. CCOs appear to have very complex views about the community relevant to further exploring the importance of viewing CCOs as boundary spanners.

After establishing how CCOs work with offenders and the community, Chapter 4 shifts to how CCOs' professional lives transpire within their own agency. Research shows that the structure of organizations directly influences their employees' experiences and how they work to achieve their intended mission. CCOs conscientiously work to balance their responsibility to the agency by following policy with their responsibility to offenders by being responsive to offenders' risks and needs. Oftentimes bureaucratic challenges such as liability, safety, sensational cases, conflicting missions and goals, and administrative policies merge to create stress for CCOs. It is clear that community corrections organizations need to be structured and administered to achieve success and can no longer be passive participants in offender management and reform. It is the professionalization of the agency to achieve success that provides the foundation for CCOs to be effective boundary spanners with the ability to directly improve correctional outcomes that result in safer communities.

Importantly, Chapter 5 builds on the previous chapter by exploring "what works" in community corrections and how community corrections must be built on a foundation of evidence-based practices, program integrity, and quality assurances. The movement to use research to inform practice has resulted in a significant expansion of our knowledge concerning effective supervision strategies and treatment interventions that reduce recidivism and enhance successful outcomes. Understanding what improves offender outcomes and what may actually do more harm than good means that CCOs must possess the expertise to properly respond to individual offenders. Sometimes this involves greater structure and accountability and at other times it means providing greater levels of support and treatment. Notably, this requires policymakers and administrators to prepare systems for change by structuring their agencies to incorporate the principles of effective supervision, make available evidence-based treatment programs, and provide CCOs with the resources to be effective in conducting their daily work. The use of evidence-based practices to manage both offender risks and needs entails an interdisciplinary and fluid approach to supervision.

Chapter 6 presents how many CCOs inherently act as street-level boundary spanners between their agency, police, mental health services, social services, faith-based organizations, employers, and public health services. Research shows many positive aspects of collaborating across agencies, but there are often shared histories of mutual distrust, ill will, and conflicting missions to hamper free-flowing relationships. These challenges are more apparent in attempts to collaborate with helping institutions such as social services and mental health services and less so in relationships with agencies that hold coercive power such as the courts, police, jail, and prison. In order for CCOs to be truly effective boundary spanners supportive of a fluid approach between control and assistance, greater attention has to be given to building linkages with helping institutions.

Finally, Chapter 7 highlights the need to reframe community supervision from a passive offender management system to a proactive boundary-spanning organization with professionals geared to achieving positive outcomes within the context of the community. This can only be achieved by reinvesting in community corrections as an agency that has the potential to do what no other agency in social services or criminal justice has the power to accomplish alone—to use an expansive range of options to manage both offenders' risks and needs to guide the entire process of change, over time and across systems, to enhance public safety. Unfortunately, this incredible resource is wasted by uninformed politicians and driven by an uninformed public and a narrow conceptualization of community corrections officers that oftentimes results in a disastrous set of policies and expectations for both CCOs and the offenders to which they are responsible. A review of the literature, combined with listening to CCOs, presents the opportunity to realistically define the utility of community corrections and to inspire policymakers and corrections leaders to meaningfully invest in community corrections to improve the success of the entire criminal justice system. It is time to remove the cloak of invisibility from community corrections officers and fully respect the importance of their work to enhance public safety.

It is my hope that students, practitioners, and policymakers will find this book useful to informing their education, supporting their professional practice, and engaging policymakers to fully invest in community corrections as a powerful tool to improve the overall outcomes of the criminal justice system. A practical purpose of this book is to bring to life the social science research about community corrections officers by connecting it to real-life examples of what CCOs think about their work in relation to the issues important to them. Existing research is brought from the abstract to reality to illustrate the complex roles, experiences, and perceptions of officers responsible for managing and integrating offenders into the community. Ideally, a comprehensive review focused on community corrections officers will inform policymakers, educators, practitioners, and the public that a narrow conceptualization of community corrections officers creates a disastrous set of expectations for both community corrections officers and the offenders to which they are responsible. By listening to CCOs and connecting their experiences to existing research, a more realistic vision evolves about the complex role CCOs perform and the importance of their work to the ultimate success of the criminal justice system.

ACKNOWLEDGMENTS

While writing this work, it became very clear that no author works alone, even though at times writing is a lonely endeavor. My interest in community corrections officers began with a call from the Washington State Department of Corrections to see whether anyone at Washington State University was interested in a researcher-practitioner partnership to study neighborhood-based supervision. Fortunately, one of my senior colleagues, Nicholas Lovrich, was interested in mentoring a junior scholar at the time through the process of applying for a national grant and sharing his extensive knowledge about research, collaboration, and partnering with state agencies to achieve mutually beneficial outcomes. I will always be grateful to him for sharing with me the importance of "face time," listening to practitioners talk about the importance of their work to inform research, and that research is as much about building relationships as it is about building statistical models. I will always be thankful to have had the good fortune to work with Dr. Peggy Smith and Ms. Doreen Gieger, both with the Washington State Department of Corrections, as my practitioner partners on this project. Their understanding of the inner workings of the Department of Corrections (DOC), insightful observations about program implementation, and willingness to embrace research and to respond to my multiple questions and requests for data will always be appreciated. They, along with Elizabeth Drake, my former student and a research analyst for the DOC at the time, will always have my gratitude. Finally, I will always be indebted to Dr. David Murphy, the graduate research assistant for this project. David conducted the majority of the interviews, completed all of the transcriptions, and worked to bring the project to fruition while I was trying to balance work with several major events in my personal life. He will always have a warm place in my heart, and I hope I can repay his kindness by passing it forward.

I also appreciate the support provided for this study through the National Institute of Justice (Grant No. 1999-CE-VX-0007), the Washington State Department of Corrections (WADOC), and Washington State University (WSU). The points of view in this book are mine and do not necessarily represent the official position or policies of the U.S. Department of Justice, the WADOC, or WSU. I am especially thankful for the access and time given to this project by the employees of the WADOC. The frankness, passion, and care given by CCOs when expressing their views gives valuable insight about the complexity of working as a community corrections professional and provides a basis to build theory, expand research, inform policy, and influence practice. I will always be grateful for their willingness to educate and to share their expertise. I also appreciate my ongoing collaboration with WADOC research managers Teri Harold-Prayer, Michael Evans, and Dave Daniels and their ongoing endeavor to use research to inform best practices.

I am thankful to my colleagues at Washington State University who have always been a source of intellectual inspiration, support, and more importantly laughter throughout my career, especially Laurie Drapela, Otwin Marenin, Martha Cottam, Tom Preston, Nöel Sturgeon, Jacqueline van Wormer, Zachary Hamilton, Melanie Neuilly, David Makin, Lisa

Janowski, Sisouvanh Keopanapay, and most recently Mary Stohr and Craig Hemmens. In addition, I appreciate Roger Schaefer's willingness to allow me to use excerpts from our coauthored work published elsewhere to support Chapter 5 on evidence-based practice and for our many impromptu intellectual exchanges. There were also a number of under-graduate students who showed great patience as they listened to my ideas regarding this book throughout classes—especially those in CJ450 (Fall 2012) and CJ424 (Spring 2013) and Katelynne Mierz and Maria Cortes, who took the time to review various chapters and give important feedback. In addition to my colleagues and students at WSU, I am also grateful to my Sage editor, Jerry Westby, who took an interest in my idea and helped me to bring this project to fruition and to Mark Bast, who made it shine. I am thankful for the external reviews conducted by Michael Brown, Mario L. Hesse, Cathy Levey, Alfredo Montalvo, and Michael Montgomery—their insight helped to strengthen the manuscript.

Of course, no book can be completed without the support and joy experienced with friends: Lael and Larry Turnbow, Charlie Gerke and Gretal Leibnitz, Jackie Helfgott and Zalia, Fran Bernat, Cherith Letargo and Ariel Malicse, Nina Gregory, Marvel Ebert, Phyllis Millan, Alice Kaste, and Diane Biby, who has become family. My whitewater river-running buddies: Jim and Janet, Jocelyn and Bill, Jen and Frank, Kath, Mark, and Mike. My fellow EMTs who always inspire me with their will-ingness to selflessly volunteer to serve our community by helping others day and night: Rick, Robin, Lynn, Mike, and Kathy. Finally, I am grateful to Abbey and Beckum for keeping me company throughout the project.

It is the love and support given by my family that brings the purest of joy to my life and whose support makes my research and writing possible. I will always be thankful for my parents Sheila and Wayne Lutze, whose belief in the value of education and the ability to fully appreciate the simple pleasures in life set me up to fully enjoy mine. Thanks to Wayne Lutze Jr., whose humor, honesty, camaraderie, and integrity make me proud to call him my brother, and to his family who always bring a smile: Bea, Wayne III, and Andy. Finally, and most importantly, it is Rick, my husband and best friend, who creates the loving and "easy silence" in my life that I am thankful for every day. Along with Rick are our children, Julia and Walker, who have brought to my life both adventure and the knowing of pure joy. Nothing is better.

NOTES

   1. The City of Spokane is located in northeastern Washington State and has a population of approximately 208,000 people. It is located in Spokane County

(SC) with a total population of about 470,000 (U.S. Census 2010). The City of Spokane has an unemployment rate of 9.6% (SC 9%) and a median income of $41,466 (SC $49,257), with 66% (SC 64%) employed in occupations related to service, natural resources, construction, maintenance, production, transportation, and material moving. For those living in the City of Spokane, 12.7% (SC 9.3%) of all families and 18.6% (SC 14.4%) of all people lived below the poverty line during the last 12 months.

    2.   The full methodology for this study is available on request by contacting the author at lutze@wsu.edu or see Drapela and Lutze (2009) and Murphy and Lutze (2009). To assure anonymity, research identification numbers are used instead of names to distinguish officer quotes from one another.

WORKS CITED

Drapela, L. A., & Lutze, F. E. (2009). Innovation in community corrections and probabtion officers' fears of being sued: Implementing neighborhood-based supervision in Spokane, Washington. *Journal of Contemporary Criminal Justice, 25*(1), 364–383.

Murphy, D., & Lutze, F. (2009). Police-probation partnerships: Professional identity and the sharing of coercive power. *Journal of Criminal Justice, 37*, 65–76.

United States Census Bureau. (2010). *American fact finder*. Retrieved from http://factfinder2.census.gov/faces/tableservices/jsf/pages/productview.xhtml?src=bkmk

ONE

THE PROFESSIONAL RESPONSIBILITY OF COMMUNITY CORRECTIONS OFFICERS

The imprisonment binge that began in the early 1980s had an unparalleled effect on the ability of both institutional and community corrections to manage an ever increasing offender population. In the frenzy to build more prisons, little forethought was given to the increase in offenders being sentenced to community sanctions or those who would eventually be released from prison and supervised in the community. Interestingly, but maybe not surprisingly with all of the focus on prison expansion, little attention was given to probation and parole officers and the complex task bestowed on them to prevent people from committing crime who are oftentimes living in dysfunctional families within stressed communities and being released from prisons inadequately prepared to cope with the transition to the community. Even as greater attention has shifted to prisoner reentry in recent years, most of the focus has been on offenders and very little on probation and parole officers, also known as community corrections officers (CCOs).

Little is known about the professional lives of CCOs in spite of the tremendous responsibility bestowed on them, a responsibility that for the most part cannot be passed off on to other parts of the system. Police officers make arrests and pass offenders on to the jail and prosecutor, judges pass offenders on to the prison, and prisons pass offenders on to community corrections. This leaves community corrections officers "holding the bag" so to speak, responsible for all the wrongs, systemic and individual, that the offender has passed through or committed. CCOs are the professionals who must deal with the entirety of the offender by developing an ongoing professional relationship that includes not just the individual but the offender's family and peers, employers, treatment professionals, educators, housing providers, and others important to supporting reentry efforts. For community corrections officers, the environment that offenders return to is not

1

some abstract place but instead one that includes real people, real poverty, real violence, real hardship, and real threats to all involved. Failure means a new victim, more harm to the community, and being held personally and professionally accountable. When offenders violently and publicly reoffend, it is not the prison or other social institutions held accountable for failure, it is the community corrections officer whose work is portrayed and criticized throughout the media. Yet when CCOs do their jobs well and offenders are successfully reintegrated into society without returning to prison, they remain invisible actors within the system and outside of the public discourse.

In spite of their responsibility and the important work community corrections officers conduct as part of the justice system, no systemic social science review has been given concerning how they manage their responsibility and the effect it has on the way they engage their work within the agency, with the offender, and within the community. Therefore, this book provides an in-depth analysis of what it means to be a probation and parole officer in the United States during a period of unprecedented growth in community corrections and change in offender supervision. Importantly it explores how CCOs believe offenders should be supervised, how they perceive the institution in which they work, how they coordinate with and use other agencies to assist in reintegrating offenders, and how they define the communities in which they work. Finally, this book presents the complex role CCOs play in spanning the professions that deliver control, sanctions, treatment, and support to bring about change in the lives of ex-convicts.

Traditionally, the working philosophy and tasks of CCOs have been conceptualized and measured along a continuum with law enforcement at one end and social work at the other. CCOs who subscribe to a law enforcement philosophy to guide their work focus on monitoring, surveillance, compliance, enforcing technical violations, sanctions, revocation, and rearrest—in other words, they focus on criminal risk and police ex-offenders to assure compliance with court-ordered conditions. Those who adhere to a social work philosophy focus on ex-offender needs and connect the offender to sources of social support, life skills, and rehabilitation or treatment—in other words, they focus on criminogenic needs and prevention strategies to assure compliance with court-ordered conditions. Based on existing research and interviews with CCOs, I argue that the professional roles of CCOs are dynamic and exist beyond the simple binary roles of law enforcement and social work. I conclude that CCOs are instead "street-level boundary spanners" who work to bridge the power and resources of corrections, police, social work, treatment, and the community to supervise and reintegrate ex-offenders. Thus, they are not, as traditionally presented, merely the end player of a long criminal justice system process but instead are the keystone to engineering the support necessary to guide ex-offenders toward successful reintegration. Failing to understand their unique role in the criminal justice system and ignoring the complex historical, political, social, and economic context in which they work results in a profession that is misunderstood, oftentimes disrespected, overburdened, and underused in its power to enhance the success of the entire system.

MISSION OF COMMUNITY CORRECTIONS OFFICERS

Community corrections has historically been driven by a rehabilitative philosophy focused on addressing offenders' needs, providing treatment, and integrating the person into conventional law-abiding society. Originally "parole officers" were viewed as mentors and friends who developed a relationship with offenders in order to guide them toward a better life free from alcohol and vice instead of going to jail (Augustus, 1852; Rothman, 1980). These origins would eventually morph into a more formal and professional relationship in which the parole officer still developed a friendly relationship with parolees but also functioned as a counselor, psychologist, or investigator, focused on diagnosing offender needs and professionally guiding the offender's reintegration into the community (Caplan, 2006; Rothman, 1980).

Parole from prison as we know it today formally emerged during the Progressive Era (1890–1920). During the Progressive Era criminal behavior was considered a disease that could be cured with appropriate treatment delivered in suitably designed prison environments and followed by support when discharged from prison on to parole (Pisciotta, 1994; Rafter, 1985; Rothman, 1980). The duration of the treatment or sentence depended on the individual's progress toward being cured from a life of crime. As outlined in the *Declaration of Principles* (1870), the state has an ongoing responsibility to ex-offenders beyond the confines of the prison reformatory:

> More systematic and comprehensive methods should be adopted to save discharged prisoners, by providing them with work and encouraging them to redeem their character and regain their lost position in society. *The state has not discharged its whole duty to the criminal when it has punished him, nor even when it has reformed him. Having raised him up, it has the further duty to aid in holding him up. And to this end it is desirable that state societies be formed, which shall co-operate with each other in this work.* (emphasis added; *Declaration of Principles*, 1870, as reprinted in Pisciotta, 1994, p. 159)

Progressive Era reformers realized that release from prison was a challenging transition and if not supported, the treatment administered in prison could quickly be sabotaged in the community. Reformers also recognized the need for the development of "state societies" to cooperate in providing the resources necessary to assure success—an awareness that former inmates needed multiple forms of aid. There was an early consciousness that for prison reformatories to be successful there must be continuity in care that spanned from the prison into the community.

Although originating from lofty ideals that recognized the difficult challenge transitioning from prison to the community could pose, parole has been one of the most highly criticized of the Progressive innovations (Rothman, 1980). Oftentimes the general public and policymakers blame parole for the coddling of offenders and being too lenient in reducing prison sentences. Rothman (1980, p. 161) insightfully asks,

> How did a procedure take hold and perpetuate itself right down through the 1960s while suffering from such popular disdain? Clearly parole, by being last in line in criminal justice practices, did pay for all the inadequacies in the system. . . . *It was the parole board that broke down prison walls and therefore deserved all blame for whatever happened next.* (emphasis added)

Therefore, in its traditional form, parole as an assessment of an offender's success along a continuum of self-reflection, remorse, and change came under severe criticism and was used as an example of the ultimate failure of the medical model of corrections. Political and public sentiments, and therefore the guiding philosophy of corrections, shifted for the first time since the discovery of the asylum from rehabilitation to punishment (Cullen & Gilbert, 1982; Cullen & Jonson, 2012). This philosophical shift also served to relieve policymakers and the state from taking full responsibility for the reform of offenders and redirected responsibility on to the offender alone. Relieving the state of the responsibility to reform laid the groundwork to abandon rehabilitation and to shift contemporary supervision tactics to surveillance, monitoring compliance, sanctions, and revocation. Ex-offenders may be directed toward rehabilitation, but the responsibility is theirs alone to succeed or fail no matter the conditions in which they live or the integrity of the programs in which they participate.

To place the entire blame for success or failure solely on the offender, the most powerless of those involved in the criminal justice system, may work well in the abstract, but it conflicts with the professional reality of CCOs put in the vicarious position of having to share the responsibility of reform and reintegration with offenders if they are to be successful in reducing recidivism and protecting the community. Although CCOs may not be held accountable for the rate of overall failure of those on their caseloads, when an offender's failure becomes public through cases sensationalized through the media, it is community corrections and the CCO that are criticized and not the failures of prisons, police, courts, social services, public education, or broader public health initiatives also responsible for the well-being of communities. CCOs are challenged to pursue the goal of community safety within a context of competing and shifting political, economic, and social expectations about how offenders should be managed. It is the political, organizational, and social realities that require CCOs to become street-level boundary spanners if they are to successfully negotiate holding offenders accountable, participating in effective case management, and establishing meaningful long-term reintegration.

DEMAND FOR COMMUNITY CORRECTIONS WORK: OFFENDER NEEDS AND CCO RESPONSIBILITY

It is important to consider the multiple and systemic conditions in which CCOs function. Their work is influenced by four primary contexts: (1) political and public punitiveness, (2) the demands placed on the agencies employing CCOs, (3) the individual needs of offenders, and (4) the community context where supervision takes place. Each of these contexts interacts to influence CCOs' professional well-being and their capacity to effectively implement desired outcomes related to offender change and long-term success.

Political and Public Punitiveness

Social, political, and legal movements in the 1970s brought about crucial changes in sentencing and incarceration rates that some have referred to as an American "imprisonment binge" (Austin & Irwin, 2003). Prior to the 1970s, the "war on poverty" provided the framework to explain many social ills and focused state power and resources on institutions that provided support for those in need of food, housing, education, and health care. Soon after the political upheaval of the civil rights movement, the women's movement, and the Vietnam War protests, however, the United States shifted its attention to what was perceived as a permissive generation out of control and thus a need to reestablish public order. Those participating in social change movements were often presented as drug users and irresponsible young adults. During this same period, crime rates were at record highs, with the rate of violent crime committed by people aged 15 to 24 among the highest (Austin & Irwin, 2003). The social context was ripe to easily connect crime to drug and alcohol abuse, and the connection set the political stage to argue that both crime and drugs needed to be addressed through the criminal justice system and not the social welfare or health care systems. In addition, the media fueled public fears about race, crime, and public disorder with continuous reports and displays of young men of color participating in violence within cities. Politicians capitalized on these fears by linking crime to a weak and lenient criminal justice system.

Very rapidly, emphasis shifted from the helping institutions that fought the "war on poverty" to the coercive institutions of the criminal justice system (police, courts, and corrections) to fight the "war on crime" and the "war on drugs." Redefining social ills as based in crime versus poverty quickly shifted domestic policy toward using the full coercive power of the criminal justice system to address social and political challenges. As a result, prison populations escalated beyond what most could have imagined and created an increasing demand for community corrections officers and their services.

For instance, prison populations in the United States remained fairly stable from 1925 to 1973, with approximately 106 people per 100,000 adults in the general population sentenced to prison each year (SCJS, 2010c). As of 2008, the number of people sentenced to state or federal prisons increased to 504 people per 100,000 adults in the general population (SCJS, 2010c). The U.S. prison population leads the world with an incarcerated population of approximately 1.5 million adults per year, equating to nearly 25% of the world's prison population (Cullen & Jonson, 2012). In addition to prison, approximately 736,000 adults are confined in county jails and detention centers, bringing the total number of people incarcerated each year to approximately 2.5 million (Glaze & Parks, 2012; SCJS, 2010a). At the current rate of incarceration, about 1 in 107 adults is housed in a prison or jail in the United States (Glaze & Parks, 2012). Even though many were astonished when the prison population reached 1 million in 1995 and prison trajectories were continuing upward, only a few scholars expressed concern about what would happen when the vast majority of this population was released from prison and returned to the community (Irwin & Austin, 1997; Petersilia, 2003; Travis, 2005). This concern has now become a reality with approximately 736,000 offenders released from prison each year, which equates to approximately 2,015 offenders per day (SCJS, 2010b).

New releases from prison occur through a number of mechanisms such as sentence completion, the parole board, good time or earned credits (mandatory parole), and prison population reduction strategies. Therefore, not all offenders released from prison are supervised. In addition, many convicted offenders (including felons) never go to prison but are sanctioned in the community through probation and other intermediate sanctions. Thus, community supervision caseloads are often inclusive of both probation and parole populations. The number of parolees has increased from approximately 220,000 offenders in 1980 to 850,000 offenders in 2011, or 3.6 times the 1980 level (SCJS, 2010a). The number of probationers has also increased significantly, from approximately 1.1 million in 1980 to 4 million in 2011, or nearly 4 times the 1980 level. This means approximately 1 in 50 adults is under probation or parole supervision.

Greater punitiveness by policymakers also went beyond the use of prisons to the use of civil sanctions to further punish offenders. Numerous laws restrict those with a felony record from receiving public assistance. For instance, those convicted of a felony drug offense may not reside in

Figure 1.1   Prison Population Growth

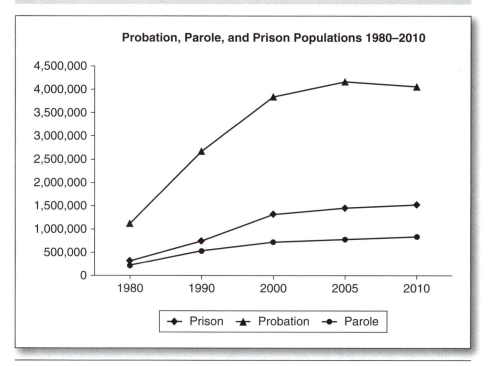

Source: Glaze and Parks (2012).

federally funded public housing, receive funding for public education, be licensed by the state for certain occupations, or vote in public elections (Mele & Miller, 2005). Sex offenders may also have additional restrictions of having to register with local police and being limited in where they may live in relationship to schools, parks, and other locations where children are commonly present (Peterilia, 2003). With most offenders being poor and returning to poor communities, these civil penalties layered upon criminal sanctions create additional burdens for families, friends, and communities to provide support to parolees at the individual and local level while in the midst of surviving poverty themselves (Clear, 2007).

Increased public punitiveness toward offenders and a withdrawal from a cross-systems approach (i.e., social services, public health, education, criminal justice) to address crime and offenders' needs instigated an increased reliance on the criminal justice system that translated into policies supporting more police and prisons while oftentimes ignoring the resulting burdens placed on courts and community supervision. The responsibility of managing such a large correctional population within a punitive and unforgiving political context often caused ongoing tension between institutional corrections (prisons) and community corrections within many jurisdictions.

Department of Corrections Context

The sheer number of offenders sentenced to prison beginning in the 1980s put extreme pressure on states to focus on expanding institutional corrections and building more prison cells. During the 1980s most states were burdened with ageing institutions, many of which were built near the turn of the 20th century and had antiquated security systems; outdated plumbing, heating, and ventilation; and inadequate space to accommodate programs. Crowding became so severe that many states were under court order to reduce their prison populations or expand their physical plant to accommodate the influx of offenders (Austin & Irwin, 2003). The combination of harsher sentencing and inadequate prison space spurred many states to try to build their way out of the correctional crisis, reflected in the overall national expenditure of an estimated $47 billion per year (Pew Center on the States, 2009; SCJS, 2006). Furthermore, political pressure pushed many departments of corrections to favor prisons over community corrections (Lehman & Labecki, 1998). This resulted in stagnated spending on community corrections since the late 1970s (Petersilia, 2002). A disparity that favors prison spending is also apparent in that only 32% of the correctional population is incarcerated, yet that same population consumes 88% of correctional costs (Pew Center on the States, 2009). The emphasis on prison spending is further highlighted by the fact that correctional spending in many states still outpaces spending on hospitals and health care, education, and public welfare (Hughes, 2006).

The political climate that inspired the need for greater prison capacity also devalued the need for prisons to provide rehabilitation programs and tended to favor security and incapacitation instead (Cullen & Gilbert, 1982; Garland, 2001; Lehman & Labecki, 1998). The increasing economic burden created by the cost of prison construction and the get-tough political climate justified the elimination of education, vocational training, life skills courses, rehabilitation programs (e.g., substance abuse treatment, psychological counseling), and recreation programs from most prisons (Cullen & Gilbert, 1982; Petersilia, 2003). These ideologically punitive and economic-driven policies have resulted in fewer inmates having access to treatment, education, or vocational programs (Lynch & Sabol, 2001; Petersilia, 2003). These changes were further justified by the belief that treatment programs were ineffective, the rehabilitative ideal had failed, and the best that prisons could hope to achieve was the safe incapacitation of convicted felons (DiLulio, 1987; Wilson J. Q., 1983).

Although prisons were relieved of the responsibility for improving the plight of offenders and preparing them for release into the community during this punitive period of social policy, community corrections was not similarly excused and was presented with the oftentimes conflicting missions of both punishment and rehabilitation. For instance, many states had no choice but to sentence or release more offenders to the community because of prison overcrowding but were hampered by the perception that community supervision was an inadequate, "soft on crime" punishment. Thus, many states developed alternatives to prison designed to be stricter and more likely to hold offenders accountable, such as shock incarceration, intensive supervision, electronic monitoring, specialty caseloads (e.g., gangs, sex offenders), and other enhanced surveillance approaches. Yet offenders returning to the community still had serious problems related to substance abuse, mental health conditions, and skill deficits that were not adequately addressed in prison and therefore needed to be treated in the community. With no new resources to deal with the increased population of offenders being released from prisons that had made few if any attempts to improve offenders' potential for success, many community corrections agencies were left with no clear mission on how to proceed except through surviving deprivation of resources and focusing on surveillance and efficiency (Harlow & Nelson, 1990; Petersilia, 2002).

Disparity in funding between prisons and community corrections, along with increasing caseloads, has also left many agencies without the ability to provide basic support to their officers so that they may better track offenders, hold offenders accountable, and provide offenders with program support (Pew Center on the States, 2009). In spite of huge increases in probation and parole populations in recent years, too little attention has been given to the size of probation and parole caseloads and how CCOs have adjusted their work. It is estimated that the average probation officer supervises 100 to 170 offenders and the average parole officer approximately 60 to 70 offenders (DeMichele & Payne, 2007; Petersilia, 2002; Pew Center on the States, 2009). In addition, high-risk offenders tend to get priority, leaving others on supervision with limited support or attention. Under these conditions, it is realistic to expect that CCOs are challenged to proactively control much of what happens to those on their caseloads.

Relatedly, the failure of community corrections can be very public and fuel existing fears of crime that lay the foundation for harsh reactionary policies by lawmakers. Sensational crimes committed by parolees reflect poorly on community corrections, CCOs, and the DOC. These public cases, oftentimes beyond the power of CCOs to prevent, bring greater scrutiny of administrative polices, accusations that community corrections is soft on crime, and calls for increased surveillance and accountability through quicker and harsher sanctions for all ex-offenders on supervision. These oftentimes heinous crimes, though worthy of investigation and scrutiny, are generally outliers when one considers the millions of offenders currently being supervised or who have passed through community supervision without committing violent crime (Griffen & Stitt, 2010). These outliers do, however, involve real emotionally laden victim stories and often drive public fear, public policy, and the decisions of CCOs to err on the side of caution with a noncompliant offender because of the publicity that may result if they select treatment instead of a sanction and the offender reoffends. A focus on reducing risk through sanctions and revocation versus managing risk through prevention and treatment locks CCOs into an ever-narrowing set of responses that defines supervision as reacting to single events at specific points versus managing supervision as a process over time that leads to long-term reintegration.

Not surprisingly given the political and economic context in which parole exists, research outcomes have not been very impressive. Nationally, for both state and federal populations, 34% of offenders returned to prison from parole in 2008 (Sabol, West, & Cooper, 2009). Additional research has also shown that within 3 years of release from prison, approximately 65% of parolees return to prison (Burke & Tonry, 2006; Petersilia, 2003). Failures tend to be those convicted of a property crime; those with greater criminal histories; those unemployed, younger, and living alone; and those who use drugs (Petersilia, 2002, 2003). Increasingly, failure of community supervision resulting in a return to prison is also due to technical violations or noncompliance (37% of all readmissions nationally) versus a new crime (Burke & Tonry, 2006; Grattet, Petersilia, Lin, & Beckman, 2009). Although these are unacceptable rates of failure, they are not surprising given the emphasis on punitive responses to offenders, the failure to adequately address offender needs, and the ongoing effects of poverty and living in seriously disadvantaged neighborhoods.

Although the political context has shifted from a rehabilitative philosophy guiding corrections to one steeped in punishment and accountability with an emphasis on prisons, the reality of offenders' life experiences has not changed. Many offenders are still undereducated, unemployed, and unhealthy due to substance abuse and the long-term effects of poverty. CCOs are often challenged by meeting expectations to hold offenders accountable by emphasizing surveillance and sanctions while knowing there is little chance of change without social support, treatment, and appropriate case management. Although the current political context may ignore the complexity of offenders' lives, CCOs understand and tend to support both offender accountability and treatment approaches within supervision (Caplan, 2006). In order to be successful, CCOs understand that both the risk offenders pose to the community and offenders' needs and behaviors most likely to sabotage their success must be addressed.

Offender Context

Poverty, and the conditions most highly correlated with it, such as unemployment, lack of education, disease, poor mental health, race, and age, is the single most common attribute of those sent to prison (Reiman, 2004). Poverty in the United States tends to be concentrated, not randomly distributed throughout the population, and it places families at a disadvantage in their ability to compete in the labor market (Clear, 2007; Petersilia, 2003; Rank, 2004). As Rank (2004, p. 30) points out, "Consequently, minorities, children and young adults, women, female heads of household, residents of central cities or economically depressed neighborhoods, and individuals with little education or a disability all face greater risks of poverty. These relationships have held steady across decades of cross-sectional yearly poverty data."

Those released from prison reflect many of these same qualities. The prison population is overwhelmingly male (93%), young (50% under age 34), undereducated (33% have less than a high school diploma), unemployed (33% unemployed in the month prior to arrest), and overrepresentative of racial and ethnic minorities (34% White, 38% Black, and 20% Hispanic) (Clear, 2007; Government Accounting Office, 2000; Petersilia, 2003; Sabol, West, & Cooper, 2009). Currently, 1 in 45 Whites, 1 in 27 Hispanics, and 1 in 11 Blacks are under some form of state control (Pew Center on the States, 2009). Black men have a 29% lifetime chance of serving at least 1 year in prison, compared to 16% for Hispanic males (of any race), and 5% for White males (Travis, Solomon, & Waul, 2001). Although men across all racial groups are 5 times more likely than women to be under correctional control, 1 in 89 women are in prison, jail, or under some form of community supervision (Pew Center on the States, 2009). In their abstract form these statistics are rather dry, and one may conclude that we have known these figures for a long time. These statistics, however, have staggering consequences when interpreted in terms of real lives lived by offenders and the professional responsibility of community corrections officers to successfully manage and integrate offenders into the community.

For instance, doing without means making daily decisions about whether the very basics of life will be available, such as obtaining food, clothing, shelter, health care, and transportation (Rank, 2004). Those living in poverty often live without a sufficiently balanced diet because they must balance the cost of food with other important expenses such as shelter. Food in poor communities is also more expensive and oftentimes does not include access to fresh produce, grains, or meats and instead consists of processed foods that are less healthy yet less likely to spoil. In addition to inadequate nutrition, little to no preventative health care often results in babies born with low birth weights, a lack of immunization, and no preventative care for teeth and eyes, all resulting in complications later in life. Life is also inhibited by being trapped in unsafe neighborhoods where resources are scant and transportation to and from work is expensive. The combination of these factors, as well as those described later, culminates in a death rate for those aged 25 to 65 who live in poverty that is 3 times that of affluent groups and a life span that is on average 9 years shorter.

Doing without also creates emotional and physical burdens that tend to inspire accumulated stress levels that influence daily decisions and personal relationships (Rank, 2004). For instance, the poor must make ongoing decisions between things such as eating or heat or paying the rent. Each decision has a negative consequence in the immediate as well as the long term, thus consistently forcing choices between life-sustaining necessities. These ongoing stressors often cause tension and stress within primary relationships that may result in greater risks of separation, divorce, family violence, and greater financial hardship and long-term poverty.

Without understanding the reality of poverty one cannot effectively manage offender reentry or understand the professional responsibility of community corrections officers. Thus, people who live in poverty for sustained periods are structurally and individually limited in their social and physical well-being (Rank, 2004). With life's focus purely on survival, it is difficult to plan ahead, envision the future beyond the current hardship, or be socially and politically involved in changing the forces that influence the well-being of the individual, family, or community. As Rank (2004, p. 45) states, "So it is with individuals who live in poverty for sustained periods of time. A lack of proper food, shelter, education, and other essential resources, coupled with the stress of impoverishment, results in stunted individual development. Sometimes this stunting is visibly apparent; often/times it lies underneath the surface." Therefore, even when opportunities are presented to ex-offenders by CCOs and others, they may not be in a position to either recognize the potential or to fully take advantage of those opportunities (Giordano, Cernkovich, & Rudolph, 2002).

When considering in the abstract statistics about offenders returning to their communities from prison, it is easy to miss the complex and harsh reality of what it means to be reintegrated into the community after serving time in prison—especially if ignoring the fact that the offender is not returning to a state of well-being and stability but to families and communities already stressed. In addition, the offender's condition is exacerbated by the additional burden of a felony conviction and a period of incarceration that has potentially strained existing primary personal relationships and hampered social and financial networks, and a prison term remiss in developing the skills necessary for success upon release. Community corrections officers are faced with the responsibility of managing and guiding the offender through all of the ills of a life put on hold by incarceration, challenged by poverty, and stigmatized by a criminal record, with the hope of preventing the victimization of those living in the community by the offenders they are responsible for supervising.

In addition, and to be blunt, some offenders really are not very nice people. Although many were put on the path to prison due to family and community hardships, they are often in prison due to the effects of drug and alcohol addiction, dishonesty, and histories of committing violence within their families and in the community. They have often so damaged their relationships, sometimes beyond repair, with those they need the most to be successful upon release that there is no "home" for them to return to. Understanding the hardships offenders confront does not excuse their behavior; it does, however, bring one to a clearer understanding, based in reality instead of stereotypes, of what it takes professionally to effectively work with this population in reducing recidivism. Therefore, community corrections officers are challenged with integrating offenders into desperate communities and working with people who have not always coped well with the conditions of their lives. The individual coping strategies, or lack thereof, are often further exacerbated from having left a prison environment where examples of mature coping are rare and the very structure of the prison may perpetuate the negative behavior that brought them to prison to begin with (Franklin & Lutze, 2007; Haney, 2001; Johnson, 1996; Lutze, 2003, 2006; Lutze & Bell, 2005; Zamble & Porporino, 1988).

The notion of developing policy or supervising offenders from a position of privilege and believing that offenders should do just as the CCO has done in his or her life, or that they should just have the willpower to pull themselves out of poverty, is rather naïve. The needs of offenders released from prison are significant and are interwoven with the needs of the community to which they return. In spite of best efforts to treat and rehabilitate the individual, without considering the condition of the places people live, the CCO's efforts are likely to fail (Clear, 2007; Currie, 1985; Kirk, 2012; Sampson, 2002; Wright, 2010). Offenders' individual needs and conditions often directly parallel the needs of the communities to which they return. Predictably, offenders may find it difficult to find the support they need, and communities may find it difficult to provide the necessary care because both are experiencing the same challenges.

Community Context

Just as poverty and incarceration are not randomly distributed throughout the population, release from prison into the community is not randomly distributed but instead is highly concentrated in impoverished communities (Clear, 2007). For instance, in some states 30% to 50% of those released from prison return to a single city—such as Baltimore, Chicago, Houston, and New York City—in the state, and within the city, approximately one-third of ex-prisoners return to only five or six neighborhoods (see Travis, 2005). In Chicago, this translated into 5,000 prisoners returned to only 6 of 77 communities within the city in a single year (Travis, 2005). Understanding the communities in which offenders live is just as important as understanding the offenders themselves. Although offenders are isolated physically from their communities while incarcerated, they are still tied to the people and places they affiliated with before prison and will be returned to those places upon release as a matter of policy in most jurisdictions.

Research has shown that where a person lives affects his or her social and economic opportunity as related to local service quality, shared norms and social control, peer influences, crime and violence, and job access (Clear, 2007; Rose & Clear, 1998; Sampson, 2002). In poor communities, the quality of services suffers from inadequate schools and limited access to health care, child care, grocery stores, and other quality-of-life businesses and institutions. Additionally, when people feel unsafe in their communities they tend to withdraw from public spaces and public engagement so that the norm in public spaces becomes narrowly represented by young people and crime. When a community is isolated due to poverty, a lack of safety, and limited transportation, access to peers and networks outside of the immediate neighborhood is stifled and culture becomes defined by the physical boundaries, relationships, and experiences of poverty. Those who live in high-crime areas are oftentimes saddled with the additional burden of avoiding victimization, dealing with the trauma of victimization, and the inability to escape the place and people that put them at future risk (see Lutze & Kigerl, 2013). When legitimate businesses abandon poor areas due to all of the factors just discussed, access to employment is limited within the community and access to work away from the community is often hampered by available and affordable transportation.

The communities to which offenders are released are also those that lack human capital, healthy social networks, social capital, collective efficacy, and informal social control (Clear, 2007; Rose & Clear, 1998; Sampson, 2002). Each of these relates to the content and availability of resources a community may draw on to respond to the needs of its citizens via private networks (e.g., family, friends, peers, employers) or public networks such as institutions (e.g., religion, education, public health, law) and specific agencies (e.g., social services, child care, police). The places in which community members experience the greatest level of incarceration, "concentrated incarceration" (Clear, 2007), are those that have the fewest individual and community levels of capital to expend on those in need (Anderson, 1999; Currie, 1985; Wilson W. J., 1987).

Due to the isolation and condition of many poor communities, the residents often lose faith that the traditional social, political, and legal institutions affluent communities rely on will serve them. Many of the services the poor do rely on are offered only under strict conditions. For instance, welfare benefits are based on the assumption that women are unmarried, living alone with their children, unemployed, and seeking work outside of the home (Raphael, 2000). The reality is that most poor women, although not married, are not single, may be living in violent relationships, and may have difficulty seeking employment due to the cumulative effects of violence, poverty, and the inability to afford child care (Raphael, 2000). Similarly, individuals on probation or parole often have curfews and may not interact with other felons, possess firearms, live in public housing, vote, or use alcohol. They may be visited in their home's at any time by a community corrections officer without a warrant who may be accompanied by a police officer (Mele & Miller, 2005; Murphy & Lutze, 2009; Petersilia, 2003; Travis & Stacey, 2010). For those living in unsafe, poor communities with a high concentration of convicted felons, it is almost impossible not to be in violation of the conditions of parole.

Although these legislative-, court-, and agency-driven conditions have a great deal of validity, they are unrealistic when placed in the context in which poor people live or, for that matter, how most people live (see Klockars, 1972). These conditions are often designed and enforced by people who do not understand the complexity and burden of poverty or who base policy on stereotypes of the poor (Rank, 2004). State institutions then become one more aspect of life to manage, evade, and possibly manipulate in order to survive the everyday intrusions of state-funded services or supervision. The intrusion of state institutions into every aspect of life, both private and public, may easily lead to the perception by those in poor communities that the state is coercive, controlling, and unjust.

In addition, given that most communities experiencing concentrated poverty and incarceration are segregated by race and ethnicity (Clear, 2007), it should not be surprising that a history of racial discrimination and disparity furthers the belief by many minorities and the poor that state agencies perpetuate injustice (Christianson, 1998; Shelden, 2001). For instance, Petersilia (2003, p. 30) argues that

> It is sufficient to say that, for prisoner reentry discussions, race is the "elephant sitting in the living room." It affects every aspect of reentry, including communities, labor markets, family welfare, government entitlements, and program innovations, which need to be culturally appropriate....Greater alienation and disillusionment with the justice system also erodes residents' feelings of commitment and makes them less willing to participate in local activities. This is important, since our most effective crime-fighting tools require community collaboration and active engagement.

Clear (2007, p. 89) argues similarly that "the state is most likely encountered as a coercive agent of control rather than a fair agent of justice, and when this perception is true, people are less likely to conform their behavior to the requirements of the law."

Understanding the political context in which the department of corrections exists and the reality of offenders' lives and the communities in which they live provides a much more realistic perspective about the complex role of community corrections in managing and reintegrating ex-offenders. Conceptualizing CCOs and their work only within the department of corrections or the criminal justice system is too narrow and sets up false expectations about what can be achieved by CCOs. Expanding the paradigm to conceptualize CCOs as street-level boundary spanners provides a more realistic picture of the importance of their position within the criminal justice system to serve as agents who cross multiple systems to effectively monitor offender risk and address offender needs by supporting the process of change necessary to achieve long-term success. As boundary spanners who capture the power of multiple systems to address complex problems, CCOs are very likely to increase the success of offenders and the criminal justice system as a whole.

CONCEPTUALIZING COMMUNITY CORRECTIONS OFFICERS AS STREET-LEVEL BOUNDARY SPANNERS

Although the concept of probation and parole was founded in principle as a boundary-spanning activity among the court, the jail, and the community (Augustus, 1852), and continued to be inclusive of a more comprehensive approach through the Progressive Era, the contemporary placement of probation and parole within the criminal justice system, and more specifically within corrections in many jurisdictions, has resulted in CCOs strongly influenced by political pressure to be tough on crime and the more coercive aspects of social control (Gregory, 2010; Petersilia, 2003; Ohlin, Piven, & Pappenfort, 1956). This has resulted in narrowing the roles of CCOs and presented a set of unrealistic expectations regarding the ability of community supervision to actually achieve community safety.

It is clear that expectations of community corrections must be aligned with the reality of the work CCOs are asked to conduct. They are understandably expected to manage the risk many offenders pose to the community. Current social and political contexts encourage that risk to be managed through surveillance, sanctions, revocation, and arrest. Although these are relevant components of supervision, a review of the deficits confronting many offenders and the stressed communities in which they live suggests that punishment alone will not achieve long-term success or safer communities. The work of CCOs must also include the resources necessary to address the criminogenic needs of ex-offenders, such as changing antisocial attitudes and providing access to life skills education, vocational training, employment, health care, and treatment for substance abuse and other conditions that inhibit success in the community (Andrews & Bonta, 2010; Cullen & Jonson, 2012). Most importantly, it is time to recognize that CCOs may be in the best position of any other actor in the criminal justice system to manage both the risks and needs of offenders due to their power to respond to noncompliance with coercive sanctions and their ability to connect individuals to the helping professions of social services, mental health, treatment, and education.

Therefore, expectations of what CCOs can accomplish need to be realigned beyond the boundaries of the department of corrections and the criminal justice system and toward the multiple networks of individuals and agencies capable of addressing the full continuum of offenders' risk and needs. CCOs must be enabled to focus their energy on being boundary spanners and organizing their power to work with the criminal justice system, social services, treatment, and the community to effect change.

Boundary spanners are those who "attempt to understand human behavior in the context of the systemic structures, operations, and barriers that exist within and between communities and prisons, seek to bridge communication, understanding, and service gaps and translate the working of one entity into the language of another" (Pettus & Severson, 2006, p. 208). Boundary spanners are usually identified in research and practice as individuals in mid- to upper-level management of organizations who build

Figure 1.2   CCOs as Street-Level Boundary Spanners

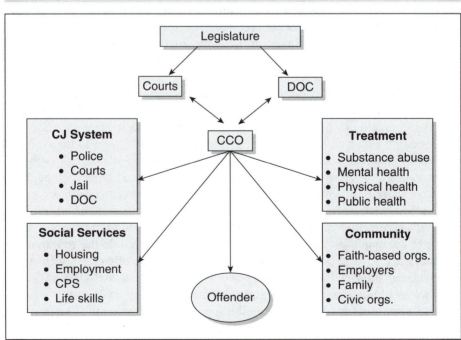

connections across independent systems to enhance the likelihood of solving common problems. These systems, although serving similar clients, may have disparate missions (e.g., public safety, social stability, health, education). Although interagency collaboration and partnerships have become popular ideas, few professional communities have permeated the boundaries at the upper levels of organizational leadership to effect lasting change. In spite of the general lack of boundary spanners at the upper levels of leadership in many fields, CCOs provide a credible example of how professionals working directly with clients with multiple needs and levels of risk often serve as *street-level boundary spanners* in order to effect change for offenders and greater success for their agencies at the macro level.

This book makes it clear that CCOs, using both surveillance and assistance, are purposeful street-level boundary spanners who without fail work in a profession built on human relationships and interdisciplinary professional networks. Given what is known through social science and from the shared professional experiences of CCOs, one needs to more fully understand the complexity of CCOs' professional roles in order to fully take advantage of their power and capacity to effect positive change within the criminal justice system and the community. To envision how to effectively empower CCOs, one needs a holistic understanding of their professional roles, including their relationships with offenders, their work within the community, their place within their agencies, how and when they use evidence-based practices, and the extent of their collaboration with other institutions. It is only within this broader understanding that one can fully and effectively invest in community corrections and value its boundary-spanning capacity to effect positive change.

WORKS CITED

Anderson, E. (1999). *Code of the street: Decency, violence, and the moral life of the inner city.* New York: W. W. Norton.

Andrews, D., & Bonta, J. (2010). *The psychology of criminal conduct* (5th ed.). Cincinnati, OH: Anderson.

Augustus, J. (1852). *A report of the labors of John Augustus* (Bicentennial ed.: 1984 ed.). Lexington, KY: American Probation and Parole Association.

Austin, J., & Irwin, J. (2003). *It's about time: America's imprisonment binge.* Belmon, CA: Wadsworth.

Burke, P., & Tonry, M. (2006). *Successful transition and reentry for safer communities: A call to action for parole.* Silver Spring, MD: JEHT Foundation.

Caplan, J. M. (2006). Parole system anomie: Conflicting models of casework and surveillance. *Federal Probation, 70*(3), 32–36.

Christianson, S. (1998). *With liberty for some: 500 years of imprisonment in America*. Boston: Northeastern University Press.

Clear, T. R. (2007). *Imprisoning communities: How mass incarceration makes disadvantaged neighborhoods worse*. New York: Oxford University Press.

Cullen, F., & Jonson, C. (2012). *Correctional theory: Context and consequences*. Thousand Oaks, CA: Sage.

Cullen, F. T., & Gilbert, K. E. (1982). *Reaffirming rehabilitation*. Cincinnati, OH: Anderson.

Currie, E. (1985). *Confronting crime: An American challenge*. New York: Pantheon Books.

DeMichele, M., & Payne, B. K. (2007). Probation and Parole Officers Speak Out—Caseload and Workload Allocation. *Federal Probation, 71*(3), 30–35.

DiLulio, J. J. (1987). *Governing prisons: A comparative study of correctional management*. New York: The Free Press.

Franklin, C., & Lutze, F. E. (2007). Home confinement and intensive supervision as unsafe havens: The unintended consequences for women. In R. Muraskin (Ed.), *It's a crime: Women and justice* (4th ed., pp. 608–623). Upper Saddle River, NJ: Prentice Hall.

Garland, D. (2001). *The culture of control: Crime and social order in contempoary society*. Chicago: University of Chicago Press.

Giordano, P. C., Cernkovich, S. A., & Rudolph, J. L. (2002). Gender, crime, and desistance: Toward a theory of cognitive transformation. *The American Journal of Sociology, 107*(4), 990–1064.

Glaze, L. E., & Parks, E. (2012). *Correctional populations in the United States, 2011*. Bureau of Justice Statistics. Washington, DC: U.S. Department of Justice.

Government Accounting Office. (2000). *State and federal prisoners: Profiles of inmate characteristics in 1991 and 1997*. Washington, DC: United States General Accounting Office.

Grattet, R., Petersilia, J., Lin, J., & Beckman, M. (2009). Parole violations and revocations in California: Analysis and suggestions for action. *Federal Probation, 73*(1), 2–11.

Gregory, M. (2010). Reflection and resistance: Probation practice and the ethic of care. *British Journal of Social Work, 40*, 2274–2290.

Griffen, T., & Stitt, B. G. (2010). Random activities theory: The case for "Black Swan" criminology. *Critical Criminology, 18*, 57–72.

Haney, C. (2001). *The psychological impact of incarceration: Implications for post-prison adjustment*. From prison to home: The effect of incarceration and reentry on children, families and communities. National Policy Conference. Washington, DC: U.S. Department of Health and Human Services.

Harlow, N., & Nelson, E. K. (1990). Probation's responses to fiscal constraints. In D. E. Duffee & E. F. McGarrell (Eds.), *Community corrections: A community field approach* (pp. 165–184). Cincinnati, OH: Anderson.

Hughes, K. A. (2006). *Justice expenditures and employment in the United States, 2003*. Office of Justice Programs, U.S. Department of Justice. Washington, DC: Bureau of Justice Statistics.

Irwin, J., & Austin, J. (1997). *It's about time: America's imprsionment binge.* Belmont, CA: Wadsworth.

Johnson, R. (1996). *Hard time: Understanding and reforming the prison* (2nd ed.). Boston: Wadsworth.

Kirk, D. S. (2012). Residential change as a turning point in the life course of crime: Desistance or temporary cessation? *Criminology, 50*(2), 329–358.

Klockars, C. B. (1972). A theory of probation supevision. *The Journal of Criminal Law, Criminology and Police Science, 63*(4), 550–557.

Lehman, J. D., & Labecki, L. A. (1998). Myth versus reality: The politics of crime and punishment and its impact on correctional administration in the 1990s. In T. Allman & R. Gido (Eds.), *Turnstyle justice: Issues in American corrections* (pp. 42–70). Upper Saddle River, NJ: Prentice Hall.

Lutze, F. E. (2003). The acceptance of ultramasculine stereotypes and violence in the control of women inmates. In B. Zaitzow & J. Thomas (Eds.), *Women in prison: Gender and social control* (pp. 183–203). Denver, CO: Lynne Reinner.

Lutze, F. E. (2006). Boot camp prisons and corrections policy: Moving from militarism to an ethic of care. *Journal of Criminology and Public Policy, 5*(2), 389–400.

Lutze, F. E., & Bell, C. (2005). Boot camp prisons as masculine organizations: Rethinking recidivism and program design. *Journal of Offender Rehabilitation, 40*(3/4), 133–152.

Lutze, F. E., & Kigerl, A. (2013). The psychology of reentry. In J. Helfgott (Ed.), *Criminal psychology* (Vols. 1–4). Westport, CT: Praeger.

Lynch, J. P., & Sabol, W. J. (2001). *Prisoner reentry in perspective.* Justice Policy Center. Washington, DC: Urban Institute.

Mele, C., & Miller, T. A. (Eds.). (2005). *Civil penalties, social consequences.* New York: Routledge.

Murphy, D., & Lutze, F. (2009). Police-probation partnerships: Professional identity and the sharing of coercive power. *Journal of Criminal Justice, 37,* 65–76.

Ohlin, L. E., Piven, H., & Pappenfort, D. M. (1956). Major dilemmas of the social worker in probation and parole. *National Probation and Parole Association Journal, 2,* 211–225.

Petersilia, J. (2002). Community corrections. In J. Q. Wilson & J. Petersilia (Eds.), *Crime: Public policies for crime control* (pp. 483–508). Oakland, CA: Institute for Contemporary Studies.

Petersilia, J. (2003). *When prisoners come home: Parole and prisoner reentry.* New York: Oxford University Press.

Pettus, C. A., & Severson, M. (2006). Paving the way for effective reentry practice—The critical role and function of boundary spanner. *The Prison Journal, 86*(2), 206–229.

Pew Center on the States. (2009). *One in 31: The long reach of American corrections.* Washington, DC: The Pew Charitable Trusts.

Pisciotta, A. (1994). *Benevolent repression: Social control and the American reformatory prison movement.* New York: New York University Press.

Rafter, N. (1985). *Partial justice: Women in state prisons, 1800–1935.* Boston: Northeastern University Press.

Rank, M. R. (2004). *One nation, underprivileged: Why American poverty affects us all.* New York: Oxford University Press.

Raphael, J. (2000). *Saving Bernice: Battered women, welfare, and poverty.* Boston: Northeastern University Press.

Reiman, J. (2004). *The rich get richer and the poor get prison: Ideolgy, class, and criminal justice* (7th ed.). Boston: Allyn & Bacon.

Rose, D. R., & Clear, T. R. (1998). Incarceration, social capital, and crime: Implications for social disorganization theory. *Criminology, 36*(3), 441–480.

Rothman, D. (1980). *Conscience and convenience: The asylum and its alternatives in progressive America.* Boston: Little, Brown and Company.

Sabol, W. J., West, H. C., & Cooper, M. (2009). *Prisoners in 2008.* Washington, DC: Bureau of Justice Statistics.

Sampson, R. J. (2002). The Community. In J. Q. Wilson & J. Petersilia (Eds.), *Crime: Public policies for crime control* (pp. 225–252). Oakland, CA: Institute for Contemporary Studies.

SCJS. (2006). *Direct expenditures for correctional activities of state governments.* Retrieved March 12, 2010, from Sourcebook of Criminal Justice Statistics Online: www.albany.edu/sourcebook/pdf/t1112006.pdf

SCJS. (2010a). *Adults on probation, in jails or prison, and on parole: United States, 1980–2006.* Retrieved March 15, 2010, from Sourcebook of Criminal Justice Statistics Online: www.albany.edu/sourcebook/pdf/t612006.pdf

SCJS. (2010b). *Sentenced prisoners admitted to and released from the jurisdiction of state and federal correctional authorities.* Retrieved March 15, 2010, from Sourcebook of Criminal Justice Statistics Online: www.albany.edu/source book/pdf/t600092008.pdf

SCJS. (2010c). *Number and rate (per 100,000 resident population in each group) of sentenced prisoners under jurisdiction of state and federal correctional authorities on December 31.* Retrieved March 15, 2010, from Sourcebook of Criminal Justice Statistics Online: www.albany.edu/sourcebook/pdf/t62822008.pdf

Shelden, R. G. (2001). *Controlling the dangerous classes: A critical introduction to the history of criminal justice.* Needham Heights, MA: Allyn & Bacon.

Travis, J. (2005). *But they all come back: Facing the challenges of prisoner reentry.* Washington, DC: The Urban Institute.

Travis, J., Solomon, A. L., & Waul, M. (2001). *From prison to home: The dimensions and consequences of prisoner reentry.* Washington, DC: Urban Institute, Justice Policy Center.

Travis, L. F., & Stacey, J. (2010). A half century of parole rules: Conditions of parole in the United States, 2008. *Journal of Criminal Justice, 38,* 604–608.

Wilson, J. Q. (1983). *Thinking about crime* (2nd ed.). New York: Vantage Books.

Wilson, W. J. (1987). *The truely disadvantageed: The inner city, the underclass, and public policy.* Chicago: University of Chicago Press.

Wright, K. (2010). Pullman, WA: Dissertation, Washington State University.

Zamble, E., & Porporino, F. J. (1988). *Coping, behavior, and adaption in prison inmates.* New York: Springer-Verlag.

BEYOND LAW ENFORCEMENT AND SOCIAL WORK

Achieving Balanced and Integrated Supervision

"The first thing I learned was that a parole officer was always walking a tightrope—that slim, wavering line between parolee rehabilitation and protection of society from further harm."[1]

Probation and parole originated on the premise that criminal offenders needed to develop relationships with healthy members of the community in order to address the causes of their criminality related to substance abuse, education, vocational training, and general prosocial behavior (Augustus, 1852). Through individual mentoring and support, offenders on probation could find their way through the process of change while living in the community instead of going to jail or prison. Relationships between community mentors and the offender remained relatively informal until the late 1800s and the emergence of the Progressive Era (1890–1920). Formal community supervision became relevant once emphasis was placed on the medical model, individual reform, and indeterminate sentencing structures that necessitated treatment in the community either before prison (probation) or after inmates were "cured" of their criminality and paroled from prison to become productive citizens (Pisciotta, 1994; Rothman, 1980). Once probation and parole became institutionalized as critical components of reform, the role of community corrections officers was also elevated to a more professional status.

A shift from informal mentor to institutionalized professional brought about significant changes to the role of CCOs. For instance, the Progressive

Era's emphasis on individualized treatment, rehabilitation, and reintegration meant that CCOs needed to become experts at recognizing the social, emotional, and physical needs of ex-offenders and identify appropriate interventions. CCOs had to understand the offender's life history, current social context, existing skills, and likelihood to reoffend in addition to knowing when to intervene to achieve positive outcomes. In short, CCOs needed to develop a professional relationship with offenders in order to advise the offender, the court, the parole board, and the department of corrections about the best plan of action for the ex-offender and his or her transition to the community.

The formal authority to manage ex-offenders through the use of both sanctions (coercion) and treatment (support) places CCOs in a unique position that holds tremendous responsibility unlike any other in the criminal justice system. For instance, police generally act to quell the immediate situation regarding a person's behavior and then remove themselves. Institutional corrections officers maintain an ongoing relationship with inmates, but they deal with offenders in a controlled environment, isolated from the broader context of the offenders' lives. Unlike the police or prison officers, CCOs need to maintain a relationship over time in order to gain the offender's cooperation throughout supervision. CCOs also have to consider the offender's overall progress, determine the severity and meaning of an offender's behavior, and decide whether the offender's family, greater social network, or community will be adversely affected by any actions taken. In other words, the CCO's actions, if not considered in the broader context of the offender's life, may affect outcomes across multiple domains. There are few positions in the criminal justice system that provide the opportunity to interact with offenders in such a holistic manner.

This broad responsibility to manage offender risk and needs is what places CCOs in the position of being street-level boundary spanners. To manage criminal risk, CCOs may need to garner resources from police, code enforcement, the court, the jail, attorneys, victim advocates, and institutional corrections. To manage treatment needs, CCOs may work with medical professionals, substance abuse treatment providers, mental health counselors, health insurers, and public health educators. To manage social support, CCOs may work with social services, employers, landlords, child protective services, faith-based organizations, community action centers, families, and educators. Most often these relationships and professional networks are created at the "street level" by individual officers or those working together in the same unit. These resources are informally shared rather than developed through administrative interagency agreements. As will become clear through a review of the research on CCOs' roles, no matter what role they may adhere to along the continuum from law enforcement or social work, they are constantly confronted with making challenging decisions that will ultimately have an impact on the well-being of multiple people in the offender's life as well as the formal institutions charged with the offender's care.

Although CCOs have always struggled with balancing the risk and needs of ex-offenders, and research has focused on whether they act more as law enforcement or social workers, CCOs are rarely bound by either role. This chapter provides a review of the research on how CCOs define their professional role and how this is influenced by social, political, and institutional characteristics. It is apparent that CCOs view their work as both simple and complex. Simple because many offenders on their caseloads share common conditions of supervision ordered by the court and often enforced through a common set of interventions outlined by policy. Their work is complex, however, because each person they supervise is unique in how he or she is affected by conditions such as poverty, addiction, victimization, histories of failure, family relationships, the prison experience, and the ability and willingness to change. CCOs do not view their work as abstract cases but as relationships necessitating the establishment of both trust and respect that flows both ways between the CCO and the offender. CCOs are well aware that they cannot always help ex-offenders achieve reintegration without spanning boundaries and going beyond the power of the criminal justice system to manage behavior. Finally, no matter what their working philosophy and relationship with offenders, they are constantly aware of having to balance offender needs with their own safety as well as the community's safety in a way that minimizes negative exposure for themselves and their agency.

SUPERVISION STYLES AND ORIENTATIONS OF COMMUNITY CORRECTIONS OFFICERS

How to manage community corrections supervision has been closely scrutinized and debated in recent decades due to the shift from the rehabilitative era that traditionally guided corrections to the more recent just deserts and crime control era (Cullen & Gilbert, 1982; Cullen & Jonson, 2012; Garland, 2001; Petersilia, 2003; Wilson, 1983). Proponents of rehabilitation as the guiding philosophy of corrections argue that the best way to achieve long-term change and community safety is to provide support, rehabilitation, and evidence-based practices informed by the assessment of both offender risk and need (Andrews & Bonta, 2010; Cullen & Jonson, 2012). Proponents of just deserts as the guiding philosophy of corrections argue that the best way to achieve community safety is by focusing on risk and holding offenders accountable through intensive monitoring and surveillance resulting in arrest or revocation for violations of supervision followed by immediate sanctions (Wilson, 1983).

The general view of community corrections as "soft on crime" and "failing to protect the community" led many community corrections agencies to prove their value to policymakers by redefining their mission to be more in line with political pressure to be tough on offenders. This shift within a punitive era was most easily accommodated by policies focused on managing risk through the use of coercion, quickly removing offenders from the community, extensively documenting the process of supervision (e.g., number, type, and content of contacts; type of interventions; urinalyses results; risk assessments) and increasing surveillance (e.g., intensive supervision, electronic monitoring, police-probation partnerships) to show that community corrections supervision is a viable intervention able to hold offenders accountable for their behavior. The demands of documenting and justifying all aspects of supervision basically shifted the work of CCOs from that of field workers to office workers (Takagi, 1973).

Even though there was a significant shift from targeting offender change to managing risk, many jurisdictions still retained some aspect of addressing offender needs while adding an emphasis on holding offenders accountable. For example, many states include an emphasis on what may be considered conflicting objectives to achieve safety by providing support and treatment to amenable offenders and holding all offenders accountable through sanctions and revocation (see Purkiss, Kifer, Hemmens, & Burton, 2003; Seiter & West, 2003; Ward & Kupchik, 2010). Without clear directives about how to achieve these oftentimes competing goals, many CCOs experience conflict over what aspects of supervision should be emphasized and with which offenders. In addition, challenges arise because what offenders need to be successful often conflicts with pressure to minimize the agency's and CCO's public exposure to offenders' failure and the resulting professional, financial, and legal consequences (see DeMichele, 2007; Lynch, 1998; Morgan Belbot, & Clark, 1997; Ohlin, Piven & Pappenfort, 1956; Surette, 2011). Therefore, the safest approach for many CCOs and the agencies for which they work is to document every element of supervision and to quickly sanction offenders or revoke community supervision rather than take the long-term risk that an offender may change over time through rehabilitation and other community-based interventions.

The formal authority to use both sanctions and treatment creates a constant state of tension between the short- and long-term goals of supervision. Both sanctions and rehabilitation can contribute to community safety (Andrews & Bonta, 2010; Cullen & Jonson, 2012), and CCOs are expected to choose wisely because both options have short- and long-term consequences. To choose a sanction may achieve short-term accountability but undermine prosocial achievements such as participation in treatment, work, education, and supporting one's family—all things likely to lead to long-term change. To choose treatment may achieve long-term change but in the immediate leave citizens vulnerable to victimization and officers responsible for managing ongoing risk. It is understandable why researchers have placed emphasis on whether CCOs tend to adhere more to a law enforcement role that focuses on surveillance, accountability, and revocation or whether they adhere to a social work role that focuses on monitoring, support, and rehabilitation.

Professional Roles and Styles of Supervision

The professional roles of CCOs generally are categorized along a continuum that includes three approaches: (1) law enforcement, (2) case manager or broker, and (3) social work.[2] Law enforcement and social work roles are generally described as polar opposites, with law enforcement perceived as punishment and crime control oriented and social work as treatment and support oriented. Case managers or brokers are considered to be someplace in the middle. These roles, however, have been generally defined based on a dichotomy between an emphasis on punishment or rehabilitation. A review of the research and observations made by CCOs reveals that these categories tend to be overly narrow conceptualizations and do not fully capture the reality of their work with offenders.

CCOs who subscribe to a law enforcement role are depicted as more concerned about offender risk and less concerned with offender need. This is often referred to as a "surveillance" role because emphasis is placed on surveillance, monitoring behavior, rule enforcement, arrest, and revocation for violations of supervision. CCOs may be more likely to partner and collaborate with police, code enforcement, and the jail rather than with social service agencies. Offenders are expected to strictly adhere to all conditions of supervision and to anticipate sanctions for failure. When treatment is a condition of supervision, offenders are expected to enroll, participate, and navigate rehabilitative services with little assistance from their CCOs. The CCO's role is primarily to make sure the offender attends programs and not focus on whether the process or experience is working for the offender. The following quote represents an example of CCOs who view their work as similar to law enforcement.

> Our job as a CCO is monitoring and supervising—we don't chase taillights—other than that, we do the same job as a police officer, except

that we get more intimate with the offenders, meaning we go in and out of their homes and have more control over their personal lives. But, the training should be the same, we should have full commissions, we should be removed from other aspects of the Department of Corrections, such as the prisons, the social-worker aspects, and become a part of the state police and the only difference in our training would be…more of what's appropriate for probation and parole. But as far as the rest of the training, arrest, search and seizure, there's no difference. And I think for safety purposes, we need to be more aligned with law enforcement. (CCO 104)

CCOs subscribing more to a social work role are depicted as being concerned with both offender risk and need. Emphasis is placed on what an offender needs to be successful, and the CCO works to provide treatment (e.g., substance abuse and mental health counseling), rehabilitation (e.g., life skills, vocational training, education), and support services (e.g., social services, employment services, housing) to address issues that may challenge or sabotage reintegration. CCOs may be more likely to collaborate with social service, treatment, and health care agencies rather than with the police alone. Risk is monitored and weighed against both safety and treatment outcomes. Therefore, risk may be minimized through increased treatment (e.g., transfer from intensive outpatient to residential), surveillance (e.g., increased drug testing, home or office visits), or temporary confinement (jail) until a broader plan can be implemented. The following quote represents CCOs who take a social work approach to supervision.

Well, first of all, I think that it's our responsibility…to keep the community informed of risk, to keep the community safe. Secondly, we have a responsibility to the offender. I feel like it's my job to help the offender be successful in life as much as I am able to influence that offender—helping them to make changes that they need to make, helping them to be successful in their supervision and also in the community. (CCO 249)

CCOs who subscribe to a case manager or broker role are most concerned with the process of supervision. Caseworkers are not necessarily attached to either the law enforcement or social worker role but instead are engaged in managing the process by making sure offenders are appropriately monitored and have access to available services and opportunities to meet the court-ordered conditions of their supervision. Sanctions are imposed when necessary in response to technical violations and new offenses. The following quote represents a case manager perspective.

I think the things they need from me is my referrals, you know, if they need treatment, I can refer them to a treatment agency that fits their needs, either it be a public funded or a private treatment agency. They need me to monitor them [so] that they are complying with the court conditions. They don't think they need that, but I think in fact they do, because they have to make sure they're complying or they'll be in violation....And I hear about a lot of good jobs, and they come to me for job sources....And just basic information on their case...because sometimes they don't know the actual conditions and I can explain to them what the conditions are and how to comply with these conditions. (CCO 107)

Although these categories are useful in conceptualizing how CCOs' roles may reflect the tension between the goals of corrections—punishment and rehabilitation—they do not necessarily reflect the reality of the work that encompasses the need to include a range of approaches in order to be effective agents of change (see Clear & Latessa, 1993; Taxman, 2002; Taxman, Shepardson, & Byrne, 2004; Whetzel, Papparozzi, Alexander, & Lowenkamp, 2011). Although it is true that some officers may strictly adhere to a particular orientation, research shows these role categories tend to be overgeneralizations that do not take into consideration the individual attributes of the officer, the types of offenders the officer supervises, the agency or unit in which the officer works, or the resources available in the community to support supervision (Clear & Latessa, 1993; Glaser, 1964; Gunnison & Helfgott, 2008; Helfgott, 1997; Klockars, 1972; Ohlin et al., 1956; Steiner et al., 2011; Taxman, 2002; Taxman et al., 2004; West & Seiter, 2004). These simplistic categorizations also ignore the importance of the working relationships that develop between officers and offenders to achieve professional and individual goals. A review of the research and examples based on the professional experiences of CCOs shows that the responsibility to enhance community safety and achieve reintegration of offenders must span boundaries, even within CCOs' own profession, in order to be successful.

Integration of Professional Roles

In terms of a general philosophy of supervision, it appears that a majority of CCOs are still supportive of rehabilitation and providing support to offenders in spite of political shifts toward greater punitiveness, but the multiple goals of supervision are more likely to coexist than in the past (Harris, Clear, & Baird, 1989; Payne & DeMichele, 2011; Quinn & Gould, 2003; Sluder & Shearer, 1991; Taxman, 2002; Whitehead & Lindquist,

1992; Wright, 1998). Studies of CCOs conducted prior to the 1980s tend to report broad support for rehabilitation with a few exceptions (see Harris et al., 1989; Quinn & Gould, 2003, for reviews of the literature). More recent studies show a more complex interaction between the environment in which community corrections agencies function and officers' attitudes toward supervision.

Even with the political focus on crime control and punitive approaches to criminal justice, research on CCO orientation shows that most officers have not abandoned rehabilitation and view it as an important part of community supervision. It is clear, however, that they must give greater consideration to concerns about monitoring and accountability than in the past (Harris et al., 1989). Interestingly, support for rehabilitation is even found in studies conducted in states that may be considered more conservative and punitive in their political ideology (see Quinn & Gould, 2003; West & Seiter, 2004; Whitehead & Lindquist, 1992). For instance, Quinn and Gould (2003) found that Texas parole officers generally supported rehabilitation in spite of a changing political climate and diminishing resources related to treatment services in the community. Similarly, Payne and DeMichele's (2011) nationwide study of probation and parole officers found that officers overall valued multiple philosophies, such as community safety (85%), rehabilitation (82%), monitoring (80%), victim protection (78%), punishment (73%), reintegration (65%), and character reformation (46%) (also see Whitehead & Lindquist, 1992). Interestingly, in Payne and DeMichele's (2011) study, officers did not consider reintegration or character reformation to be as important as other goals of supervision. This may suggest that CCOs are more concerned about things they have direct power to influence, such as providing access to rehabilitation or protection of the community by sanctioning high-risk behaviors, rather than character reformation and reintegration, which are much more dependent on the offender's desire to change.

One might expect that individual characteristics of officers may also influence their approach to supervision. Research findings are mixed about the importance of CCOs' individual characteristics and adherence to any particular philosophy or style of supervision. Although some studies have found that personal characteristics tend to be unrelated to specific roles or to decisions related to punishment or treatment interventions (Kerbs, Jones, & Jolley, 2009; Lopez & Russell, 2008), several studies suggest that some characteristics are significantly associated with support for rehabilitation, assistance, and casework. For instance, it appears that women, those who are older, have greater seniority, and possess higher levels of education, have more prosocial personalities, are moderate to liberal in their political ideology, and more likely to be supportive of rehabilitation and related activities (Quinn & Gould, 2003; Sluder & Shearer, 1991; Trotter, 2000; Ward & Kupchick, 2010; West & Seiter, 2004).

Although research shows there is still broad support for rehabilitation, there is evidence that CCOs generally implement some level of all three categorical approaches to supervision. For the most part, their very position of having the power to coerce and the mandate to reintegrate offenders places them in the professional position to use a multitude of approaches not available to either law enforcement or social workers alone. For instance, CCOs have leverage to motivate offenders to attend programs that treatment providers do not, and they have access to a range of interventions short of arrest that police officers do not. Officers tend to take full advantage of their unique position when the opportunity presents itself to use support and/or coercion to bring about change for the offender and to enhance community safety.

Many CCOs draw on the various professional roles with flexibility when addressing specific types of offenders and their behavior (Clear & Latessa, 1993; Gunnison & Helfgott, 2013; Klockars, 1972; Ward & Kupchick, 2010; West & Sieter, 2004; Whetzel et al., 2011; Whitehead & Lindquist, 1992). For example, some officers appear to be more rigid in choosing a specific role that will then be applied to specific categories of offenders while other officers appear to follow a more fluid philosophy that changes depending on the offender's behavior and needs at the time. The following quotes are from officers who tend to more rigidly categorize offenders into amenable and nonamenable and then choose a specific role-related strategy.

> If I see an opportunity for treatment for someone who's willing or even may be cajoled into treatment, then I use that and behave in more of a treatment professional direction. If I see people who are resistant, who are criminally oriented, then my philosophy is that of law enforcement—that they are not fit to be amongst us and if they need to be locked up, that's where they need to be. (CCO 227)

> I mean, there are some people that I supervise where all I do is monitor. All I do is lock them up when they get in trouble because they are not willing to make change, or whatever the case may be. And there are other people that I go out here on the edge with and do other things. I'll avoid locking them up to be able to make sure that they're hooked up with mental health and hooked up with chemical dependency and hooked up with other agencies and, you know, it depends on the person. (CCO 236)

These CCOs demonstrate that some offenders are just not worthy of attempts at reform and that the best type of supervision is a strict law enforcement approach and revocation to a secure facility. Clearly, however, these CCOs are willing to support the treatment efforts of those who are amenable or who just need a little encouragement to get the process of change started. It is unknown how quickly CCOs make the judgment about what approach will be used to supervise a particular offender and once an orientation is chosen the likelihood of switching strategies.

Research also shows that many CCOs attempt to balance coercion and support with all offenders before making clear categorizations (Paparozzi & Gendreau, 2005; Seiter & West, 2003; Ward & Kupchick, 2010; Whitehead & Lindquist, 1992). The following quotes provide examples of a more fluid philosophy that changes depending on the circumstances and clearly indicates a willingness to move from a treatment, to a resource broker, to a law enforcement philosophy as needed within the supervision of any particular offender.

> My general philosophy has always been that I am willing to work with the offender to identify what their issues are and help them to address those issues. If I am unable to address specific issues, then I'm that resource and I can direct that offender to the appropriate agency to get the help that they need to address that behavior. If they fail to do that, and they continue with their criminal activity and violating the conditions of their supervision as outlined by the court, then we have to protect the community and in doing that, the only other alternative then is to incarcerate that individual so that we're assured that they're not going to go out and cause harm to themselves and to innocent folks in the community. (CCO 114)

This same CCO continues later in the interview:

> I think you've got to be right in the middle. You've got to be able to be a social worker. You've got to be able to be the cop. If the offender understands that, I think you are going to have more respect and you're going to have more success with the offender. The offender has to know what the boundaries are, what the guidelines are, and you know, what's going to happen if they do certain things.

An officer from Kentucky in West and Seiter's (2004, p. 49) study indicates a similar approach when stating that the role of a probation or parole officer is "two-fold...we've got two primary concerns. One is obviously the protection of the community and I think the other one is rehabilitation of a client....One is a law enforcement and one is social work and you have to kind of come to a nice mesh."

Similarly, Ward and Kupchick (2010, p. 58) conclude, "In short, punishment and rehabilitation do not appear to be regarded as two sides of the same coin, but rather, flexible and situational response options" (also see Clear & Latessa, 1993; Whitehead & Lindquist, 1992). Therefore, it is apparent that CCOs are in the unique position to role shift depending on the situation and on understanding where the offender is within the process of change and reintegration. They have a broader perspective than other professionals in criminal justice, which may indicate whether an offender's current behavior is merely a one-time relapse or whether the behavior is a complete failure and indicative of a continuation of criminal behavior.

A balanced and fluid philosophy also appears to be the most effective supervision style in reducing recidivism and increasing the successful completion of supervision. Supervision strategies that provide treatment to high-risk offenders, provide more contacts, consistently enforce conditions, address the needs of high-risk offenders before problems occur, employ CCOs with balanced law enforcement–social casework orientations, and are implemented in supportive organizational environments reduce recidivism from 10% to 30% (Paparozzi and Gendreau, 2005). Paparozzi and Gendreau (2005) argue that the success of a balanced approach by officers is most likely due to being both firm and fair in their approaches, thus providing the structure needed for offenders to understand and meet expectations and the certainty of the impending consequences for noncompliance. For instance, Wodahl and colleagues (2011 p. 400) found that "offender management strategies that incorporate both sanctions for noncompliant behavior and rewards for conforming behavior will be most effective in improving supervision outcomes." Their study showed that a ratio of four rewards to every one sanction (4:1) substantially increased the likelihood of successfully completing the intensive supervision program (ISP) with a 71% probability of completion.

The following quote reflects the notion of a firm yet fair approach to supervision.

> They need me to be consistent and they need me to be honest with them. They need to know what the expectations are and they need to absolutely know and absolutely understand what my role is and the fact that I am going to consistently supervise those conditions, and that individual, and that I am a resource. As long as they are doing what they need to do or as long as they are trying to get from point A to point B, I am there to

help them out, but I am also going to confront them on all kinds of negative behavior, even outside of what conditions might be. So, fairness, consistency, and acting as a resource, I guess. (CCO 103)

It also appears that officers who overemphasize law enforcement strategies place too much significance on surveillance and structured activity that tends to target failure with too little attention on treatment needs (Paparozzi & Gendreau, 2005). Similarly, those who overemphasize social work may be too nondirective, unstructured, and permissive, which fails to give offenders adequate guidance and boundaries necessary to stay in compliance with supervision. One CCO captured this exactly:

> There are some that are just really, really harsh on them. I think they need to go back and work in prison. And there are some that are very, very lenient with them. That puts the community at risk. It puts other CCOs at risk.... But, you're always going to have that. Because, no matter what area of corrections you're dealing with, everybody has their own style. (CCO 101)

It is clear that all three professional roles, law enforcement, case management, and social work, are employed in community supervision, but it is often a fluid combination that is most effective in achieving correctional goals related to both offender change and community safety.

Building Professional Relationships
With Offenders: The Human Side of Supervision

Too often CCOs are viewed as mere observers of offender behavior who react only when there is a problem versus being active participants who understand and engage those on their caseloads (Taxman, 2002). Similar to other human service professions, CCOs interact with offenders in ways that not only make their work easier but also more enjoyable. It is important to understand how CCOs' activities are connected to offender outcomes and whether building professional relationships with offenders enhances the quality of their work. Differences of opinion about how offenders should be treated result in conflict, not just related to offender behavior but also among colleagues, in the court's conditions of supervision, and in DOC policy. Exploring the connection between CCOs' philosophy of supervision and how they conduct their work makes it apparent that the quality and content of CCO-offender interactions is central to achieving successful supervision outcomes.

Supervision activities. An important shift in research has occurred from focusing on offender attributes and their likelihood to fail to consideration of how CCOs' professional approaches and practices may have both positive and negative influence on offender outcomes (Dowden & Andrews, 2004). This line of inquiry focused on the content and quality of CCOs' professional behavior reinforces the need to balance and integrate supervision styles to fully address offenders' risk and needs.

It appears that an officer's supervision philosophy is related to time spent on activities such as counseling, making referrals, providing classes, monitoring behavior, surveillance, home and office visits, paperwork, and other activities related to supervision. Seiter and West (2003) considered whether CCOs' surveillance or casework style is related to how officers spend their time supervising offenders. They found that "officers who rated themselves...as having more of a casework than a surveillance style, actually do spend a majority of their time doing casework-categorized activities than surveillance-categorized activities" (Seiter & West, 2003, p. 68; also see Payne & DeMichele, 2011). Seiter and West (2003) also report that officers in their study spent about 56% of their time on casework and 41% on surveillance activities, regardless of whether they supervised a traditional or specialized caseload, and that 41% of officers' time was spent on primarily three activities: counseling offenders (16.4%), writing violation reports (13.6%), and conducting assessments of offenders (11.4%).

West and Seiter (2004, p. 47), in a follow-up study, report that "officers who perceived themselves as more casework oriented...spent the same amount of time engaged in surveillance activities as officers who perceived themselves as more surveillance oriented." In addition, DeMichele (2007) found that officers spent most of their time taking care of administrative tasks (36 out of 120 hours per month), followed by home visits (20 hours per month) and motivational interviewing (18 hours per month), with collateral contacts, court appearances, technical violations, and presentence investigations each clustering from 10 to 14 hours per month. These findings give insight on how much time and emphasis are placed on office work that establishes an administrative record of supervision versus time spent on offender-related activities that directly affect outcomes related to risk or need (also see Dowden & Andrews, 2004).

CCOs' emphasis on surveillance and assistance also appears to influence the degree to which CCOs use sanctions, revocation, or rewards with offenders. For instance, a recent study of Ohio parole officers' attitudes toward supervision shows that officers' adherence to authoritarian and assistance supervision styles is related to their likelihood of applying sanctions or pursuing revocation (Steiner et al., 2011). Steiner and colleagues found that officers classified as high authority/low assistance and high authority/high assistance were more likely to be enforcement oriented. They also found it "worth noting, however, that high-authority/high-assistance officers were the only type of officers that were more inclined to both enforcement and reward behavior. High-authority/low-assistance officers were only more inclined towards enforcement behaviors, while low-authority/high-assistance officers were not disposed towards enforcement or reward behaviors" (p. 919). Those who scored higher on the high-assistance measure were more likely to reward offenders who completed supervision goals, and those who scored higher on the authority measure were more likely to pursue revocation hearings (Steiner et al., 2011). These findings show that officers' adherence to a supervision style influences their supervision activities (also see West & Seiter, 2004).

In addition to the influence of supervision style on practice, researchers have also considered how professional orientation may interact with the orientation emphasized (assistance or control) by the agency at which the CCO works. Based on a small sample of CCOs working in three separate intensive supervision units (two assistance and one control oriented), Clear and Latessa (1993) report that CCOs' tasks are driven both by personal role identity and organizational philosophy. They found that "preference for the authority role does not suppress selection of support tasks with cases, nor does preference for assistance suppress selection of control tasks with cases" (p. 445). They conclude that law enforcement and social work approaches are not incompatible.

Importantly, recent studies have moved beyond the measurement of tasks to quantify the content of CCO-offender meetings. Not surprisingly, the topics CCOs focus on during their meetings with offenders matter in reducing recidivism (Dowden & Andrews, 2004; Taxman, 2002; Trotter, 2000). For instance, Bonta and colleagues, while studying the content of CCO meetings with offenders, discovered that most meetings averaged 22 minutes and included both conversation with the offender as well as clerical work related to the offender's case (Bonta, Rugge, Scott, Bourgon, & Yessine, 2008). They discovered that marital and family issues, substance abuse, and housing were the issues most often discussed while employment, antisocial attitudes, and criminal peers were the least often discussed. Interestingly, Bonta and colleagues (2008) found that the more time spent by CCOs addressing ex-offender criminogenic needs (e.g., antisocial attitudes, peers) the more likely recidivism decreased, and the more time spent on the conditions of supervision, the more likely recidivism increased (also see Dowden & Andrews, 2004).[3]

A clearer understanding of what leads to success for those on supervision and evidence from related fields have led to considering how CCOs may be able to motivate offenders to change and directly influence positive outcomes (Taxman, 2002; Trotter, 2000). Trotter (2000), in a study of Australian probation workers, found that those trained to model prosocial values and work through problem-solving processes focused on offense-related issues significantly reduced recidivism in comparison to officers who did not. Similarly, many agencies are adopting motivational interviewing (MI) with the intention of changing the tone and content of CCOs' meetings with offenders from negative compliance-centered exchanges to an emphasis on optimism and change (see Andrews & Bonta, 2010; Walters, Alexander, & Vader, 2008; Walters, Vader, Nguyen, Harris, & Eells, 2011). Taxman (2002) argues that CCOs need to have technical skills, full engagement in the process of change, communication skills, and the ability to manage offenders' new strategies of change. Unfortunately, based on a study of how CCOs communicate with offenders, she reports that fewer than one-quarter used open-ended questions so offenders could provide an explanation for their behavior; agents did not use communication techniques to engage offenders in the change process; and agents' overall communication skills were fairly minimal (Taxman, 2002).

It appears important that offenders have the opportunity to discuss issues of psychological and emotional relevance versus simply what will happen to them if they do not comply (see Gunnison & Helfgott, 2013). Obviously, knowing the rules of supervision is important, but compliance is much more about receiving guidance and support related to resolving conflict and coping maturely with challenges, whether they are personal or process related (Gunnison & Helfgott, 2013; Lutze, Johnson, Clear, Latessa, & Slate, 2012; Lutze & Kigerl, 2013). Therefore, viewing community corrections as a human service profession "that combines accountability and support with the intention of reducing ex-offenders' feelings of stress, anxiety, fear and other psychological needs is important to success for both the ex-offender and the criminal justice system" (Lutze & Kigerl, 2013; also see Gregory, 2010). In order for offenders to expose their weaknesses concerning personal issues and living conditions, they must have a relationship with their CCO built on more than the technicalities of case management and impersonal surveillance, monitoring, and accountability.

Building relationships within supervision. There is some debate about whether building meaningful and professional relationships with clients assists with the process of change and improves counseling outcomes for offender populations. Some argue that building meaningful relationships enhances the trust and respect necessary to lay the foundation for change while others have argued that professionals who possess coercive power within treatment settings violate the basic premise of equality-based relationships necessary for clients to feel safe while going through vulnerable periods of change (see Dowden & Andrews, 2004; McCleary, 1992; Ohlin et al., 1956; Taxman, 2002; Van Voorhis, Braswell, & Lester, 2000).

CCOs certainly hold coercive power over the offenders they supervise. They have the power to revoke supervision and return offenders to prison, to implement intermediate sanctions including curfews and jail time, to admit individuals to residential treatment facilities, and to initiate the arrest of those who commit new crimes. In addition, the offender is ultimately coerced by the state to comply with supervision, including treatment. Shapiro and Schwartz (2001) argue that typically, parolees do not consider their interactions with parole officers as relationships. They argue that "each distrusts the other because of the inherent power imbalance. . . . Relationships like these do not encourage compliance or promote change—they are adversarial, controlling, and fraught with resistance" (p. 59).

One can imagine that many offenders may be unlikely to trust others to follow through with promises because they have been betrayed by "the system" before or they live in dysfunctional families and dangerous communities that are consistently unreliable. Similarly, officers may have put trust in offenders who have then failed by causing professional problems or, worse, committing new crimes. It is easy to understand how each side may be cautious or unwilling to place trust in the other no matter how good their intentions (see Lutze & Murphy, 1999, for a similar discussion about institutional corrections officers).

In spite of these challenges presented by an authoritarian relationship and social distance, there is a sense that CCOs can develop meaningful relationships with offenders characterized by respect, rapport, collaboration, and trust, and there is evidence that such relationships can be very helpful to offenders attempting to navigate the legal, social, and emotional aspects of reentry (Dowden & Andrews, 2004; Gregory, 2010; Gunnison & Helfgott, 2013; Ireland & Berg, 2008; Shapiro & Schwartz, 2001; Taxman, 2002; Van Voorhis et al., 2000; Whitehead & Lindquist, 1992). Offenders on supervision have reported that a positive relationship with their community corrections officer was helpful in successfully negotiating reentry into their families and the community (Cobbina, 2010; Leibrich, 1994). Ex-offenders report that having someone to talk to about their problems, being treated as an individual, having conditions connected directly to the type of crime they committed, being clear on expectations, and being connected to services that provide for basic human needs helped to appropriately resolve many of the challenges confronted during the process of reentry (Leibrich, 1994; Lutze & Kigerl, 2013).

CCOs are motivated by interacting with offenders whom they like and believe they can help, even if there are specific challenges along the way

(Gregory, 2010; Whitehead & Lindquist, 1992). In addition, CCOs believe having a relationship based on respect and rapport enhances compliance and provides greater safety for the officer (Ireland & Berg, 2008; West & Seiter, 2004). The following quotes reflect community corrections as truly a human business that conflicts with a purely "warehousing" or "assembly line" form of justice:

> Because they are an addict doesn't mean they don't have a personality. We all have those people, that in my job, I might be arresting a guy, but I look forward to the day that he comes in and sits in my office because he's got an engaging personality. He challenges [me] to think. He's intelligent; he's got a sense of humor, whatever. So, you see the person as a person and that's ultimately what we come down to, is we are working with people. If these were just cattle, it'd be easier. But you're working with people, with human beings, what are you trying to do? (CCO 226)

Another CCO commented,

> With me, I try to listen. I want them to be successful. I mean, even if they violate, you know,...but "I'll work with you if you just hang in there with me, I'll hang in there with you."...I have offenders that move—or like they're gonna move—and they ask me, "Well, where's your area? I want to make sure I stay in your area." They don't want to leave because they've had bad experiences with other officers and, you know, makes me feel good because I think it says a lot for my supervision style. And those that are like that, usually, they'll slip up a little bit and I've even put them in jail and they come back and say, "Well, I admit, I screwed up. But you were fair and you told me up front that you'll do that." (CCO 102)

Similarly, Gregory (2010, p. 2287), based on interviews with probation officers in the United Kingdom (UK), concluded that "the other person in these circumstances is not a separate other, upon whom a solution can be imposed, but is a fellow human being with whom the solution is jointly created."

In addition to the general perspective that community corrections is a human business, and therefore offenders should be treated respectfully, it is clear that many officers believe building trust and respect also increases officer safety (Ireland & Berg, 2008). For instance, officers expressed that, for the most part, if they developed a rapport and treated individuals in a "firm, fair, and consistent" manner, then CCOs were more likely to defuse volatile situations and be less likely to engage in physical conflict even when making an arrest. For instance, when asked about conflict with offenders, the following officers responded that conflict was most likely to occur if they treated offenders badly.

> Kind of the Gestapo tactics where officers that don't do anything [but] roust guys, always shaking guys down. And then they wonder why guys don't want to report or why guys give them a bad time or threaten them or whatever.... So, like I said, you can treat people with respect and still arrest them. I can respect the hell out of a guy for trying his damnedest, but, you know, he slips back into dealing dope, I can be nice to a guy while I am searching his house or while I am taking him to jail have a pleasant conversation about how the guy's got to change his ways. You know, the biggest conflict is when people don't treat offenders with respect and only look at the negatives. (CCO 103)

> You know, you've heard of people power tripping; I think a lot of people get into this career field for the wrong reasons—they enjoy power, they enjoy pushing people.... There are certain people that I will not go out with. We go out and something goes bad, you know, they start running their mouth, they actually agitate the person and start to cause problems, um, it's not a safe environment for the rest of us. And I think that's getting rarer, especially in our unit. (CCO 106)

Similarly, in a qualitative study of female parole officers by Ireland and Berg (2008, p. 485), a majority reported "the belief that respecting a parolee (through words and actions) resulted in cooperative parolees. Conversely, disrespecting parolees (e.g., using degrading terms, embarrassing them in front of their families) resulted in uncooperative and even combative parolees." An officer in their study reported,

> I have encountered situations where a parolee has actually been protective of me, either against people in the neighborhood or other individuals in the home. I think it all boils down to the respect you have garnered as a result of the relationship you develop with this individual. (p. 487)

It is also clear that not all officers are comfortable with thinking about their interactions with offenders as relationships built on mutual trust. Many officers wanted to create clear professional boundaries and make offenders feel as if they were always present, even when they were not, and to create a constant feeling of doubt so that offenders would be afraid to get into trouble. For instance, the following officer is clearly grappling with the expectation that offenders need to trust enough to comply with supervision, but the interaction with many offenders is laden with an expectation of dishonesty and a lack of trust by the CCO.

> The most important thing, I think, is for them to be able to trust me. For one, know that I will hunt their ass down. Any time of the night or day, I will hunt them down if they don't comply with certain minimal things. So, it is very important for me not to lie to my offenders. Now, that doesn't mean that I won't tell a lie to someone to get a very dangerous person off the street. But then I've burnt that. I have lost that piece with them. Somehow, I have to establish this relationship that they trust me, so that they come in here—it doesn't mean that they won't lie to me—I might be vague with them about things, I might just not tell them things, and I expect them to lie to me—let me back that up—I don't expect them to lie, but I am not surprised when they do. I try to set expectations like I would with anybody else. (CCO 227)

This CCO is not alone in expressing concern about trusting offenders. For instance, Whitehead and Lindquist (1992), in a study of CCOs in Alabama, found that 51% agreed that you cannot ever completely trust an offender, and 60% agreed that leniency leads to being taken advantage of by offenders. Reasonably so, with most CCOs it appears a lack of trust is directly related to issues of personal safety, being "conned," and uncertainty about what the offender may do to violate public safety. Trust and safety are closely intertwined with the issue of whether CCOs should carry firearms as a part of their work and how carrying guns might alter the working relationship between CCOs and offenders.

Not surprising, the debate about whether CCOs should carry guns is a powerful flash point regarding supervision styles, building trusting relationships, and ensuring officer safety. Some officers strongly believe guns increase their safety in the field, while others strongly believe they decrease safety and the ability to build relationships with offenders. Interestingly, this debate also gets mixed in with relational issues such as trust and the ability to communicate effectively with offenders, and where CCOs stand represents differences in how they perceive their role working with offenders. (The firearms issue is discussed more in Chapter 4 regarding CCOs' perceptions of DOC policy.)

The firearms debate has been heightened for several reasons. First, as community corrections populations began to shift from lower-risk nonfelons to higher-risk and -need offenders during the 1980s, CCOs began to debate the need and pursue the ability to carry firearms (Lindner & Bonn,

1996; Petersilia, 2003; Sluder & Shearer, 1991). Second, Petersilia (2003) suggests that CCOs began to consider carrying firearms as their orientations shifted from an education based primarily in social work in the 1980s to contemporary officers most often educated in criminal justice, a discipline that stemmed from the need to professionalize law enforcement officers. This shift in the educational background and expertise of CCOs has helped drive more law enforcement–oriented approaches to community supervision. Research appears to support the relationship between CCO orientations and their desire to carry firearms. For instance, Sigler and McGraw (1984), in a survey of Alabama probation and parole officers, found there was little conflict between those who take a treatment role and those more law enforcement oriented, but law enforcement–oriented officers were significantly more likely to carry weapons than treatment-oriented officers (also see Sluder & Shearer, 1991).

Based on a national survey of probation and parole officers, Lindner and Bonn (1996) reported field officer safety and carrying guns as important to field officers. In the open-ended portion of their survey, officers responded both in support of and opposition to carrying guns. For instance, one officer wrote, "In recent years attitudes have turned 100 percent and most probation officers would prefer to carry guns." Another wrote, "Probation officers may not want to carry as it may interfere with [the] social services/rehabilitative role" (Lindner & Bonn, 1996, p. 21).

Interestingly, another study based on interviews with female CCOs in California found that most officers did not believe firearms were necessary (also see Sluder & Shearer, 1991) but carried weapons either because they were mandated to do so or because they felt that carrying a gun gave them credibility with male officers (Ireland & Berg, 2008). One of the subjects stated,

> When I was first a parole agent, we did not carry weapons. When I left, it was an option [*pause*]; it was also a part of my decision to leave. I did not feel that carrying a weapon was good for the job. We had not done that; you learned to talk your way through things; you learned to look at things differently [*pause*] in order to resolve your problems....When I came back, it was mandatory to carry a weapon....I became comfortable with it. I've never had to use it for protection or because I was in fear (Ireland & Berg, 2008, p. 484).

While the comment from the California study suggest a contemplative acquiescence to firearms as a mandated part of the job, the following comment indicates that carrying guns symbolizes the conflict about whether community supervision is about law enforcement or assistance and the ability of officers to choose.

> So now if we are armed, we have to go out looking like a SWAT team: Kevlar vests, fanny pack, the big belts, the big coats,...It's like, you know, you show up looking like ROBOCOP going, "Hi, I am here to help you." Well, the whole thing, kind of, the picture doesn't make sense with the sound....The rule of thumb is always when you strap metal on your hip, your mouth stops working. And there is a certain amount of psychology applied to it, that when you are the biggest bully on the block, you don't have to talk anymore. (CCO 234)

In the previous two comments, firearms are perceived as inhibiting verbal communication and the building of rapport to resolve conflict through cooperation. The perception is that carrying a gun begins conflict resolution with the threat of force. Fogel (1992, p. xiv) colorfully summarizes this point by stating,

> a parole officer can be seen going off to his/her appointed rounds with Freud in one hand and a .38 Smith and Wesson in the other hand. It is by no means clear that Freud is as helpful as the .38 in most areas where parole officers venture—at least in the great urban areas of the nation. Is Freud a backup to the .38? Or is the .38 carried to "support" Freud?

Yet not all CCOs believe carrying a gun changes their relationship with those they are supervising. For instance,

> In fact, it's funny. They go, "Geez, we thought you were crazy that you didn't! I wouldn't do your job without one!" [laughing]. I've never heard anybody that ever felt it changed anything and never has and never will, in my view. (CCO ---)

The debate over guns and their influence on supervision strategies highlights that differences in supervision styles and how offenders are treated may cause tension between CCOs (for an exception, see Sigler & McGraw, 1984). Although most research has considered the conflict between what policymakers and administrators expect of CCOs and CCOs' individual styles, little, if any, research has considered possible role conflict when CCOs with more fluid philosophical approaches to supervision are at odds with their more-rigid peers, those either too treatment oriented or too law enforcement oriented (Ohlin et al., 1956; Sigler & McGraw, 1984). For example, the following CCO expresses frustration with peers' rigidity and behavior that conflicts with their primary style, whether it is law enforcement, social work, or case management. Once again, issues related to the importance of building relationships and safety are key.

> That's one of the reasons why I walked away from the caseload that I was on, is that I didn't want to do what they perceived should be done. What they want to do is something that will not work and I can't do that. The gangsters were fine. But I saw a lot of different agendas—as opposed to being for community safety.... We would run the gauntlet of, we need to put these people down, we need to hammer them, put the boot to these people, you know, hurt them and run them out of town. Okay, well, that doesn't work obviously—it's been around for what, a thousand years?—crime.... So I would go out there and I would talk to them like I am talking to you. A couple of times I'd even go in the morning, one of them would say, "Hey [name], let me get you a cup of coffee." "Cool, why not." That happened twice. I consider that a good thing that we can still treat them in such a way that they are not going to want to put a dagger in you. The dagger comes from the people behind you going, "What, are you friends with them?"... "Don't be nice to them! These guys are gangsters, these guys are just like ...!" So? I can run them out of town, but law enforcement can't run them out of town? So you get that—you start to be friendly to them because you are what? Nice? Nice means complicit all of a sudden here? And so we see a lot of that stuff and it was too much. (CCO ---)

These comments regarding safety, carrying guns, and building relationships suggest the possibility that officers' role conflict may be driven by their peers' rigidity and the frustration with singular approaches to supervision at the expense of all others. They also reflect that not building relationships and interacting, even with the worst offenders, in a respectful and humane fashion is detrimental to achieving the goals of community supervision and enhancing officer safety. Gregory (2010, p. 2287) also found that many of the officers in her sample "are conscious of their feelings of continued responsibility towards clients, even when the clients are difficult and dangerous people." Unnecessary authoritarianism as well as leniency or passiveness with offenders is perceived as detrimental to both the offender and other CCOs. Therefore, building relationships was generally viewed as positive and necessary to enhancing offender compliance with supervision, making the quality of interaction more enjoyable and increasing safety for all involved. Interestingly, but not surprisingly, the decision to carry a gun or not magnified the issues related to the type and quality of relationships CCOs should have with offenders and ultimately what philosophy should drive the profession.

CCOs, no matter their supervision style or perspective, must adapt to external forces that dictate the parameters of their responsibility and directly influence the quality of the time they spend with offenders. Although many of the laws and policies that guide the work of CCOs and mandate particular behaviors of offenders are generally created with good intentions, they often sabotage the potential for successful outcomes for both staff and offenders and ultimately the system.

Organizational Attributes and Their Influence on Supervision

Regardless of the professional orientation held by CCOs and their beliefs about how best to interact with and supervise offenders, they work within a larger system that has the power to influence how they manage their work with offenders. For instance, CCOs may believe in a particular orientation but feel the need to manage offenders differently due to external pressures such as court-imposed conditions, DOC administrative policy, and practical issues such as caseload size. These influences on supervision tend to be outside of their immediate control and often cause conflict due to the disconnect between the reality of offenders' lives and the expectations imposed on them by the courts or the reality of the CCOs' workload compared to the expectations of the agency. These conditions appear to create tension that interferes with CCOs' potential to build close working relationships with offenders or to conduct their work in ways they believe more productively serve the court, the DOC, the community, and offenders.

Court-ordered conditions. Although CCOs hold full responsibility for supervising offenders, in many states they may only hold offenders accountable for the conditions ordered by the judge during sentencing. Many of the conditions imposed by the court are standard, such as abiding by all laws, staying away from criminal peers, remaining within the jurisdiction, reporting to the CCO, seeking and maintaining employment, and participating in treatment (Petersilia, 2003; Travis & Stacey, 2010). If, for instance, a CCO identifies an offender need not listed in the court's conditions, the CCO cannot subject the offender to additional conditions without returning to court for the judge to modify the conditions of supervision.

This can make it difficult for a CCO who may identify that a particular offender, for example, needs substance abuse or mental health treatment to support successful reintegration. The CCO cannot make an offender participate because it has not been imposed by the court. In addition, court delays can also cause a CCO to miss an opportunity to get an amenable offender into treatment in a timely manner.[4] The following quote provides an example of an officer attempting to problem-solve the difference between court orders and the offender's real problem in a meaningful way.

> I mean, I've had somebody who the judge has said that this individual needs to complete an anger management class and a parenting class and it has nothing about drugs or alcohol, nothing about any of this other stuff. And yet, this guy came into my office and finally said, "You've gotta help me out, I've been smoking pot for seven years every day and when I don't smoke pot, that's when I get angry." That is kind of like the baseline issue. So, you know, he needs to do these other things, but these other things aren't gonna matter until he gets clean and sober. So, I mean, you are conflicted with it, but I also have no problem doing a report to the court explaining what I am doing and why I am doing it. I guess why I am deviating from their order [is] because the way the sentencing laws are, if he wasn't drunk or under the influence when this happened, then they couldn't have made a drug and alcohol condition. But it came out and this is somebody who's actually taking charge and being motivated to take care of it on his own. (CCO 226)

A CCO may also believe the conditions imposed by the court are unnecessary or unrealistic and are likely to lead to noncompliance for justifiable reasons. For instance, this may happen when offenders are subjected to treatment unrelated to their risk and need or when they are required to comply with conditions they cannot adhere to due to physical or mental handicaps. It is evident that the court has direct influence over the potential quality of supervision and the direction taken by CCOs (DeMichele, 2007; Seiter & West, 2003). The following quote captures the frustration of having to go along with court-ordered conditions that are very likely setting up the offender to fail.

> I mean, we have judges who are sentencing [people] who are developmentally disabled, mentally ill, and chemically addicted and they think they are giving them a break or the public defender is working to give them a break by dealing community service hours. I mean, that person's chances of doing community service hours are nil and then you look

down the road at the idea of, now you're gonna have to convert those back to jail time because you have no other option, and, depending on who their CCO is, they can do up to 60 days in jail for a violation on that and some of that is just not fair. (CCO 226)

Similarly, another CCO commented on conditions set by the court that are likely to result in ongoing failure.

. . . they are placed on a telephone reporting system, they can't afford to make the 1-900 calls, they don't have phones, and they're pretty much told they will do it, there's no other way. To prevent a conflict, I just have them mail it in. Again, the court order mandates them to go into treatment, they live 50 miles up on top of a mountain, no public transit system, no vehicles—most of them have had their license suspended for three lifetimes—it's just not realistic. There are so many unrealistic orders—more unrealistic orders from the court than unrealistic policy. . . . [Interviewer: So how do you resolve that?] You have to go back to the court and try to convince the court that that's not realistic. And sometimes the judges will not bend, and so it's really difficult to tell an offender that you understand his reasons for not attending treatment, but the court insists and all I can tell them [is] "If you don't do it, I have to report to the court, and if the court throws you in jail, that's their prerogative. It's pretty much out of my hands." I have to report the violation, even though I don't see it as a willful violation. I think there's mitigating circumstances there. So, that's the majority of the conflicts that we have. (CCO 104)

Unrealistic expectations set by the court were also viewed as a problem in interviews of probation officers conducted in the United Kingdom by Gregory (2010, p. 2282). For example, one of her subjects responded, "I often have said that one of the stressful things is that we have to negotiate between the reality of their lives and the kind of expectations that the organization places on them, and that is stressful" (also see Klockars, 1972; Ohlin et al., 1956).

A focus on how the courts may be in conflict with officers' styles is important because it redefines what drives CCO decision making that is beyond the scope of the CCO's or the DOC's influence. No matter what CCOs know about proven evidence-based practices, and regardless of their professional experience and knowledge of working with offenders in the community, they are bound by court-ordered conditions that may be disconnected from what works for the offender or CCO. This may be of greater concern for officers who emphasize treatment rather than surveil-lance because it requires officers to go beyond basic rule enforcement and instead focus on directing resources and energy that may conflict with policy or run against the normative grain to produce outcomes (Ward & Kupchick, 2010; also see Kern & Bahr, 1974).

Conflict between the court and CCOs also reflects a disconnect between the court (i.e., judges and attorneys) and those who live in poverty and do not have access to common means such as phones, reliable trans-portation, and expendable resources beyond providing for the basics of survival. As discussed shortly, failure to comply with supervision then results in additional penalties on top of the existing penalties offenders haven't been able to complete due to legitimate life circumstances. Thus, the accumulation of penalties does not engender change but instead sabo-tages the ability of offenders to ever move forward. The CCO quoted earlier (CCO 226) suggested later in the interview that judges, prosecutors, and defense attorneys need to be educated on what works and what is realistic for offenders to achieve while being supervised in the community.

DOC policy. In addition to mandated court conditions, the department of corrections may set policy that dictates the parameters for supervision. Policy often determines the number and type of contacts CCOs have with offenders each month based on an offender's level of risk and need; deter-mines the level of documentation necessary to manage risk if an offender fails; and limits what programs may be used to provide treatment or other services. Administrative policy can at times make CCOs feel very limited in their choices related to supervision and may conflict with what they believe is best for the offender (also see Chapter 4). Kerbs and colleagues, in a study of sociodemographic, occupational, and organizational charac-teristics, found that "the PPOs' discretionary decisions were predomi-nantly affected by organizational characteristics beyond the PPOs' daily control" (Kerbs et al., 2009, p. 435). They argue that, given how "agency policies mandated or inhibited response to certain violations, one must question whether such policies are diverting line officers from making discretionary decisions that they feel are in the best interests of community safety and offender rehabilitation" (Kerbs et al., 2009, p. 438; also see Ohlin et al., 1956).

For example, many CCOs may feel restricted by administrative policy but are reluctant to divert too far away because of the potential negative consequences. This is illustrated by the following comment:

> I would like to be more in their lives than I am right now. There are some boundaries that we can't cross...not supposed to be out there sabotaging

them either. But there are some choices that I would like to make about how I set up a supervision plan. It might be a little different than what case management wants. It might be a little different than what LSI-R[5] is. I might want to be out in the community 6 times a month instead of what they say I have to do. I mean, I guess you have the discretion to go out and to do those things, but that's not what you'd be held accountable for. You'd be held accountable for "did you do what they told you you had to do?" So, you have to balance those. Do I want to do what I think is a really good job and really have an impact on the community and the offender or do I want to make sure I always follow the policies? Well, if I don't follow the policies, I can get fired. I can't do this anyway. And a lot of people war with that. (CCO 223)

CCOs may, however, go beyond policy because they feel it will make a difference.

I have this kid who comes in on supervision and I did an LSI and he scored minimum and we as a department have had to make a decision where we're not gonna focus our energy on the minimums because there's just not enough resources to do that. Well, dumping the minimums hadn't happened yet, so I hung on to this kid's case because he's somebody who didn't have a criminal record before this at all, has very supportive parents at home, a good support system, been involved with church most of his life—I mean, everything was there, he's a smart kid, got a high IQ. . . . And so the closer I looked, what I realized is what was going on, he had some drug and alcohol issues, mostly alcohol and part of that had to do with depression . . . specifically sent him to a place where they would do a dual diagnosis, and sure enough, he was diagnosed as being clinically depressed. They got him on Paxil and got him going to treatment and he now is financial only. . . . But it took a lot of extra energy and typically he would be a minimum that we wouldn't spend any time with. . . . He could have gone either way, and had somebody not paid attention and just caught the little stuff. . . . You know, we will probably never see him again. (CCO 236)

Yet another CCO expresses frustration about a system that keeps people on supervision for extended periods who are not dangerous to the community and who will remain a burden to the system because of an inescapable cycle of harm interwoven into sanctioning practices.

Policy probably more than statute dictates the way we do business. I feel, for instance, someone's been through so many treatment programs, they've been counseled to death, and I don't feel that further beating a dead horse is appropriate, and sometimes I don't feel that more jail time is appropriate. There again, mostly I feel that way in cases where someone has been on for...a lengthy period of time, they already owe like $50,000–$100,000 restitution and they're kept on supervision—they won't work or can't work, or for some reason, can't come up with the money, they're not paying, warrants are issued, they go back into court, and so many courts just give them another 30 days or 60 days, tell them to make payments or they'll be back, and it's just a revolving door. I feel sad for the victims,...and I think you have to come to a point where you just terminate the individual—meaning, like, discharge NOT the other meaning of the termination [laughing]. (CCO 104)

The point that these CCOs make is important because it cuts to the core of recent movements, whether focused on punishment or rehabilitation, to limit officer discretion. The focus of both ideologies is often about how to limit discretion in a way that moves front-line workers to be more punitive or supportive or legalistic. Although limits on discretion are good when attempting to remove bias or abuse of authority from the system, they may also unintentionally stifle innovative problem solving that favors both the offender and the agency. Instead of focusing on discretion, it may be more important to clearly develop officers' expertise about what constitutes success, what evidence demonstrates success, and what tools are most effective in achieving success. This allows CCOs to reach their goals in a measurable way with each offender.

Understanding what offenders need or how they may best be managed comes from knowing the offender, the offender's life circumstances, and whether he or she is making legitimate attempts to comply with and complete supervision. Basically, CCOs need to know and build professional relationships with offenders in order to effectively use their expertise and discretion. Providing CCOs with the professional discretion necessary to effectively manage both risk and need has to be supported through organizational structure and planned implementation of a continuum of options to both support and sanction offenders (see Chapter 4 and Chapter 5). This can only be achieved, however, if caseloads are kept within manageable limits. As discussed in the next section, managing large caseloads creates stress and influences the depth of the relationships CCOs have with offenders and the extent they may help with the process of change through the application of sanctions, rewards, and assistance.

Caseloads. There has been ongoing concern that large caseloads (number of offenders) and increased workloads (time to manage tasks) may decrease the number of face-to-face contacts necessary to get to know offenders and their needs, which may lead to fewer services to avert potential failure (Grattet, Petersilia, Lin, & Beckman, 2009; Gunnison & Helfgott, 2011; Weber, 1958). Whitehead and Lindquist (1992, p. 22) provide some support for this concern by reporting that "officers reporting greater hours of client contact tended to be less punitive while those reporting larger caseloads tended to be more [punitive]." Although some argue that 30 to 50 offenders is the ideal caseload depending on the risk and need level of those being supervised, most caseloads grossly exceed this range (DeMichele, 2007; Grattet et al., 2009; Kerbs et al., 2009; Lutze, Smith, & Lovrich, 2004; Petersilia, 2003; Taxman, 2002; West & Seiter, 2004). In a nationwide survey of community corrections officers conducted by DeMichele (2007), he reports that slightly over 70% of officers indicated their workloads were either slightly or much too large. On average, officers suggested that 77 offenders was the correct number to adequately supervise but that general caseloads were 30% larger (mean = 106) than the suggested size. It is difficult to imagine how officers are to achieve any success in holding offenders accountable or relating to their needs when face-to-face meetings are rare and incredibly short when they do occur.

Interestingly, most of the research on caseload size and recidivism shows no difference in outcomes (Taxman, 2002). Much of the recent research on caseload size has been conducted using intensive supervision programs (ISPs) where caseload size is capped and high-risk offenders are subjected to increased levels of supervision through greater surveillance, monitoring of behavior, and contacts (see Taxman, 2002). Most of the research on ISPs shows that reduced caseloads do not reduce recidivism and generally increase the chances for failure due to technical violations (see Taxman, 2002). There is evidence however that ISPs can be effective in reducing both recidivism and technical violations when a balanced approach is taken between surveillance and programs that meet offender needs and follow proven practices (Dowden & Andrews, 2004). For example, a recent study by Jalbert and colleagues (2010) found that an ISP designed to rely on evidence-based practices inclusive of both surveillance and treatment, and comprised of caseloads that were 30% smaller (30 vs. 50), reduced recidivism for all offenses by 25.5% after 6 months.

For traditional caseloads, however, it is difficult to imagine that CCOs have adequate time to meet with offenders, assess their needs, and intervene in anything but superficial interactions short of arrest. For instance, Grattet and colleagues (2009) report that 80% of parolees in California have fewer than two 15-minute face-to-face meetings with their parole officer each month, and these nearly always happen at the officer's office (also see Bonta et al, 2008; DeMichele, 2007; Petersilia, 2003; Takagi,

1973). Takagi (1973) argues that because CCOs have so few contacts and so little time with those on supervision, they must rely on others to gather information, usually the police. This is an important observation because it shows how the working relationships of CCOs become structurally skewed toward the police, which enhances the surveillance and accountability aspects of supervision while ignoring other important collaborations with helping organizations such as social services, mental health services, and treatment providers (Murphy & Lutze, 2009). Structural influences are also evident in Seiter and West's (2003, p. 70) study, where they found "some officers believe a casework orientation to be most effective in the long term, but that caseload size and paperwork requirements sometimes 'force' them to adopt more surveillance-type activities to move offenders through the system" (also see West & Seiter, 2004). For instance, the following quotes illustrate how caseload size directly influences the quality of supervision.

> So, it's frustrating knowing that I think I have the skills to make a difference and to intervene. But, given the number on my caseload and the requirements on me, I'm almost prevented from doing that. And it's basically you address the squeaky wheel. (CCO 210)

> I can't do—I could be sitting in a cop shop now and with 80 people on my caseload, I still can't do good service to that neighborhood based on that. You know, something's got to be done either about the number of people [CCOs] we have or the number of cases we supervise because, I mean, otherwise, nothing's gonna change. (CCO 2--)

Large caseloads limit the ability of CCOs to build relationships based on face-to-face contacts that include the exchange of useful information and understanding about how the offender is coping and how the officer may help. Without knowledge about the offender, officers may find it best to err on the side of caution and sanction an offender because it is easier and less likely to be criticized if something goes wrong later. Although there is no direct evidence to support this, there are some findings to indicate that this does happen. For instance, a national study of special probation mental health units showed that those with larger caseloads were significantly more likely to endorse revocation and jail and less likely to endorse problem solving (Skeem, Emke-Francis, & Louden, 2006). It may be that most CCOs monitor caseloads that far exceed their capacity to either consistently sanction, reward, or support offenders, and therefore the finding that larger traditional caseloads result in fewer technical violations is due to a lack of time and resources to do anything well.

BENEFITS OF UNDERSTANDING CCO ORIENTATIONS AND PROFESSIONAL RELATIONSHIPS IN THE CONTEXT OF BOUNDARY SPANNING

The goal of community supervision to ensure community safety necessitates both surveillance and assistance. Given what we know about offenders' risk and needs it is naïve to believe community safety will only be achieved through law enforcement or social work alone. Some offenders are dangerous people who pose a direct threat to the community. These offenders need to be closely monitored as they begin the process of change because their failure will inflict the most harm. Others, however, are at risk of failure because they have extensive needs and encounter challenges beyond their ability to cope as they navigate their way through supervision. It is this broad diversity of offenders and the complexity of their lives that requires fluid responses from CCOs versus singular, narrow approaches that neglect either risk or need. The benefit of understanding CCOs' orientation and relationship with offenders is to realize that community supervision is about integrated approaches and relationships with offenders that inform responses based on the situational needs of the offender and the expertise available to deal with issues in the short and long term. Most importantly, CCOs tend to acknowledge that risk and need are interrelated and not isolated conditions—managing risk builds the foundation for addressing need, addressing need reduces long-term risk—and therefore must be balanced to achieve the ultimate goal of community safety.

It is time to give up the polarizing and mostly ideological debate about whether community supervision should be driven by a law enforcement or social work philosophy and begin to respond to research that clearly shows more fluid approaches as the most effective in increasing compliance, reducing recidivism, and therefore increasing community safety. Identifying community corrections officers as street-level boundary spanners who take advantage of multiple strategies and resources to negotiate successful outcomes has the potential to transform community supervision.

Conceptualizing CCOs as street-level boundary spanners gives them the professional space to acknowledge and engage their capacity to effect multifaceted change for offenders. What we learn from the research and from listening to CCOs speak directly about their work with offenders is their desire to serve the community by both holding offenders accountable to the conditions of their supervision and by helping offenders to help themselves related to employment, housing, transportation, education, and treatment. Importantly, when CCOs speak about accountability and assistance, these are not abstract concepts but tangible, realistic, and achievable services with measurable outcomes. These outcomes meet the needs of multiple stakeholders, including the CCO's agency, the community, and the offender.

Much of what offenders need, beyond risk management, is found outside of the criminal justice system and therefore inherently motivates CCOs to be boundary spanners. Although some may decide their job is to remain within the coercive confines of the criminal justice system, and therefore their role is strictly surveillance, monitoring, rule enforcement, and processing offenders, the majority of CCOs still believe rehabilitation, support, and assistance are important aspects of their jobs. CCOs must grapple with finding a means to balance surveillance and assistance when working with offenders in spite of the challenges presented by some of their coworkers, the courts, and the DOC.

Many CCOs express the importance of building meaningful professional relationships with offenders in order to effectively and efficiently manage both risk and need. They make it clear, however, that community supervision is built on relationships delicately balanced on coercion and cooperation. The ability to build rapport with offenders and relationships that are honest expressions of the CCO's combined role—enforcing compliance while simultaneously promoting opportunities for success—needs to be recognized as a critically required expertise to be fully exploited by the criminal justice system to produce positive outcomes. It is this expertise that makes CCOs pivotal to spanning the boundaries among the agencies of the criminal justice system (police, courts, jails, prisons) to harness the resources necessary to manage offender accountability while at the same time working cooperatively with offenders and with helping agencies (social services, mental health, public health, education) to garner the resources required to provide assistance. Analyzing the importance CCOs place on building relationships with offenders helps to identify the boundaries that may be spanned to prevent negative outcomes and increase opportunities for success.

For instance, one place CCOs express their role as boundary spanners is with the court. CCOs willing to advocate on behalf of the offender with the court often help to promote success by keeping the system from sabotaging itself. CCOs recognize that chronic sanctioning of offenders who cannot comply with conditions because they are challenged by poverty, transportation, mental illness, and other circumstances that inhibit full compliance merely culminate in offenders who constantly cycle through the system. The "revolving door" is not because offenders are actively defiant, have committed new crimes, or are a threat to the community but because the cumulative effects of new fines, jail time, and loss of driving privileges inhibit them from ever moving forward. Without CCOs working with the court, the prospects for success are dismal.

Another place CCOs span boundaries is when working with police to make an arrest and take offenders to jail. Many CCOs attempt to control the context of how those on their caseload are treated when arrested because they are conscious of the fact that because someone has failed in the immediate situation does not mean the offender is going to discontinue the process of change. Therefore CCOs are selective about who they will partner with from within their agency and, if possible, outside of their agency when searching an offender's house, conducting an arrest, or transporting an offender to jail. Many CCOs expressed that officer safety is tied to the consideration of the overall relationship a CCO has with an offender. CCOs oftentimes have to continue working with offenders even after an adverse event and therefore acknowledge that sustaining the relationship may promote positive outcomes in the future.

Listening to CCOs also indicates that boundary spanning is important to providing offenders with the necessary services to address real needs. CCOs are able to provide services or connect offenders with a ready list of treatment providers, employers, and community resource centers. They oftentimes share contacts, use existing professional relationships to expedite services, and direct offenders to people and places where they are most likely to be successful and least likely to be rejected because of their criminal record. In order to connect the right offender to the appropriate services, CCOs need to know the offender's life circumstances and what challenges need to be resolved to gain compliance and successful reintegration.

Even though most CCOs articulate a desire to span boundaries and create opportunities for offenders, they often feel overwhelmed by the size of their caseloads and the demands placed on them to justify their decisions and activities. Getting to know offenders and managing their risk and needs is nearly impossible when caseload size dictates short, superficial meetings focused on case management instead of criminogenic needs and other issues related to solving life issues. Large caseloads and the associated documentation necessary to meet agency record-keeping requirements provides little time to problem-solve on behalf of the offender or the agency. Officers appear to be put in a situation where they must decide what is best for the agency and what is best for the offender, turning inward to satisfy the immediate needs of the agency and outward to address the needs of the offender and the community. When workload forces an overemphasis on managing the process versus the offender, then CCO responses are going to be skewed toward DOC and criminal justice options that emphasize sanctions more likely to cover a CCO's professional "ass" (CYA) than respond to offender need (see Clear, 2005). On the other hand, providing adequate time and resources to the offender allows for the implementation of strategies along a full continuum inclusive of sanctions, incentives, rewards, support, and treatment.

When CCOs are encouraged and given the time to span boundaries then the responsibility for offender change will be shared across institutions, professions, and multiple domains of expertise. The knowledge gained from understanding the experiences of CCOs is that they fully appreciate what it takes to be successful working with offenders and need to expand beyond the boundaries of the criminal justice system to enhance positive outcomes. Shifting to a new paradigm that offenders can and will be successful instead of an expectation that they will most likely always fail allows CCOs the professional freedom and direction to implement a multitude of approaches.

What can be achieved in community supervision is not just dependent on what formal institutions of control and support can provide or how individual officers conduct their work; it is also dependent on the informal controls and support networks of the community. Much about what works in community supervision is focused on offenders and their engagement in specific programs, but what works in community supervision must also be placed in the context of the community in which offenders live. Just as CCOs do not conduct their work in isolation from the court or their home agency, they also do not work in isolation from the community. Therefore, it is important to explore how the community influences supervision outcomes. Corrections initiatives may be simultaneously supported and sabotaged by the communities in which offenders live and CCOs work. Success in community corrections cannot be acknowledged without understanding the individual relationships developed between CCOs and offenders and how both groups are explicitly interwoven with the community.

NOTES

1. Berson, 1952, p. vii
2. Most authors discuss some variety of these three roles with various nuances along a continuum of surveillance and assistance. See Glaser, 1964; Klockars, 1972; Ohlin, Piven, and Pappenfort, 1956; Seiter and West, 2003; and Steiner, Travis, Makarios, & Brickley, 2011 for various configurations of officers' roles and orientations.
3. Bonta and colleagues (2008), however, also found that having a relationship with the offender was not significantly related to outcomes.
4. Some states, such as Washington and Oregon, have begun to address this issue by allowing community supervision officers to adapt conditions based on offender risk and need as long as the added conditions are directly related to criminal conduct and the likelihood of future criminality (Lehman, 2001; Petersilia, 2003; Reddick, 2001).
5. The Level of Service Inventory-Revised (LSI-R) refers to the risk assessment tool implemented by the Washington State Department of Corrections at the time of this study.

WORKS CITED

Andrews, D., & Bonta, J. (2010). *The psychology of criminal conduct* (5th ed.). Cincinnati, OH: Anderson.

Augustus, J. (1852). *A report of the labors of John Augustus* (Bicentennial Edition: 1984). Lexington, KY: American Probation and Parole Association.

Berson, F. (1952). *After the big house: The adventures of a parole officer.* New York: Crown.

Bonta, J., Rugge, T., Scott, T.-L., Bourgon, G., & Yessine, A. K. (2008). Exploring the black box of community supervision. *Journal of Offender Rehabilitation, 47*(3), 248–270.

Clear, T. R. (2005). Places not cases?: Re-thinking the probation focus. *The Howard Journal, 44*(2), 172–184.

Clear, T. R., & Latessa, E. J. (1993). Probation officers' roles in intensive supervision: Surveillance versus treatment. *Justice Quarterly, 10*(3), 441–462.

Cobbina, J. E. (2010). Reintegration success and failure: Factors impacting reintegration among incarcerated and formerly incarcerated women. *Journal of Offender Rehabilitation, 49,* 210–232.

Cullen, F. T., & Gilbert, K. E. (1982). *Reaffirming rehabilitation.* Cincinnati, OH: Anderson.

Cullen, F., & Jonson, C. (2012). *Correctional theory: Context and consequences.* Thousand Oaks, CA: Sage.

DeMichele, M. T. (2007). *Probation and parole's growing caseloads and workload allocation: Strategies for managerial decision making.* Lexington, KY: The American Probation & Parole Association.

Dowden, C., & Andrews, D. A. (2004). The importance of staff practice in delivering effective correctional treatment: A meta-analytic review. *International Journal of Offender Therapy and Comparative Criminology, 48*(2), 203–214.

Fogel, D. (1992). Foreword to the first edition. In R. McCleary, *Dangerous men: The sociology of parole* (2nd ed., pp. xi–xviii). New York: Harrow and Heston.

Garland, D. (2001). *The culture of control: Crime and social order in contempoary society.* Chicago: University of Chicago Press.

Glaser, D. (1964). *The effectiveness of a prison & parole system.* New York: Bobbs-Merrill.

Grattet, R., Petersilia, J., Lin, J., & Beckman, M. (2009). Parole violations and revocations in California: Analysis and suggestions for action. *Federal Probation, 73*(1), 2–11.

Gregory, M. (2010). Reflection and resistance: Probation practice and the ethic of care. *British Journal of Social Work, 40,* 2274–2290.

Gunnison, E., & Helfgott, J. B. (2011). Factors that hinder offender reentry success: A view from community corrections officers. *International Journal of Offender Therapy and Comparative Criminology, 55*(2), 287–304.

Gunnison, E., & Helfgott, J. B. (2013). *Success on the street: Creating opportunities for offender reentry.* London: Lynne Rienner.

Harris, P. M., Clear, T. R., & Baird, C. S. (1989). Have community supervision officers changed their attitudes toward their work? *Justice Quartely, 6*(2), 233–246.

Helfgott, J. B. (1997). Ex-offender Need Versus Community Opportunity in Seattle, Washington. *Federal Probation, 61*(2).

Helfgott, J. B., & Gunnison, E. (2008). The Influence of Social Distance on Community Corrections Officer Perceptions of Offender Reentry Needs. *Federal Probation, 72*(1), 2–12.

Ireland, C., & Berg, B. (2008). Women in parole: Respect and rapport. *International Journal of Offender Therapy and Comparative Criminology, 52*(4), 474–491.

Jalbert, S. K., Rhodes, W., Flygare, C., & Kane, M. (2010). Testing probation outcomes in an evidence-based practice setting: Reduced caseload size and intensive supervision effectiveness. *Journal of Offender Rehabilitation, 49*, 233–253.

Kerbs, J. J., Jones, M., & Jolley, J. M. (2009). Discretionary decision making by probation and parole officers: The role of extralegal variables as predictors of responses to technical violations. *Journal of Contemporary Criminal Justice, 25*(4), 424–441.

Kern, A. G., & Bahr, H. M. (1974). Some factors affecting leadership climate in a state parole agency. *Pacific Sociological Review, 17*(1), 108–118.

Klockars, C. B. (1972). A theory of probation supevision. *The Journal of Criminal Law, Criminology and Police Science, 63*(4), 550–557.

Lehman, J. D. (2001). Reinventing community corrections in Washington state. *Corrections Management Quarterly, 5*(3), 41–45.

Leibrich, J. (1994). What do offenders say about supervision and going straight? *Federal Probation, 58*(2), 41–46.

Lindner, C., & Bonn, R. L. (1996). Probation officer victimization and fieldwork practices: Results of a national study. *Federal Probation, 60*(2), 16–23.

Lopez, V., & Russell, M. (2008). Examining the predictors of juvenile probation officers' rehabilitation orientation. *Journal of Criminal Justice, 36*, 381–388.

Lutze, F. E., Johnson, W., Clear, T., Latessa, E., & Slate, R. (2012). The future of community corrections is now: Stop dreaming and take action. *Journal of Contemporary Criminal Justice, 28*(1), 42–49.

Lutze, F. E., & Kigerl, A. (2013). The psychology of reentry. In J. Helfgott (Ed.), *Criminal Psychology* (Vols. 1–4). Westport, CT: Praeger.

Lutze, F. E., & Murphy, D. (1999). Ultra-masculine prison environments and inmate adjustment: It is time to move beyond the "boys will be boys" paradigm. *Justice Quarterly, 16*(4), 709–733.

Lutze, F. E., Smith, R. P., & Lovrich, N. P. (2004). *A practitioner-initiated research partnership: An evaluation of neighborhood based supervision in Spokane, Washington (Grant #: 1999-CE-VX-0007).* Final Report, National Institute of Justice, Washington, DC.

Lynch, M. (1998). Waste managers? The new penology, crime fighting, and parole agent identity. *Law & Society Review, 32*(4), 839–870.

McCleary, R. (1992). *Dangerous men: The sociology of parole* (2nd ed.). New York: Harrow and Heston.

Morgan, K. D., Belbot, B. A., & Clark, J. (1997). Liability issues affecting probation and parole supervision. *Journal of Criminal Justice, 25*(3), 211–222.

Murphy, D., & Lutze, F. (2009). Police-probation partnerships: Professional identity and the sharing of coercive power. *Journal of Criminal Justice, 37,* 65–76.

Ohlin, L. E., Piven, H., & Pappenfort, D. M. (1956). Major dilemmas of the social worker in probation and parole. *National Probation and Parole Association Journal, 2*, 211–225.

Paparozzi, M. A., & Gendreau, P. (2005). An intensive supervision program that worked: Service delivery, professional orientation, and organizational supportiveness. *The Prison Journal, 85*(4), 445–466.

Payne, B. K., & DeMichele, M. (2011). Probation philosophies and workload considerations. *American Journal of Criminal Justice, 36*, 29–43.

Petersilia, J. (2003). *When prisoners come home: Parole and prisoner reentry.* New York: Oxford University Press.

Pisciotta, A. (1994). *Benevolent repression: Social control and the American reformatory prison movement.* New York: New York University Press.

Purkiss, M., Kifer, M., Hemmens, C., & Burton, V. S., Jr. (2003). Probation officer functions—A statutory analysis. *Federal Probation, 67*(1), 12–24.

Quinn, J., & Gould, L. (2003). The prioritization of treatment among Texas parole officers. *The Prison Journal, 83*, 323–336.

Reddick, C. (2001). Oregon provides probation officers with authority to impose sanctions directly on offenders who violation probation. *Community Corrections Report, 8*(2), 17–18.

Rothman, D. (1980). *Conscience and convenience: The asylum and its alternatives in progressive America.* Boston: Little, Brown and Company.

Seiter, R. P., & West, A. D. (2003). Supervision styles in probation and parole: An analysis of activities. *Journal of Offender Rehabilitation, 38*(2), 57–75.

Shapiro, C., & Schwartz, M. (2001). Coming home: Building on family connections. *Corrections Management Quarterly, 5*(3), 52–61.

Sigler, R. T., & McGraw, B. (1984). Adult probation and parole officers: Influence of their weapons, role perceptions and role conflict. *Criminal Justice Review, 9*, 28–32.

Skeem, J. L., Emke-Francis, P., & Louden, J. E. (2006). Probation, mental health, and mandated treatment: A national survey. *Criminal Justice and Behavior, 33*(2), 158–184.

Sluder, R. D., & Shearer, R. A. (1991). Probation officers' role percpetions and attitudes toward firearms. *Federal Probation, 55*(3), 3–9.

Steiner, B., Travis, L. F., III. Makarios, M. D., & Brickley, T. (2011). The influence of parole officers' attitudes on supervision practices. *Justice Quarterly, 28*(6), 903–927.

Surette, R. (2011). *Media, crime, and criminal justice: Images, realities, and policies* (4th ed.). Belmont, CA: Wadsworth, Cengage Learning.

Takagi, P. (1973). Administration and professional conflicts in modern corrections. *The Journal of Criminal Law and Criminology, 64*(3), 313–319.

Taxman, F. S. (2002). Supervision: Exploring the dimensions of effectiveness. *Federal Probation, 66*(2), 14–27.

Taxman, F. S., Shepardson, E. S., & Byrne, J. M. (2004). *Tools of the trade: A guide to incorporating science into practice.* Washington, DC: National Institute of Corrections.

Travis, L. F., & Stacey, J. (2010). A half century of parole rules: Conditions of parole in the United States, 2008. *Journal of Criminal Justice, 38*, 604–608.

Trotter, C. (2000). Social work education, pro-social orientation and effective probation practice. *Probation Journal, 47*, 256–261.

Van Voorhis, P., Braswell, M., & Lester, D. (2000). *Correctional counseling & rehabilitation.* Cincinnati, OH: Anderson.

Walters, S. T., Alexander, M., & Vader, A. M. (2008). The officer responses questionnaire: A procedure for measuring reflective listening in probation and parole settings. *Federal Probation, 72*(2), 67–70.

Walters, S. T., Vader, A. M., Nguyen, N., Harris, T. R., & Eells, J. (2011). Motivational interviewing as a supervision strategy in probation: A randomized effectiveness trial. *Journal of Offender Rehabilitation, 49*, 309–323.

Ward, G., & Kupchick, A. (2010). What drives juvenile probation officers? Relating organizational contexts, status characteristics, and personal convictions to treatment and punishment orientations. *Crime & Delinquency, 56*(1), 35–69.

Weber, G. H. (1958). Explorations in the similarities, differences and conflicts between probation, parole and institutions. *The Journal of Criminal Law, Criminology, and Police Science, 48*(6), 580–589.

West, A. D., & Seiter, R. P. (2004). Social worker or cop? Measuring the supervision styles of probation and parole officers in Kentucky and Missouri. *Journal of Criminal Justice, 27–57*(2), 27.

Whetzel, J., Papparozzi, M., Alexander, M., & Lowenkamp, C. T. (2011). Goodbye to a worn-out dichotomy: Law enforcement, social work, and a balanced approach: A survey of federal probation officer attitudes. *Federal Probation, 75*(7), 7–12.

Whitehead, J. T., & Lindquist, C. A. (1992). Determinants of probation and parole officers' professional orientation. *Journal of Criminal Justice, 20*, 13–24.

Wilson, J. Q. (1983). *Thinking about crime* (2nd ed.). New York: Vantage Books.

Wodahl, E. J., Garland, B., Culhane, S. E., & McCarty, W. P. (2011). Utilizing behavioral interventions to improve supervision outcomes in community-based corrections. *Criminal Justice and Behavior, 38*(4), 386–405.

Worrall, J. L., Schram, P., Hays, E., & Newman, M. (2004). An analysis of the relationship between probation caseloads and property crime rates in California counties. *Journal of Criminal Justice, 32*, 231–241.

Wright, C. E. (1998). The relationship of case management strategies to probation officer personality types. *Perspectives, 22*(1), 36–38.

❧ THREE ❧

CCOs AND THEIR RELATIONSHIP WITH THE COMMUNITY

"Becoming relationally focused, as opposed to offender centered, means that new ways of supervising and working with offenders and the communities must be invented."[1]

In order to fully understand the work of CCOs, equal consideration must be given to the "community" portion of their title and how their work is influenced by the ecology of the broader community. Community corrections work often takes place with offenders who live in dire circumstances. Many communities experiencing high rates of reentry are mired in poverty and crime and have few local resources to ease the hardship of transitioning from prison to home (see Clear, 2007). Considering the broader conditions of the community is important because, even when community corrections successfully implements offender-centered supervision, community-level pressures continue to pose challenges and work to sabotage long-term success. Thus, "corrections of place" needs to be more fully integrated into the conceptualization and evaluation of community corrections as it coincides with offender-centered strategies to enhance the well-being of communities (Clear, 1996).

Surprisingly, little is known about how CCOs interact with the community beyond their work with offenders. It is well established that successfully addressing offender needs requires going beyond the criminal justice system and engaging other agencies and service providers in the community (see Lattimore, Visher, Winterfield, Lindquist, & Brumbaugh, 2005). Yet inadequate attention has been given to how CCOs perceive the broader community and more specifically the neighborhoods in which concentrated reentry is most likely to occur. Although more is known about CCOs' understanding of offender needs and how they correspond with existing resources in the community (Gunnison & Helfgott, 2011; Helfgott, 1997; Helfgott & Gunnison, 2008; Hipp, Jannetta, Shah, & Turner, 2011), it is not clear whether CCOs want to work more closely with community stakeholders, such as faith-based groups, landlords, and business owners, or how closely they care to work with offenders' families, friends, and neighbors. In addition, if CCOs do want to work more closely with community stakeholders, or are required to, consideration must be given to how they incorporate these activities into their overall workload and responsibility for offender-centered supervision strategies.

This chapter explores how CCOs span the boundaries between offender-centered supervision and the broader community. First, the concept of corrections of place is defined, as well as what community attributes are most likely to support or hinder successful reintegration. Second, a review of the research shows CCOs are well aware of the challenges communities and neighborhoods present to ex-offenders, but little is known about how this influences their supervision strategies or work in general. Finally, the importance of CCOs' roles as boundary spanners within the community and their potential to enhance the success of criminal justice outcomes while engaging the community is discussed.

ACHIEVING CORRECTIONS OF PLACE

Most of the attention by corrections policymakers and planners is dedicated to the "corrections" side of community corrections officers' work, whether that is surveillance or assistance, and little attention has been given to the "community" side of the profession. *Community* in *community corrections* has traditionally meant the work takes place outside of prisons and in the community but not as an inherent part of the community (Clear, 1996; Lehman, 2001). Even as the mission of community corrections has broadened to include community safety, the strategies have continued to be narrowly defined as reducing recidivism through offender-centered approaches that incorporate some variation of surveillance, support, treatment, and sanctions.

Corrections of place refers to a subtle shift toward broadening community corrections work from interacting with offenders as isolated individuals who happen to live in the community instead of prison (offender-centered approaches) to relating to offenders as integrated members of a broader community network that includes both informal (families, peer groups, churches, neighborhoods) and formal (criminal justice, social services, public health, education) networks (Clear, 1996; Drapela & Lutze, 2009). Clear (1996, p. 53) contends that "incorporating a place orientation takes the offender out of the center of the picture and inserts instead a concern for community safety." When offenders are considered members of a larger community instead of isolated cases, then community corrections strategies can be broadened to include CCOs, offenders, and the community as partners sharing the responsibility of successful integration. To achieve corrections of place there must be a clear understanding about what constitutes a community, what attributes of communities relate to successful reintegration, and how CCOs, offenders, and the community may develop partnerships to enhance positive outcomes. It becomes clear that spanning the boundaries between offender-centered strategies and community-level stakeholders is likely to result in innovative approaches that build on shared responsibility for both the success and failure of offenders.

COMMUNITY AND REENTRY

It is well established that the environment in which offenders live influences the likelihood of their success and therefore the success of community corrections. Those that leave prison for communities with greater social and economic resources are significantly more likely to achieve long-term reintegration than those returning to disadvantaged communities (Kirk, 2009, 2012; Kubrin & Stewart, 2006). Communities may be defined in two primary ways (Sampson, 2002; Travis, 2005). First, they are often identified by their geographic location, such as specific neighborhoods or broader boundaries such as cities. Spatial definitions of communities generally consider the area's demographic characteristics, such as its socioeconomic condition, racial and ethnic identity, existing institutions, education level, employment, incarceration, and crime. Second, communities are defined as a set of complex social and kinship networks that include individuals, families, neighbors, community members, businesses, organizations, and government institutions. Social networks function to structure communities within a set of common values used to maintain effective social control (Sampson, 2002).

Young, Taxman, and Byrne (2002) argue that the definition of community should be functional and include those most affected by and influential in engaging offenders in the community. They reason that "community is best viewed as people who, by virtue of their natural (extralegal) relationship with the offender, have the greatest potential impact on the offender's behavior, or are most affected by the behavior" (Young et al., 2002, p. 9). Both the general and functional definitions of community present relationships as primary to solving individual- and community-level problems and supporting a functional prosocial environment. Communities often differ dramatically in both their spatial and social network characteristics, and their ability to assert both formal and informal social control to encourage conformity and prevent crime.

The capacity for citizens to organize in response to risks and to effectively problem-solve threats to their well-being is related to the level of social capital and collective efficacy within a community. Social capital and collective efficacy relate to similar conceptual frameworks that observe how social networks and citizen involvement in collective action result in social change (Bazmore, Nissen, & Dooley, 2000; Lutze, Smith, & Lovrich, 2000). For instance, Portes (1998, p. 6) contends that "social capital stands for the ability of actors to secure benefits by virtue of membership in social networks or other social structures" and may serve as a source of social control and family support and provide benefits through access to extrafamilial networks. Sampson (2002, p. 232) defines collective efficacy as the "linkage of mutual trust and the shared willingness to intervene for the common good that defines the neighborhood context." Thus, the level of social capital and collective efficacy in a community affects the capacity of citizens to mobilize social networks to advance their own interests or the community's (Rose & Clear, 1998; Travis, 2005, p. 296). Sampson (2002, p. 230) argues that social disorganization presents "the inability of a community to realize the common values of its residents and maintain effective social controls." Therefore, collective efficacy tends to be weakened in neighborhoods that experience concentrated disadvantage, including poverty, racial segregation, family disruption, residential instability, concentrated incarceration, forced mobility, and dense population concentration (Clear, 2007; Dhondt, 2012; Rose & Clear, 1998; Sampson, 2002).

Many of the disadvantaged neighborhoods in which offenders live tend to have greater levels of social disorganization and lower levels of social capital and collective efficacy. They therefore lack the capacity to prevent crime, support victims, or assist in the reform efforts being made by those released from prison. Offenders who return to disadvantaged neighborhoods, generally the same places where they encountered trouble before prison, are significantly more likely to recidivate than those who move away from where they lived before prison or those who return to more advantaged communities (see Kirk, 2009, 2012; Kubrin & Stewart, 2006). Individuals returning to disadvantaged communities are more likely to be challenged by the absence of opportunities related to employment, education, safe housing, and family support. Returning to the community may also reunite offenders with criminal peers and networks, putting them at a greater risk of returning to crime and therefore prison (Dhondt, 2012;

Kubrin & Stewart, 2006). It is also common for ex-prisoners to live in just a few neighborhoods within large urban areas where concentrated disadvantage and incarceration occur simultaneously (see Clear, 2007; Kirk, 2012; Travis, 2005).

Ecological challenges are especially harsh for Black and ethnic minority populations overrepresented in both disadvantaged communities and in prison. Racial and ethnic minorities are significantly more likely to be living in communities without the social capital or collective efficacy necessary to provoke a broader response to crime other than the ongoing cycle of arrest and incarceration (see Clear, 1996; Rank, 2004; Wilson, 1987). Without the ability to garner collective action to effect change related to both community-level risks (crime, disorganization, poverty) and needs (social support, economic resources, education, health care), responses to community problems are dominated by formal institutions such as the criminal justice system and social welfare organizations instead of informal social controls such as religious organizations, community cohesion, and families. Formal institutions are often distrusted by minority communities because they frequently promise help laden with conditions considered to be intrusive, controlling, and coercive (see Anderson, 1999; Clear, 2007; Petersilia, 2003; Rapheal, 2000). The rules attached to offers of help from formal institutions often conflict with the realities of living in poverty and the ability to rely on intimates and peer relationships to reestablish stability.

Many of the policies designed to protect the poor or to get tough on crime generally mean well but often have disparate effects on disadvantaged and minority communities resulting in unintended consequences that may actually undermine the social capital and collective efficacy necessary to prevent crime. For instance, excluding drug offenders from public housing was enacted to reduce drug-related victimization of law-abiding citizens living in government-sponsored low-income housing. This is a noble and worthy cause, but it also prevents offenders, even those who are reformed, from rejoining their families who live in public housing and receiving the social and family support necessary to sustain sobriety and reintegration (see Geller & Curtis, 2011; Roman & Travis, 2006). Similarly, social welfare benefits attempt to relieve the hardships of poverty by favoring poor single women with children, but strict rules regarding "single" women without a male partner in residence serve as a disincentive for fathers to legally return to their families because it may jeopardize the benefits currently supporting their children until they can rejoin the labor force (Roman & Travis, 2006; Sampson, 2002; Travis, 2005; Wilson, 1987). Attempts to reclaim economic independence by offenders are also aggravated by a shortage of low-skill, well-paying jobs in many poor urban areas and policies that prevent many ex-felons from being licensed or bonded by the state in better-paying professions related to medicine, education, cosmetology, and other skilled trades that provide a livable wage (Mele & Miller, 2005; Travis, 2005). Many of the outcomes related to these well-intended policies contribute to the destabilization of informal social networks that could be relied on by offenders and used by CCOs to reduce recidivism and provide the resources necessary to enhance stability in the community (see Clear, 2007; Sampson, 2002; Travis, 2005).

In addition to numerous policies that restrict offenders from using support services in the community, recent attention has also been given to the effects of concentrated incarceration on the destabilization of social capital and collective efficacy in many communities (Clear, 2007; Dhondt, 2012; Rose & Clear, 1998). The term *coerced mobility* refers to the residential instability caused by mass incarceration and the effects of prison admissions and releases on communities (Frost & Gross, 2012; Rose & Clear, 1998). Civil penalties that limit access to public benefits and residency can also force individuals and families to move (Mele & Miller, 2005). Those experiencing coerced mobility represent a critical mass of citizens in some communities where as many as one in three young Black men are under some form of state control, and approximately 10% of the overall population is entering jail or prison and another 10% is returning to the community from jail or prison (see Clear, Hamilton, & Cadora, 2011). Incarceration of a household member eliminates the financial contributions of that person and may lead to the entire family having to move from their current residence into shared housing with family or friends or public housing and may even lead to homelessness. This may lead to school disruptions for children, missed work for partners, increased costs for transportation, and other familial, social, and economic hardships (Travis, 2005). Therefore, coerced mobility affects the offender as well as family members (see Clear, 2007; Dhondt, 2012).

Clear (2005, p. 179) argues that coerced mobility creates "concentrated disruption" in which formal social controls (incarceration) interfere with social networks and supports that "weakens the capacities of those support systems to perform functions of informal social control, with ominous implications for inter-generational involvement in the criminal justice system" (also see Dhondt, 2012; Frost & Gross, 2012; Rose & Clear, 1998). The churning of a significant portion of the community's population, especially young males, in and out of prison over time creates both social and economic instability that is difficult to address through professional action by CCOs or to overcome by offenders even when their intention is to go straight. As Kubrin and Stewart (2006, p. 189) observe,

> Although providing inmates with an education or vocational training or preparing them for a life outside prison are all steps in the right direction, skills matter little if the communities to which ex-offenders return offer few jobs or opportunities. In short, by ignoring community context, we are likely setting up ex-inmates for failure.

One can also argue that this same dynamic sets up community corrections officers as well as other service providers for failure in achieving long-term outcomes other than returning violators to jail or prison.

When crime control policies exclusively focus on the individual, they ignore the broader ecological issues such as the severity of urban poverty, unemployment, family disruption, and the desperate conditions highly correlated with both race and crime. Too often a person's race is perceived as a cause of both crime and poverty while conveniently failing to understand how many community conditions are shaped not by the individual but by structural inequality and planned government policies resulting in inequities in critical institutions relevant to the health and safety of communities (Clear, 2005; Rank, 2004; Wilson, 1987). Policymakers' decisions regarding public school funding, tax incentives for new businesses, zoning laws, distribution of public services (police, garbage, street repair), welfare benefits, attaching civil penalties to criminal penalties, and policies that return prisoners to the county of their conviction all directly affect many communities' ability to mobilize for the greater good of their members (Sampson, 2002; Sampson, Morenoff, & Gannon-Rowley, 2002; Travis, 2005). Whether intended or not, the outcomes of such policies serve to structurally benefit and sustain the safety of some communities while perpetuating instability and a lack of safety in others. These differences mean CCOs and other service providers need to be culturally aware and competent in understanding how race, sex, and class intersect to result in different experiences for different groups of people. Relevant responses purposefully crafted to improve the success of those who live in disadvantaged communities are required. A failure to fully realize how social, political, and economic policies work to support or sabotage certain groups directly affects CCOs' success in managing the long-term integration of offenders.

For instance, even the best of intentions are oftentimes compromised in disadvantaged communities because of the overwhelming need for services. Disadvantaged and concentrated-incarceration communities tend to have a significant number of services available to address the social and economic hardships of community members, but the agencies are unable to adequately respond to demand (see Hipp et al., 2011). Hipp and colleagues (2011) report that the average parolee in their California sample had approximately 5

social service providers, 10 self-sufficiency providers, and 400 other parolees within 2 miles of the parolee's residence. Parolees tend to have a number
of services available to them, but due to high concentrations of offenders and
others in the community in need of these services, helping agencies are often
overburdened (Hipp et al., 2011). Correctional treatment programs located
in less affluent communities are also less likely to incorporate the principles
of effective treatment and are less effective in serving clients and reducing
the risk of recidivism and improving prosocial behaviors (see Wright, Pratt,
Lowenkamp, & Latessa, 2012). As a consequence, the lack of capacity and
inadequate services combine to create serious challenges for both the providers and the clients in poor communities.

Although reentry initiatives often identify the serious challenges confronting offenders upon reentry, the recommendations for success often
focus on the offender's individual needs and not those of the community.
As Kubrin and Stewart (2006, p. 189) comment on the relevance of neighborhood context in predicting recidivism and the shortcomings of policy,
"In this long list of recommendations, one arena of change is completely
left out of the equation: changing communities. None of these suggestions
focus on fixing the (disadvantaged) communities to which released
inmates disproportionately return." Concentrating responses on offender-
centered strategies deals with only one element of the reentry dilemma and
leaves CCOs in the difficult position of managing offenders without the
resources, shared power, and responsibility of the community and its
stakeholders to support reintegration.

Given the stressed communities in which CCOs work, it is surprising
how little appears to be known about how CCOs interface with community
members and stakeholders to promote integration and support safe communities. Although social capital and collective efficacy are directly
related to social context and recidivism, very little is known about the
degree to which CCOs engage these broad concepts in their everyday
work. It is difficult to fully consider CCOs' effectiveness without a clear
understanding of how they define community, how they perceive the
strengths and weaknesses of the community, whether they want to engage
community members as a part of their work, and what they offer beyond
offender-centered supervision.

COMMUNITY CORRECTIONS OFFICERS'
PERCEPTIONS OF COMMUNITY

Community corrections officers clearly understand the many challenges
confronting offenders living in the community. They are quick to identify

offenders' needs important to achieving success such as housing, employment, treatment, transportation, child care, and social support (Gunnison
& Helfgott, 2011; Helfgott, 1997; Helfgott & Gunnison, 2008). They also
understand how, even when basic needs are met, there are still challenges
posed by a lack of trust and concern by families, landlords, and employers
in reengaging the offender (Clear, 2007; Helfgott, 1997; Quinn & Gould,
2003). Little is known, however, about how CCOs envision their work with
the community as a "client" broadly defined and how addressing community needs influences their working role. Few studies address this topic.
Due to the absence of published studies on CCOs' perception of the community, unlike other chapters in this book where CCO quotes are used as
real-life examples to support existing research, in this chapter quotations
are presented as original research (see Drapela & Lutze, 2009; Lutze,
Smith, & Lovrich, 2004; Murphy & Lutze, 2009).

CCO Definition of Community

Although CCOs obviously work in the community supervising
offenders, it is rare that their perspectives about what actually defines community are studied. CCOs define community in terms inclusive of the
formal definitions of the word by including spatial boundaries; functional
interactions between offenders and community members; and the interconnectedness of people, organizations, and places reflecting aspects of social
capital and collective efficacy. Not surprisingly, CCOs do not directly
speak of social capital or collective efficacy, but they do provide working
examples of these concepts in their descriptions of community.

When asked, "How do you define community?" CCOs shared an array
of responses. Most began with spatial boundaries as the foundation for
community and then extrapolated their description to the groups of people
living and working within the community's borders. For example,

> Well, I tell you, it's a given neighborhood probably with similar socioeco-
> nomic standing. It may cover a couple of blocks or it could be very simi-
> lar for a couple of square miles. But, it, the given community, has similar
> values, similar economics, and similar things going on. (CCO 112)

> Well, I think it's anybody that lives in the area where we supervise
> offenders. Whether that be a business, a social service agency, a church,
> a neighbor, storeowner, offender, volunteer—whoever. I mean, that's the
> community—where we work. (CCO 111)

Others started with relationships, networks, and the interconnectedness of people living within a geographical location. These observations

generally combined space, function, and networks into a definition that often included people having a stake in the neighborhood and a sense of belonging. For example,

> I'd say it's kind of a sense of belonging to something.... If you do something wrong, it's going to come around to your parents and they're going to find out. That's something that's tight like that, and everybody knows somebody that knows another person, every third, fourth, fifth, tenth person, they know of that person. I guess that would be a tight-knit community—somebody that calls themselves the community. People that know each other, help each other, like deal with problems. (CCO 108)

Others thought about the community more globally and about the interconnectedness of different communities in the same city or region.

> For me, community is...made up of hundreds of different communities. There's the community in which I live, there's the community in which I work and my contacts to my work, through volunteer work, through my church. I tend to think the mentality of Spokane is—"If it doesn't impact my South Hill [high socioeconomic area] community [laughing], then it doesn't impact me." And I think we're—as a city—we're starting to get away from that. "If it impacts East Valley, it impacts me. If it impacts, you know, North Spokane or the Spokane Valley, it impacts me." And I think people are starting to see that—you know, the domino effect. (CCO 231)

Interestingly, a few CCOs bluntly expressed not giving it much thought. The following quote clearly illustrates that the demands of the job do not allow for many philosophical indulgencies.

> How do I define community? I don't have a definition for community [laughs]. I don't give my job a lot of thought other than to come in and deal with whatever fires need [to be] put out for that particular day.... I don't usually sit down and work out philosophy or definitions of community or anything else. I could probably find Joe Lehman's [Secretary of DOC] definition of community somewhere in my paperwork, but it's basically just the people in the neighborhood, the people who work there, live there, um that's who I see as the community. (CCO 201)

To varying degrees, many of the definitions of community, from the most simple to the most complex, included some aspect of the three attributes outlined in the literature: spatial boundaries, social networks, and functionality (Sampson, 2002; Travis, 2005; Young et al., 2002). Importantly, many CCOs viewed community as inclusive of those living in a particular area, including individuals, families, and offenders and organizations such as schools, community centers, churches, and businesses. In addition, although not as often, criminal justice professionals, including community corrections officers and the police, were also identified as a part of the community. Therefore, community tended to be defined as inclusive of both law-abiding citizens and offenders and the social institutions, both formal and informal, most often used in their everyday lives.

When delving deeper into CCOs' views about the problems facing the community and what they could do to help, CCOs often referred to attributes of the community related to concentrated disadvantage, especially poverty, and issues related to the absence of social capital, collective efficacy, and social organization. CCOs were asked, "What do you consider to be the most significant problems of the community in which you work?" Their answers included crime, lack of knowledge about community corrections, poverty, apathy, family dysfunction, lack of resources for offenders, and not enough police or CCOs to serve the community. Of all the problems identified, most often cited were crime, lack of knowledge about community corrections, and poverty.

Drug use and violent crime were often grouped together, as in this CCO's comment:

> I'm going to say crime. Both within their own dwelling, expand it out to their neighborhood, including downtown ....And that incorporates a lot of things, you know, drug use, petty stuff, destruction of property, major crimes. And then I think probably the next thing would be probably employment, economy, taxes. (CCO 210)

> I think they're concerned for their safety—especially violence and drug-related things. They want the meth houses out. I think that's kind of where they're coming from. (CCO 252)

A lack of education was also voiced by many CCOs as a problem confronting the community. This education gap showed up most prominently as a lack of knowledge regarding community corrections but also in the traditional sense, as a lack of schooling. This lack of education concerning community corrections may be due to the time at which these interviews were conducted. Systemwide, the DOC was working to move community corrections out from obscurity and into public view, much like police had during the community-oriented policing movement. Therefore, CCOs were being directed to engage the community more often and to tap the public in achieving community corrections' goals (Lehman, 2001; Lutze et al., 2000). Many CCOs described an important movement away from being an "invisible" agency and "anonymity" to being a visible partner with other agencies and community stakeholders to meet their vision statement of "working together for safe communities." Thus, it may have been difficult for CCOs to make the shift from framing education as a lack of knowledge about the role of CCOs in the community to the problems directly affecting the community due to social, political, or economic conditions.

In spite of the context in which CCOs were interviewed, evidence from other research suggests that concern about the public's lack of knowledge about community corrections is not unique to this sample of CCOs. When asked what CCOs needed from the community, Quinn and Gould (2003) found that 80% of CCOs said public education or knowledge of community corrections, while 40% reported a need for greater respect and understanding from the community. It may not be unusual for CCOs to identify the greatest problem facing the community as a lack of knowledge about their work. The following quote gives a fair representation of this perspective.

> Lack of understanding I think of what we do and [what] law enforcement [does] and the scope of our ability to make changes and to deal with offenders. (CCO 206)

Although most of the comments in this vein were fairly neutral, one CCO expressed a much more hostile response toward the DOC's new policies and how the community's lack of knowledge was really a political issue. It is unknown to what extent this CCO's perspective was shared by others.

> I think it could very well be that the citizens have trusted us as an agency to make appropriate decision in handling [this] population group, and they're being let down.... If we were to pull a typical citizen, a typical taxpayer on the street, to ask him... [describes violent crime and violation of conditions] "What do you think I should do taxpayer?"...And I guarantee you, praise circles, movie tickets, [written essays about feelings], and all that shit that we're seeing... is absurd and it spits in the face of the taxpayers who don't have any idea. They assume that we're doing our job in a conservative manner.... The public can only buy off on that so far, and then all of a sudden it's like "wait, wait, wait, throw all this horse shit out! This person did this, they're a threat to me and my family. Go fucking

find 'em, put him in jail, and keep me safe. That's why I pay you! I pay you good money. Alright, I give you group health and dentistry, all this bullshit! Do your job!" And they have a real, closer to law enforcement, perspective of what their expectation of us is. (CC0 ---)

A few CCOs contemplated how a lack of education and isolation was a problem for the community. For instance, one CCO commented,

Okay, the significant problem in the community in which I work is I think people are undereducated, underemployed, underpaid, whatever. They have very small worlds, very small minds. A lot of the offenders and their families have never been outside of Spokane. (CCO 201)

Poverty was also noted as a problem for the communities CCOs served. Comments about poverty often included many of the attributes tied to disadvantaged neighborhoods described in the literature, such as the high concentration of offenders, unemployment, low levels of home ownership, and a transient population. The following quotes identify problems associated with concentrated disadvantage.

The most significant problems are low-income, high-offender population, then, sort of the [community name] is the home to all the dope dealers and crack whores. Mostly, I would say, because a vast majority of this neighborhood is poor. There's hardly anybody in this neighborhood that's got any money. Retired folks, fixed-income people, welfare folks, and low-income people. (CCO ---)

Another CCO identifies the problems of the community as an ongoing process of economic transition.

Well, in my community that I work, it's just poverty. It used to be a logging, mining community, and they're struggling. Now it appears that they are trying to revamp the tourism, and it's going to take a long time. (CCO ---)

The following CCO viewed the primary problems of the community as poverty and a lack of home ownership, which leads to instability that then causes other problems.

Well, here, we're the poorest legislative [district] in the state of Washington. There's a lot of different problems as I see it—the other one is absentee landlords. A lot of these people don't live here that own these homes that they rent out.... Of course, drug use will always be there—that happens to any community. And just managing a caseload where there's a lot of transient population moving in and out—the school over here.... I think they said it's a 65% turnover per year. That's very high and it's tough for those kids to, you know... I don't know how you really resolve that—it's a problem that exists. (CCO ---)

Yet another CCO considered poverty an individual failing that causes problems for taxpayers.

I think one of our biggest problems is drug abuse. I think poverty is a problem. But I also see poverty as self-propelled. I think that people should work for what they have. I don't believe in welfare. I don't believe in legalizing drugs so that you can go out and use all the drugs you want so that I, as the taxpaying citizen, can pay for your drug treatment. I don't believe in it. I had to do it all on my own. Maybe I was given better skills in coming from a decent family, but when you get to be an adult, those excuses don't work anymore. You're the only one that can do it. You know, I see too many people claiming, for example, that they can't pay their legal financial obligations or they can't pay their bills. Yet they do have enough money to buy a 6- or 12-pack of beer every day and four cartons of cigarettes in a month. That's not acceptable. (CCO 235)

Although most CCOs identified living in poverty as a context for hardship, it is unknown how many CCOs believe poverty and other community problems are the result of individual failure versus community-level ecological factors.[2] This dichotomy may be an important aspect of understanding how CCOs approach their work. CCOs who believe community problems are due to individual behavior versus structural inequality may be less likely to engage the broader community to resolve supervision issues and overemphasize offender-centered approaches.

CCOs also reported other community problems such as apathy, dysfunctional families, and too few criminal justice resources for both offenders and the community. The following quotes capture how a sense of apathy and the belief that others will take care of the problems in the neighborhood cause problems for the community related to a lack of collective efficacy.

I think a lot of times they just have that apathy that, you know, someone else should do it and I'll complain about it and stuff. Someone else go do it. So, they don't volunteer here, or they don't go to their teacher/parent conference. It's all a ripple effect. (CCO 105)

Most people, like I said, are so busy with their own lives...that they don't have the inclination to worry about what's going [on] within their neighborhood or who's living down the street. If the community knew exactly what was going on in certain circumstances, there would be a little more community involvement. (CCO 239)

In addition to apathy, family dysfunction also was identified as a problem facing communities. The primary issue related to families was a lack of caring between members and severe disruption within the family unit that undermined the stability necessary for offenders to move forward. For instance,

I think that's one of the biggest problems that I find in the community, is that some of the families have become so dysfunctional that they don't even like each other let alone care for each other or be concerned or be supportive or back each other up, or you know, the family unit is so deteriorated that it really affects a lot of the people that we supervise. (CCO 236)

There's a huge breakdown of the family. More often than not, anybody, man or woman, who I have, has a stepfather, no father, no mother around, stepmother, working on their second stepfather and the first stepfather was a drunk. Dad's not in the picture, Mom's not in the picture. Breakdown of the family. (CCO 229)

Finally, some CCOs commented on the diminished capacity of the criminal justice system to respond to offender needs or community safety. For instance, the following comment identifies a lack of resources as detrimental to the offender and thus the community.

I think one thing that is very frustrating for me is not being able to supervise and/or provide resources for offenders who may be approachable and who may be at a level where they're still treatable. That is frustrating. And I think is, or will be, equally frustrating to the community. (CCO 231)

Similarly, concern was also expressed about there not being enough police or community corrections officers to adequately engage the community to solve problems, investigate crime, and enhance safety.

Well, I don't think we have enough police. I don't think they can respond to what's going on. I don't think they have enough manpower to do some of the public meetings that I think they could do—visit Cop Shop meetings and things like that. Or arrest offenders or investigate crime. I don't think we have enough CCOs who are supervising the offenders that we have now. I don't think—as far as the balance—I don't think offenders should just come out and rely on social services. But, on the other hand, they have really been cut off from some services and so that's resulted in them committing more crime. (CCO 223)

In general, CCOs clearly define many of the problems within the community as shortcomings related to social capital, such as poverty, lack of education, and residential instability, that make it difficult to create change. CCOs also describe a lack of collective efficacy, such as people unwilling to be involved in the neighborhood and dysfunctional families who fail to provide any kind of stability or support. As may be expected, most CCOs' suggestions about how best to resolve community problems were directly related to what they defined as the primary problem of the community.

Educating the community about the DOC's role was prominent, and CCOs gave multiple examples of how they attempt to solve this problem by attending community meetings, educating individual citizens, helping victims, participating on block watches, working with employers to hire offenders, and, when possible, working with the media to accurately depict their work to the general public. Doing their job well was also viewed as an immediate way to help communities to address crime and enhance community safety. Doing their job well included obvious things like closely supervising offenders and connecting them to support services, but it also included sharing information with other agencies and the community about offenders, building relationships with stakeholders to help offenders, establishing block watches and block revitalization projects to develop connections among neighbors, working with landlords, working on issues concerning diversity, and encouraging interagency collaborations.

It is evident that many of these efforts to address community problems are directly related to building social capital within the community and enhancing a sense of collective efficacy. For example, the importance of building support and social networks to achieve success is illustrated through the following comment.

Um, I don't know that there's a whole bunch that I can accomplish as a CCO, per say, but as a human being,... I think that there's some ways that I can try to work with the people that I supervise to encourage them to create that support system that apparently doesn't exist for them now in terms of a family unit.... But there are other things that I try to do out

in the community to enrich the whole family unit that really isn't necessarily tied to being a CCO, although I think, sometimes, purely by acci-
dent, that my input may have [influence because of my] credentials [and]
the job that I do. (CCO 236)

Another example demonstrates the building of collective efficacy at
the neighborhood level through doing one's job supervising offenders and
collaborating with police.

Speaking simply from being a CCO, you know, I can't open a day care,
BUT I can certainly help out with the crime issue and I can help out with
bad, negative houses, which I've done. We had the one negative house
and I went out with the SWAT team on one of my guys...there must have
been 30 SWAT members, and it was just wild, I mean, I've never been
part of that before. It was just a real experience for me. But, when it was
kind of calming down, like 25, 30 minutes later, I'm turning around,
there had to...have been dang near 300 people that were standing around
applauding because they were complaining for a long time. They were
literally applauding, they were drinking beers—I think somebody had
rolled out a barbecue and started flipping burgers. I looked around and
just started laughing. I said, "Man, look at this." It was just nothing I had
ever seen before, you know. (CCO ---)

These quotes illustrate that CCOs have a sense of how they can help
with community problems both at the individual and community level.
Although they do not use terms such as *social disorganization, disadvantaged communities, concentrated incarceration, social capital,* and *collective efficacy,* they touch on each of these things in real-life terms and
understand the importance of issues that concern the community and influence their work and how these problems may be solved through their
individual and collective efforts.

CCO Role and Desire to Work With the Community

Although CCOs supervise offenders in the community, little is known
about how they perceive their role working with the community to achieve
supervision goals. Most community corrections agencies promote a dual
mission of promoting community safety and holding offenders accountable
through both supervision and support (Purkiss, Kifer, Hemmens, & Burton
Jr., 2003). It is unknown how this mission translates to CCOs' work beyond
the offender in engaging the community to achieve what is assumed to be

shared goals between the community and community corrections. Several studies theorize about how CCOs should engage the community (Clear, 1996, 2005; Lehman, 2001; Lutze et al., 2000), and many evaluate the outcomes of coordinating offender-centered approaches upon reentry (see Chapter 6), but no known studies have directly investigated what CCOs believe their role to be and whether they enjoy working with the community. CCOs were asked, "What is the primary role of a community corrections officer in dealing with the community?" Overall, CCOs responded that community safety (46%) and educating the public (44%) were their primary roles, with neighborhood-based supervision (NBS) officers more likely to cite community education (59% vs. 38%) and traditional CCOs more often citing community safety (52% vs. 33%) as their primary role in working with the community (Drapela & Lutze, 2009).

Across all CCOs, educating and protecting the community were often tightly interwoven. Many CCOs were succinct and direct in their responses regarding their role in working with the community.

> I think we need to make the community aware of what our job entails. But we also need to protect them. (CCO 217)

> I think we're here to serve the community and keep the community safe. (CCO 233)

Others gave more in-depth responses by providing examples of how the community did not fully understand their role. For example,

> Community safety—keeping them informed of what our limits are, too. You know, we don't have authority over people that are not on supervision. People that are on supervision, I think the community thinks that we have unlimited authority to do whatever. If they're sitting there yelling obscenities at their neighbor or something, you call the PO. The PO can come in and haul them off to jail and get them out of my hair. But we don't have unlimited authority, and people have trouble understanding that. (CCO 243)

Similarly, another CCO, when educating the community about offenders' behavior and the power of CCOs, simply states, "Just being a jerk really isn't a violation" (CCO 107).

Elaborations on CCOs' role oftentimes reflected how they overcome the limitations of their power and authority through a broader philosophy of supervision and how they span boundaries by using social capital, collective efficacy, and the formal and informal networks in the community.

For instance, the following quote represents the importance of supporting offender change as a form of protecting the community.

> Well, naturally, the routine answer is that we're here to protect the community. The question is, HOW do we protect the community? Well, the only way that you protect the community is if you contribute to the change in the offender that is at risk....We can motivate them, we can enlighten them, we can give them tools to fix themselves, help create a venue for them to want to change and be able to change. But it's all about our capacity of seeing the offender change and become part of the community. And so that's what our job is. (CCO 251)

The following quote reflects the need to engage the community in the process of supervision in order to enhance surveillance.

> My primary role as a CCO would be to make sure that none of the offenders on my caseload create another victim in the community. But that's not always possible. You can't watch them 24/7. So, I rely on part of the community—family members—to let me know if they're not coming home. Employers if they're not going to work—but I don't want them to have to be considered some guardian.[3] I want to utilize them the way that we always have without a title attached to them. (CCO 245)

One CCO, however, keenly expressed mixed emotions about the role of CCOs and whether working closely with the community was a help or hindrance to the DOC's mission and the supervision of offenders. This CCO expressed the importance of working with the community to develop resources to support offenders but did not believe it necessary to build a personal relationship with those in the community to protect them or do business with them.

> I've got all these things in my head right now. I want to say, first of all, I don't know that dealing with the community is a necessity for us. I want to say it IS a necessity for us. Personally, I see it as almost more of a hindrance for me. [I see it] two ways. First of all, me having a positive relationship with community members is positive for my offender in that if I know that Mr. Landlord over here is willing to rent apartments to offenders, I need to build a relationship with him so that when my offenders get out, they can go there. But at the same time, while I'm here to protect him, I'm here to make sure that my offender don't hurt him. I don't need to necessarily get involved with him personally to do my job. (CCO 235)

This CCO viewed interactions with the community as purely business relationships and not personal ones that involve knowing more about the person than what is necessary to supervise the offender and protect the community.

Other comments, mostly by CCOs working in neighborhood-based supervision, reflected a role firmly embedded in creating a sense of "corrections of place" (Drapela & Lutze, 2009). The following quotes describe the CCO's role as using the community as a means to achieve better supervision but also as a place where CCOs can use their position to assist people to improve quality of life.

> The primary role, I think, is to, number one, educate the community about who we are, what we do, what our authority is, and how educating them on how they can assist us and how we can assist them in improving the quality of life in their neighborhood. (CCO 114)

> Our job is to assist them in solving problems, basically whatever that might be. If it's cleaning up the alley with garbage, if it's helping some elderly person change a filter in their furnace, whatever it is....We're here to assist them, NOT say, "Here's what you need to do, here's how you need to deal with these issues or problems." (CCO 111)

Therefore, CCOs primarily considered their roles as inclusive of educating the public about their work and enhancing public safety by supervising offenders through surveillance, treatment, networking with key community stakeholders, and getting to know the people surrounding the offender at the neighborhood level. While some viewed their work with the community more narrowly than others, nearly all understood the value of including community stakeholders to manage both the risk and needs of offenders. They tended to include functional examples of the importance of using social capital and collective efficacy within the community while attempting to support them when weak or absent. Not surprising, the need to educate the community and to enhance public safety were also themes that flowed through the joys and frustrations of directly working with the community.

Desire to work with the community. When asked, "Do you enjoy working with the community?" overwhelmingly CCOs expressed that they liked working with community members, while at the same time pointing out that some aspects are very difficult and at times frustrating. The positive features of working with the community revolved around professionally representing the DOC to the community, actively involving the community in supervision, and, for some, being more involved in the community itself. The negative parts of working with the community generally included dealing with complainers or those who enable offenders to continue their negative behavior.

In general, CCOs enjoyed building relationships with community stakeholders and incorporating family and neighbors into supervision to provide extra surveillance and support. For instance, the following quotes represent many of the positive responses given by CCOs.

> I love it. I love it. It lets me go out and hopefully present a positive image of our agency...I'll do this routinely. Here's a brand new guy, he gets out of jail next week or maybe he's been released for a week and I go to visit. Well, a lot of times he won't answer the door. What if I talk to this neighbor, this neighbor, and this neighbor, AND I left him a card. And I said, "You know what? You can call Crime Check and be put on hold for 45 minutes, or you can call me and I'll come out and you tell me what the problem is with this house. If there's no problem, that's good too. That's wonderful. I would hope it goes that way. But sometimes, based on this person's history, we think there might be." Instead of that, you know what, maybe I'll come out with the neighborhood resource officer [police officer]. And it'll be a good deal. These people are effectively being supervised by this, this, this, this—[gesturing]—it's wonderful. (CCO 227)

> Yeah. I guess I like keeping abreast of what resources are out there and keeping a real strong relationship with these resources for the next guy that you want to plug in there. And if you have a guy that blows the thing apart, you want to have a solid enough relationship that they're not going to say, "Get out of here, we dealt with your last guy and he destroyed our program!" [laughs] (CCO 243)

Some of the CCOs also expressed how being embedded in the community helps change the neighborhood context by working with citizens to empower the community and to take ownership and pride in their neighborhood. This was viewed as a true benefit to the individual CCO and to the DOC overall. For example,

> Oh, this is the way it should be [speaking about NBS]. To me, and of course I am only speaking for myself—and you are going to interview some people that say, "Hey, man, that's just, pfft, that's not my job...I

mean, I take pride in the fact that THEY take pride in their neighborhood. They take pride when they live in [this neighborhood], [this particular quadrant of] Spokane. And if I can help them gain more pride and more empowerment that makes ME feel great. You know, I mean, I think it's a wonderful thing. (CCO 105)

Even though CCOs enjoyed working with the community and identified the benefits of a close working relationship, they also expressed the ongoing burden of dealing with complaints and at times wished the community and family members would take greater responsibility in problem solving. For example,

Yeah I like meeting new people, I like getting their input, hearing what they have to say. That's one of the nice parts about my job, but then the other side of that is I get tired of listening to complaints. I get tired of all the blame being placed on DOC rather than the offender, rather than the community looking at what they could do to make things look different, take some responsibility. (CCO 201)

Yeah, the only exceptions are like enablers. They're part of the problem. In fact, they ARE the problem. You arrest somebody and you get five calls afterwards. And you were trying to get a hold of those people for two weeks and they wouldn't return your phone call.... You've got to deal with it. It's not fun, it's not nice. But at least you've got somebody keeping you on your toes. (CCO 252)

Many CCOs were also challenged by having to manage conflict or concerns from the community not based in fact or a clear understanding of CCOs' authority over offenders on their caseloads.

Uh, usually. Usually. It depends on potential conflicts based on very limited information or based on just the fact that they've got their thing to do, I've got my thing to do—the trick is trying to meet each other half way and accommodate and get done what you need to get done. (CCO 238)

Yeah. The learning curve is pretty steep. [laughing] I mean, you get whiners that come in that you can't do anything for. They just want to yell at you and they don't want to listen to what you have to say. Then you have other people that don't know how to ask a question that you've got to help get to the point where you even know what they are talking about and they have reasonable and legitimate concerns, so. It's been just a real learning experience—how to talk to folks, getting to know who you are dealing with. (CCO 103)

CCOs were also asked, "Do you believe that the average citizen respects what you do for a living?" The majority of CCOs (57.9%) believed that the general public did respect them professionally, but they often made a distinction between citizens who actually understood their role and those who did not and law-abiding citizens versus felons. Of those who felt they were not generally respected (23.7%) or didn't know if they were respected by the community (18.4 %), their reasons ranged from community ignorance about their work to pure disrespect. The following are examples.

Probably not. They don't even know what we do. (CCO 233)

No. I think while we are considered professionals, and we need to have a four-year degree to do this job, I think we are seen more as blue-collar workers, as a lower form. (235)

I have no idea. I've had people tell me, "I'd rather be a garbage carrier than a parole officer! Jesus Christ! You're a what?!?" (CCO 251)

One CCO felt she was disrespected because she was a woman doing what was perceived by the community as a man's job.

Okay, I think the average citizen respects what a male community corrections officer does. But I think the average citizen looks at me and thinks,...so, "Oh, you work with females?" "No." "You work with juveniles?" "No." So, I don't think they understand it. And, "Wouldn't you be scared to work with them? Well, how could YOU arrest somebody?" Not understanding the concept if a person is not going to be arrested, a male's not going to arrest them either. So, I don't think that they really understand—in Washington State—I don't believe they do. (CCO ---)

It appears that, for the most part, CCOs believe the average citizen respects their work, but they realize the community's perception is skewed because CCOs work with a population that is not always respected or accepted and the CCO's professional role is not as visible or as well understood as the role of police in society.

Overall, it appears that CCOs embrace the notion of working with the community and understand that the negative aspects of their encounters are an inherent part of their job as public servants. They delineate their role into protecting the community from offenders on supervision and educating the community about how and when CCOs may use their power to respond to community concerns about offenders. Although to varying degrees, CCOs clearly see the benefit of tapping into the social capital and collective efficacy within the community to enhance the quality of life for all involved. As is made clear in the next section, CCOs don't think working with the community is a one-sided affair but instead clearly expect the community to be involved in the well-being of their neighborhood and to work with the DOC as well as other criminal justice and social service providers.

Community Involvement in Community Corrections

Corrections of place requires CCOs to partner with the community in ways based on mutual respect and networking with individual citizens, community groups, and offenders to achieve mutually beneficial goals that increase the quality of community life and enhance public safety (Clear, 1996, 2005; Lehman, 2001). Although corrections of place requires CCOs to develop relationships with community stakeholders to identify problems and to work together to develop solutions, it also requires the community to proactively engage community corrections either as an outcome of their social capital and collective efficacy (community driven) or as a part of the community's social capital and collective efficacy (community based). This section explores how CCOs perceive the public's involvement in community corrections, how engaged citizens should be in the development of policy and determination of supervision plans, and how the community can specifically help offenders or be in any way responsible for community corrections. CCOs appear to have mixed opinions about the level of involvement the community should have in their work, but they strongly agree that the community needs to be actively engaged in their neighborhoods in order to safely reintegrate offenders.

To garner a global sense about CCOs' working relationship with the community, CCOs were asked whether their work is community driven or community based. *Community driven* means the community defines the problems that the agency then works to resolve. *Community based* refers to working in partnership with citizens to solve problems (Drapela & Lutze, 2009; Lutze et al., 2004). As Drapela and Lutze (2009) report, of the CCOs in the Spokane study, 42.5% reported their work as community driven, 27.5% believed it was both community driven and community based, 17.5% reported it to be community based, and 12.5% believed it was neither or really didn't know.[4] Those who perceived community corrections as community driven tended to report their work as reactionary, as seen in this quote:

> Community driven at this point. Yeah, because we're still responding to any given situation—and more after the fact—not as much ahead of time. I wish we could be more community based, I think that's the goal, but I think we're more community driven at this point. (CCO 248)

Another CCO described it as both; community based because of the reliance on many community resources and community driven because public demands drive legislative action.

> In many ways, it's both. I think it's community based in that there's so many pieces and parts of the community that I have to utilize to really make a good plan for somebody. . . the nonprofit, smaller resources that I might hook them up with, there's friends, neighbors, employers, family, that sort of thing. But then, the flip to that is that in lots of ways, we end up being community driven also at the legislative level because community outcry drives the legislators to make decisions about how they're gonna deal with our offender population. A good example of that is three strikes, you're out. (CCO 236)

Another CCO reflected that it was community based because of the personal relationships formed in working more closely with the community in a COPS Shop (Community-Oriented Policing Substations).

> I think it's more community based. You know, as I say, we assist them and they have a pretty good idea from education on what our job is, what our role is, what we do, what we can't do, and we feel like—at least I do—like we are a part of the community because you are here, you get emotionally involved with a lot of the volunteers, they see us as their friends, we feel the same way, you hear about problems.... So there are a lot of examples where you just feel like you are more a partner. (CCO 111)

It appears that community corrections tends to be more reactionary and community driven rather than partnership oriented and community based. Even CCOs assigned to work directly in partnership with the community were as likely as traditional CCOs (42% vs. 43%) to view their work as community driven or as a combination of both (25% vs. 28%). As expressed in the previous quote, however, NBS officers were more likely to view their work as purely community based (33%) compared to traditional officers (11%). Therefore, CCOs generally believe the community is driving their work, whether that is through legislative action or day-to-day requests for service.

To get a better idea of how involved the community should be in community corrections, CCOs were also asked about whether the community should have a say in how offenders are supervised and in determining DOC policy regarding community corrections. Overwhelmingly, CCOs thought the community should have a say, with some consistent concerns about justice and fairness, while a minority of CCOs disagreed, with justifications similar to those voicing agreement. Most who thought the community should have a say in policy believed citizens have influence through voting, public meetings, and the legislative process. For example,

> Well, I guess in a roundabout way, they do. You know, they elect the representatives that make laws that deal with the amount of jail time, anyway, or sanctions. I think, yeah, they should. They are the constituents, they are the people inevitably affected by what offenders do—positive or negative—because of that, I think, yeah, they should have. (CCO 111)

Other CCOs expressed mixed feelings about community members having a say in the treatment of offenders or in DOC policy. They could envision it being helpful as well as presenting challenges to the fair treatment of offenders. For example,

> It depends on the individual in that community. If the community member has no idea who this person is and is telling us that we need to slam him, throw him in jail forever and ever, you know, throw away the key type thing [then no]. If the person is like a neighborhood grandmother, a neighborhood family, that says, "That kid's a fairly decent kid, he just screwed up a few times and these are the areas that we think you ought to focus on to get this kid turned around," then to me, that gives a lot of value. (CCO 228)

For those not in favor of community involvement in supervision and DOC policy, it was primarily because they believed the community did not know enough or was too biased to be objective in its decision making regarding how offenders should be treated to inform DOC policy. The following quote is a fair representation of those who felt this way.

> That's a tough one to answer because I don't think they can give an educated guess because they don't really have an understanding of what

offenders' behaviors and needs are. I think they should feel free to give their input, but I don't think we should ever make decisions based on what community members tell us. (CCO 217)

CCOs were not asked specifically about race, ethnicity, or cultural competency, but a few did spontaneously mention race and diversity when asked about whether citizens should be involved in the decision making related to offenders. For example, the following CCO believed that citizens should have input and that understanding diversity was important to being accepted by and working effectively with an ethnically diverse community.

I think so. Especially if you are in a neighborhood where you are a white guy and a lot of the folks that you are dealing with are of a different ethnic background. Yeah, then I think you need to understand that diversity and be willing to listen to those folks because if you're not and if you don't, then you may as well just pack up and head out. Because they will drive you out. (CCO ---)

Thus, CCOs believed citizens should have influence concerning supervision and community corrections policy, but their input needed to be based on knowledge and tempered by a sense of justice and fairness. The themes that flowed through the CCOs' comments about the community having a say in policy were also evident in their ideas about what the community could do to help offenders or support community corrections. These experiences are similarly reflected in other research.

For example, Quinn and Gould (2003) asked Texas parole officers what they needed from the community. POs listed the following: public education/knowledge about their work (80%), respect/understanding for officers (40%), tolerance for releasees (31%), services for releasees (28%) and stricter policies/laws (10%). The needs listed by the Texas POs are similar to what CCOs in Spokane, Washington, noted in regard to public education (discussed earlier), tolerance for releasees, and the provision of services. Spokane CCOs differed, however, in identifying a need for the community to set standards for offenders living in their neighborhoods. Although Spokane CCOs did not identify a need for stricter policies and laws, they did identify a need for community members to get involved by providing CCOs with information about offenders so that they could more effectively intervene when necessary.

To gain a sense of how CCOs envisioned the role of the community in supervision, they were asked, "What do you believe the community can do to help offenders?" and "What is the community's responsibility to community corrections?" In terms of what the community could provide to the offender, CCOs' responses ranged from "nothing" to total involvement. The most-often cited topics by CCOs were related to providing basic resources (34%) and setting standards of acceptable behavior (34%) for those living in their neighborhoods. Others thought the community could provide more information about offenders to CCOs (29%), and one CCO reported that the community could do nothing to help offenders (2%).

Similar to other research, the resources mentioned by CCOs most often referred to employment, treatment services, housing, and support from family and friends (Gunnison & Helfgott, 2011; Helfgott & Gunnison, 2008; Lattimore et al., 2005). For instance, many CCOs appreciated employers' willingness to hire offenders on their caseload and at times seemed almost surprised that anyone would give offenders a chance by hiring them.

> You know, surprisingly, our community hasn't been too bad. They hire our people. They're pretty cooperative with the disclosure rules, and we can work with an employer to make sure that this is an employment where they're never left alone with minors and that no one's at risk and so on. And so I think overall the community's been pretty darn cooperative. Of course we've got the two residential hotels downtown that don't discriminate against our sex offenders. (CCO 205)

> I think people would be surprised at the number of employers that are willing to give offenders chances. I mean, I wouldn't hire half of these guys if I were an employer, but there are employers that will. I think maybe then [it is important] for the community to give them a chance. (CCO 219)

Others mentioned community support more specific to treatment and to offenders' emotional needs. For instance,

> Different aspects of the community deal with the offenders differently. I mean, the offender's family and friends can be supportive of them in terms of reinforcing positive behavior that they have and not reinforcing negative behavior. Treatment agencies in this community can provide treatment for offenders when they need it. (CCO 216)

> It depends on who you are talking about in the community. You know, the most dysfunctional people that I work with are typically the ones...that don't have any emotional support from family, friends, significant others,

anybody.... When they get attention, it's typically when they behave badly, you know, when they go and they get drunk and they hurt somebody or they commit a new crime.... It's so sad. I think one of the other things that both the department and the community could do for these folks is looking at providing them some education on just life skills in general. (CCO 236)

An equal number of CCOs perceived a need for the community to set standards for acceptable behavior and to hold offenders accountable for their behavior in the neighborhood. CCOs admitted that it took courage and respected those community members who actively confronted bad behavior by their neighbors. For instance,

To say, "You are living in my neighborhood, you are living down the street from me. Loud parties every single night of the week, and tons of short-stay traffic is not acceptable in my neighborhood. You want to live here? Great! You know, live like the rest of us. Go to work every day. Mow your lawn. Don't be smoking crack on the front porch and running hookers out of your basement. You know, that's not okay." And if people are consistent about that and they don't just close their eyes to it, it makes a huge difference. (CCO 103)

I really had to give some of these people credit because they would stand right up and tell somebody that runs a drug house, I'm going to close you down, I'm going to work with the cops, DOC and code enforcement.... The point they were making, and a number of them were retired, I own my house, I've lived here all my life, and I'm not moving, and you're not going to destroy this neighborhood. And I really had to give those people a lot of credit. I don't live there at night. I could go home. (CCO 112)

Lock the doors so that they can't get through [laughing]. No, ... it's kind of like, you know, I am willing to help you, I am willing to be involved in my community, but don't screw me. You know, that means don't come and steal out of my backyard then. (CCO 226)

In each of these descriptions of the need for the community to set standards for offenders, CCOs recognized that community members were willing to accept offenders as part of the community as long as they were willing to be good neighbors living prosocial, law-abiding lives. This is important because the community is often portrayed as taking a hard line against all offenders living in their neighborhood (NIMBY, not in my backyard) when the DOC attempts to place a community-based facility (halfway house or day reporting center) or when high-profile sex offenders are released to a neighborhood. Based on the observations of these CCOs, communities may be more flexible than traditionally believed and can live with average offenders as long as they have the support of others, formal and informal, to confront negative behavior.

CCOs also identified a need for the community to provide information about offenders when CCOs are unavailable to observe their behavior. Offenders' families and neighbors are witness to offenders' lives and therefore more likely to know when things are going well and when they are beginning to go bad again. For instance,

> The community helps me supervise the offenders. If an offender's coming home late at night or there's a noticeable drug action going on in the house, they're helping me supervise the offender by pointing out to me that this guy is relapsing. They're my ears and eyes to the court...they have a strong interest too because it's their community they're trying to protect. So, they're doing it for me too, but they're helping the community as well. (CCO 107)

> That whole community idea of an offender being supervised by neighbors, by guardians, it's a healthy way to do it. You know, I've got 91 people. I could use some help. You know, if I've got a nosy neighbor down the street that's keeping tabs on this guy, please, call me. I love you guys....I mean, if you're going to do what you can with limited resources to make this person truly supervised and answerable to the imposed conditions of the court, what do you do? You reach out and you get help from those other community members. (CCO ---)

Similar responses were given by CCOs when asked, "What do you see as the community's responsibility regarding community corrections?" All of the comments involved some level of citizen involvement (67%), followed by a willingness to provide information (24%) and to hold offenders accountable for their behavior (9%). CCOs' perception of the community's responsibility for community corrections tended to move beyond the individual to more global approaches. Responses included things like holding the DOC accountable, working to inform policy, contacting the legislature to enact change, engaging the criminal justice system through service on community boards, and actively being a partner to create change.

> Their responsibility is to hold us accountable as we do our jobs. Their responsibility is also to get involved on the legislative end of things if they don't like what it is we're doing and to make changes, not just to sit back and whine. (CCO 103)

I think their responsibility is to support the courts and the criminal justice system in terms of dealing with offenders and trying to make them accountable and trying to recover goods and services from them that they've taken from people. (CCO 216)

Other CCOs viewed the responsibility of the community as a "quid pro quo" (this for that) relationship where if the DOC is actively providing support to the community to solve problems, then the community needs to respond by helping the DOC. Likewise, if the community is being proactive, then the DOC needs to respond accordingly. For example,

I would say that they have to be willing to be part of it. They have to be willing to accept the partnership that we're offering. If we go out of the way to let them know what we do, who we have, how we operate, where we are, and who we are, basically, they should be willing to reciprocate that by informing us or giving us whatever information they have about these offenders. Just by saying, "I didn't see it. I don't want to talk about it," that's not going to cut it. (CCO 240)

Recognizing community safety is a collaborative effort. (CCO 231)

CCOs appear to believe that globally their work is driven by the demands of the community and the community should have influence concerning community corrections' policy and how offenders are supervised. They expressed caution, however, about whether the community is knowledgeable enough to inform policy without bias or with a thorough understanding about the risks and needs of most offenders living in the community. They also had clear ideas about how the community can help individual offenders and thought the community has a responsibility to assist with community corrections by being actively engaged in their neighborhoods. CCOs understood it takes a certain level of social capital and collective efficacy to sustain a healthy community and to address the needs of offenders. When social capital and collective efficacy were absent as described through examples of apathetic people in the community, absentee landlords, residential instability, or dysfunctional families, then everyone suffered—law-abiding citizens, offenders, and CCOs working with offenders.

CCOs want to more fully engage the *community* portion of their title based on their willingness to form professional relationships with offenders and their perceptions that the community can be helpful to both offenders and CCOs. Given that CCOs readily identified the community's importance to community corrections, it is important to consider how the community's social capital and collective efficacy may be effectively incorporated into community corrections work to reduce recidivism and increase community safety. More fully engaging the community further enhances the need to identify CCOs' role as boundary spanners with the power and position to become part of the community's social capital and collective efficacy and to work to enhance the community attributes necessary to effect change.

Working With Offenders and the Community as Boundary Spanners

Emphasizing *community* as equal to *corrections* in the CCO's title means community-centered strategies are as important as offender-centered strategies in achieving the goals of community corrections. Community-centered strategies require CCOs to understand the offender's needs and to give full consideration to whether the community is prepared to meet those needs, is willing to integrate the offender back into the community, and has the social capital or collective efficacy to leverage the support or control necessary to increase the likelihood of success. Importantly, although the intent and the importance of working more closely with the community varied among CCOs, nearly all understood the importance of engaging the community to be more effective in supervising offenders. Therefore, evidence shows CCOs have the fundamental desire necessary to bridge the power of the DOC to the strengths of the community to leverage the social capital and collective efficacy essential to achieve both control of and support for offenders.

A few CCOs captured the important role CCOs could play as boundary spanners due to their position and capacity to leverage the power and resources across a multitude of agencies, groups, and community stakeholders to provide a holistic response to supervision. For example, the following quote captures this broader vision of how CCOs can enhance social capital and collective efficacy through their position and the power of the DOC.

> You know, just to use a metaphor here, I would say to be the hub for the community. We are going to be connected in the process of transitioning these people from the institution.... We are going to be in contact with various agencies that, by their nature, they will have a positive impact on this offender's life upon release. No matter whether we talk about treatment providers, law enforcement, volunteers in the community, the basic guardians that we have recruited, or the natural people in the community, like employers or family members, all of these people are maintaining

contact with the DOC. And the department is represented by the CCO because the CCO has the ultimate authority in interacting with the offender and monitoring progress. So it is the CCO that's the hub of that whole operation. It's a very important role. It's a very complex role. It's a role that involves a lot of skill because, oftentimes, I'm sure you've heard this before, the CCO wears many hats. (CCO 240)

This CCO captures the entirety of the role of street-level boundary spanner and how such a person can effectively tie the formal and informal institutions of social control together to provide effective supervision, full integration, and community engagement.

Similarly, another CCO placed the CCO position, as well as the power of the DOC, within a boundary-spanning framework by identifying the DOC as uniquely positioned to understand the entirety of what is happening with the offender and community. When asked about what CCOs can do to solve problems within the community, the following CCO began with an offender-centered approach and then transitioned into a broader understanding of where the DOC is positioned to engage the community.

Okay, what we can do and what I can do is I can, number one, hold offenders accountable. I can do that. I can offer them and refer them to resources. And as to whether it takes or not, it's up to the offender.... But,...if this were to be us [DOC], and this is the community—all the community's ailments—whatever—generally end up with us. And I think we sit in a very unique position to understand what happened. Most of the time we know how these people got here. Where this particular segment [of the community] may not, or this one, but we're here—and we know how—I think we do see how we need to embrace, or be embraced by, the whole, so I think that we have an influence on offenders. (CCO 219)

Observations that place the DOC in a central position to assist offenders and the community capture the complexity of managing the individual offender within a broader community context. Placing CCOs purposefully in the center of providing offender-centered supervision and community-oriented engagement is important and complex. It means CCOs have to balance the individual risks offenders pose to the community with time spent working directly with community stakeholders to receive, monitor, and support offenders. In more affluent communities this may mean simply tapping into the existing social capital and becoming a member of the broader community to effect change. It may, however, be more complicated in disadvantaged communities where CCOs may have to work to enhance social capital and organize the collective efficacy necessary to join formal and informal social controls to reduce recidivism and enhance public safety. The complexity of such a role, however important it is to supervision and community corrections, requires consideration of how CCOs can incorporate this broader responsibility into their current workload.

Concerns about time were spontaneously expressed by several CCOs (18%) when talking about their role or desire to work more closely with the community. Although CCOs were not directly asked how greater involvement in the community might be incorporated into their work, many shared that, although they agreed with the DOC's initiative to more fully embrace the community as part of their jobs, they did not perceive it being possible given their current caseloads and responsibility for offender-centered supervision.[5] These concerns about how to both supervise the offender and build relationships with the community arose for both those assigned to neighborhood-based supervision as well as those working from more centralized state offices. For instance, the following NBS officers expressed these concerns:

> Well, I get paid by the state to be a community corrections officer. I mean, I am in the community and I am taking input from the community in how I can best adjust my job to reflect some of what the community needs and...I also have to be cognizant the state's paying me to supervise these people, so a lot of my community activity I just have to limit in order to get the job done,...I can't be here to go to everybody's meeting. I don't have enough time. (CCO 112)

> I wish we had more time—because we are community based—I wish we had more time to interact with the community. You know, we try to be there as much as we can, but because of the high caseloads and just because of the work, we can't, I mean, we've established rapports with apartment managers around here, business owners, and stuff like that, but there's a lot of them we haven't....It sucks [laughing]. (CCO 101)

Similarly, a traditional, state office–based CCO personalized the experience by indicating that work with the community was expected to take place beyond the 40-hour work week and that this was unreasonable.

> It's a good thing, only the real truth is it's something we have to do in addition to our job. And at a certain point, you really only want to go to work for 40 hours and go home....We do have a life in addition to DOC

and we have a right to that life. Some of us are better at guarding the piece that's ours than others. I'm probably a little pissed about it because I don't do a very good job of guarding it. I wind up getting caught up in this style and working more hours than I should. Sometimes I don't mind, sometimes I do mind. (CCO 251)

Another expressed the notion that if working with the community were really important to the DOC, then they would designate time for it to happen.

Not in this building. Maybe in a COP Shop. But then again, it depends on how many items are coming through the conveyor belt and if you give me the time to do those, because if you don't, then to me it's not important. It's not really critical. You can talk about it, but in reality it's not very important. If it were important, then you'd give me the time to do that. The only way to do that is to give me fewer offenders, less paperwork, less database requirements. (CCO 210)

Another CCO's comments suggest innovation may be stifled in working with the community because there just is not enough time.

I think there's always things that I can do, there's just not always the time to do it. There's always a community meeting or somebody calling with a question or somebody that you wish you could spend time with and talk. Or you have similar ideas and "oh, couldn't we develop this? Wouldn't this be a great program?" It's just time, the time to do those things. It's very complicated. You have enough work to do every day and then your own time in trying to fit all that in. (CCO 223)

It is unknown whether these comments reflect the majority of CCOs or just those who spontaneously shared the issue of time restraints related to community involvement. Given the number of CCOs who expressed not having enough time to manage their caseloads and develop closer working relationships with offenders (see Chapter 2 and Chapter 4), their time to work directly with the community may also be limited.

Time to work with the community and commitment by the organization were important concerns expressed by CCOs in their expectation to more fully engage the community in their work. These comments offer insight on how the broader department of corrections may have to adapt its expectations in order to support CCOs' work in the community beyond offender-centered approaches to supervision. The inability to move beyond

offender-centered strategies and record keeping burdens may hamper innovation on multiple levels and stifle opportunities for CCOs to be effective
boundary spanners.

INTEGRATING OFFENDER-CENTERED
AND COMMUNITY-CENTERED SUPERVISION

Research shows that communities matter to the success of offenders
(Clear, 2007; Frost & Gross, 2012; Kirk, 2009, 2012; Kubrin & Steward,
2006; Sampson, 2002; Travis, 2005). Many offenders return to disadvantaged communities challenged by poverty, crime, concentrated incarceration and reentry, residential instability, and social disorganization. Such
communities struggle to sustain the social capital and collective efficacy
necessary to control the behavior of offenders or to provide them with the
support needed to achieve long-term reintegration. Community corrections
officers are confronted with this reality when attempting to create offender-
centered plans that adequately address both the risk and needs of offenders. They also readily identify the importance of the community to
supervision and their success in working with offenders.

Although community corrections officers do not use the terminology
of that in the literature, they readily identify the important attributes of
communities related to spatial boundaries, social and kinship networks,
and structure around a common set of values. They clearly understand that
individuals, families, neighbors, community members, businesses, organizations, and government institutions are all important to the community
and to their work supervising offenders and enhancing community safety.
They have very clear expectations that the community can directly help
offenders and that it has a responsibility to set standards for offenders and
to be proactive in the overall well-being of their neighborhoods. Community
corrections officers recognize through their shared working experiences
the importance of tapping into the community's social capital and collective efficacy to successfully reintegrate offenders into the community.
They also understand that when a community is disorganized, CCOs may
be influential in strengthening a neighborhood's social capital and collective efficacy and ideally improving the quality of life and well-being of
offenders on their caseloads and the citizens in the community.

CCOs generally enjoyed working with the community, but they were
not naïve about the challenges and complexity of being directly involved
in the community. While the majority of community corrections officers
were willing to fully engage the community in their work, they recognized

that this often left them vulnerable to complaints from citizens and having to explain the extent of their power and authority to deal with the negative behavior of offenders. They also acknowledged that to more fully engage the community may impinge on their already limited time to focus on offender risks and needs and their responsibility for enforcing individual supervision plans (Drapela & Lutze, 2009). They were also concerned that the time dedicated to building relationships with the community was to be conducted in addition to their existing responsibilities and outside of their traditional work schedule, thus impinging on their personal time.

CCOs viewed working with the community as important to their over-all mission to hold offenders accountable, provide support, and ensure safe communities. Understanding community corrections officers' views about working with the community may help structure their work in the future. For example, the findings of this chapter closely parallel the findings in the previous chapter regarding CCOs' willingness to develop professional relationships with offenders. It became clear that a purely surveillance or social work approach was less effective than a balanced approach to supervision that included accountability and support. A clearer understanding about CCOs' regard for the community reflects similar findings related to the dichotomy between offender-centered versus community-centered approaches. CCOs appear to believe that a combination of the two approaches is most beneficial in achieving successful integration. In other words, they must work to hold individual offenders accountable by creating offender-centered plans of supervision, but they must also treat offenders not as isolated cases but as integrated members of the community. It is apparent that the CCO role is not well served by isolation but is enhanced when undertaken as a member of the community.

Conceptualizing CCOs' work as embedded in the community and not as "other than prison" acknowledges the important role they play as street-level boundary spanners. As boundary spanners they are able to bridge the gap between offender-centered supervision and the community. They become pivotal keys to the ultimate success of the criminal justice system by bringing together the necessary components of successful reintegration and formal and informal social control to address the complex challenges confronting offenders and the communities in which CCOs serve. Fully understanding community corrections as part of a broader ecological context opens up opportunities for innovation and the importance of interdisciplinary approaches to corrections (Bazemore, Nissen, & Dooley, 2000). It recognizes the power and position of community corrections as central to the success of offenders instead of as a weak afterthought to police, courts, and institutional corrections.

NOTES

1. Lehman, 2001, p. 45

2. Rank (2004) presents a convincing argument that many in the United States believe poverty is due to individual failure versus systematic structural inequality. Therefore, CCOs may identify the conditions of the community as presenting hardships but view the causes of poverty as individual.

3. This CCO's reference to people in the community being used as "guardians" refers to a WA State DOC initiative that recruited volunteers to serve as formal guardians to offenders being supervised in the community. The CCO cited here obviously did not see a need to formalize or change the existing relationships with individual community members. Others quoted later, however, embraced the idea.

4. Drapela and Lutze (2009) reported on the differences between neighborhood-based supervision (NBS) and traditional CCOs. The NBS and TRD groups were similar in believing community corrections was community driven (42% vs. 43% respectively) and in holding mixed views (25% vs. 28%) but differed in their beliefs on whether it was community based (33% vs. 11% respectively) or neither/do not know (0% vs. 18%). These differences are not surprising given that NBS CCOs were located in "Community-Oriented Policing Substations" (COPS Shops) located in neighborhoods around the city with a mission to be more involved in the community. In spite of different assignments, there was a great deal of overlap in their views.

5. CCOs expressed their concerns about a lack of time to work with the community primarily in response to a question about whether there was anything they could accomplish through their position as a CCO to address community problems. One CCO (101) response is from a question in the interview about time management.

WORKS CITED

Anderson, E. (1999). *Code of the street: Decency, violence, and the moral life of the inner city.* New York: W. W. Norton.

Bazemore, G., Nissen, L. B., & Dooley, M. (2000). Mobilizing social support and building relationships: Broadening correctional and rehabilitative agendas. Corrections Management Quarterly, *4*(4), 10–21.

Clear, T. R. (1996, August). Toward a corrections of "place": The challenge of "community" in corrections. *National Institute of Justice Journal, 231,* 52–56.

Clear, T. R. (2005). Places not cases? Re-thinking the probation focus. *The Howard Journal, 44*(2), 172–184.

Clear, T. R. (2007). *Imprisoning communities: How mass incarceration makes disadvantaged neighborhoods worse*. New York: Oxford University Press.

Clear, T. R., Hamilton, J., & Cadora, E. (2011). *Community justice* (2nd ed.). New York: Routledge.

Dhondt, G. (2012). The bluntness of incarceration: Crime and punishment in Tallahassee neighborhoods, 1995–2002. *Crime, Law and Social Change, 57*(5), 521–538.

Drapela, L. A., & Lutze, F. E. (2009). Innovation in community corrections and probation officers' fears of being sued: Implementing neighborhood-based supervision in Spokane, Washington. *Journal of Contemporary Criminal Justice, 25*(1), 364–383.

Frost, N. A., & Gross, L. A. (2012). Coercive mobility and the impact of prison-cycling on communities. *Crime, Law and Social Change, 57*(5), 459–474.

Geller, A., & Curtis, M. A. (2011). A sort of homecoming: Incarceration and the housing security of urban men. *Social Science Research, 40,* 1196–1213.

Gunnison, E., & Helfgott, J. B. (2011). Factors that hinder offender reentry success: A view from community corrections officers. *International Journal of Offender Therapy and Comparative Criminology, 55*(2), 287–304.

Helfgott, J. B. (1997). Ex-offender need versus community opportunity in Seattle, Washington. *Federal Probation, 61*(2), 12–24.

Helfgott, J. B., & Gunnison, E. (2008). The influence of social distance on community corrections officer perceptions of offender reentry needs. *Federal Probation, 72*(1), 2–12.

Hipp, J. R., Jannetta, J., Shah, R., & Turner, S. (2011). Parolees' physical closeness to services: A study of California parolees. *Crime & Delinquency, 77*(1), 102–129.

Kirk, D. S. (2009). A natural experiment on residential change and recidivism: Lessons from Hurricane Katrina. *American Sociological Review, 74*(3), 484–505.

Kirk, D. S. (2012). Residential change as a turning point in the life course of crime: Desistance or temporary cessation? *Criminology, 50*(2), 329–358.

Kubrin, C. E., & Stewart, E. A. (2006). Predicting who reoffends: The neglected role of neighborhood context in recidivism studies. *Criminology, 44,* 165–197.

Lattimore, P. K., Visher, C. A., Winterfield, L., Lindquist, C., & Brumbaugh, S. (2005). Implementation of prisoner reentry programs: Findings from the Serious and Violent Offender Reentry Initiative multi-site evaluation. *Justice Research and Policy, 7*(2), 87–109.

Lehman, J. D. (2001). Reinventing community corrections in Washington State. *Corrections Management Quarterly, 5*(3), 41–45.

Lutze, F. E., Smith, R. P., & Lovrich, N. P. (2000). Premises for attaining more effective offender accountability through community involvement: Washington State's new approach. *Corrections Management Quarterly, 4*(4), 1–9.

Lutze, F. E., Smith, R. P., & Lovrich, N. P. (2004). A practitioner-initiated research partnership: An evaluation of neighborhood based supervision in Spokane, Washington (Grant #: 1999-CE-VX-0007). Final Report, National Institute of Justice, Washington, DC.

Mele, C., & Miller, T. A. (2005). *Civil penalties, social consequences*. New York: Routledge.

Murphy, D., & Lutze, F. (2009). Police-probation partnerships: Professional identity and the sharing of coercive power. *Journal of Criminal Justice, 37*, 65–76.

Petersilia, J. (2003). *When prisoners come home: Parole and prisoner reentry*. New York: Oxford University Press.

Portes, A. (1998). Social capital: Its origins and applications in modern society. *Annual Review of Sociology, 24*, 1–24.

Purkiss, M., Kifer, M., Hemmens, C., & Burton, V. S., Jr. (2003). Probation officer functions—A statutory analysis. *Federal Probation, 67*(1), 12.

Quinn, J., & Gould, L. (2003). The prioritization of treatment among Texas parole officers. *The Prison Journal, 83*, 323–336.

Rank, M. R. (2004). One nation, underprivileged: Why American poverty affects us all. New York: Oxford University Press.

Rapheal, J. (2000). Saving Bernice: Battered women, welfare, and poverty. Boston: Northeastern University Press.

Roman, C. G., & Travis, J. (2006). Where will I sleep tomorrow? Housing, homelessness, and the returning prisoner. *Housing Policy Debate, 17*(2), 389–418.

Rose, D. R., & Clear, T. R. (1998). Incarceration, social capital, and crime: Implications for social disorganization theory. *Criminology, 36*(3), 441–480.

Sampson, R. J. (2002). The community. In J. Q. Wilson & J. Petersilia (Eds.), *Crime: Public policies for crime control* (pp. 225–252). Oakland, CA: ICS Press.

Sampson, R. J., Morenoff, J. D., & Gannon-Rowley, T. (2002). Assessing "neighborhood effects": Social processes and new directions in research. *Annual Review of Sociology, 28*, 443–478.

Travis, J. (2005). *But they all come back: Facing the challenges of prisoner reentry*. Washington, DC: The Urban Institute.

Wilson, W. J. (1987). The truly disadvantaged: The inner city, the underclass, and public policy. Chicago: University of Chicago Press.

Wright, K. A., Pratt, T. C., Lowenkamp, C. T., & Latessa, E. J. (2012). The importance of ecological context for correctional rehabilitation programs: Understanding the micro- and macro-level dimensions of successful offender treatment. *Justice Quarterly, 29*(6), 775–798.

Young, D., Taxman, F., & Byrne, J. (2002). *Engaging the community in offender reentry*. Unpublished manuscript. Washington, DC: U.S. Department of Justice.

❦ FOUR ❦

WORKING WITHIN COMMUNITY CORRECTIONS AGENCIES

State-level corrections agencies are large bureaucracies managing thousands of employees responsible for the safe and secure confinement and community supervision of thousands of convicted felons. The magnitude and complexity of supervising and reintegrating offenders provides many opportunities and challenges to contemporary corrections. The multifaceted goals of using community corrections for punishment, surveillance, support, and treatment creates a dynamic professional environment. Both administrators and CCOs are encouraged to structure the organization and their practice to focus on interventions effective in reducing recidivism and increasing the likelihood of long-term reintegration. CCOs are expected to understand and implement evidence-based practices (EBP) that require proactively engaging the offender, understanding the extent of the risk they pose to the community, and addressing the needs that may defeat their reintegration. The way agencies are structured, managed, and implemented directly influences outcomes for both CCOs and offenders.

This chapter considers what it is like to work for community corrections agencies and how CCOs are inspired and challenged by the implementation of EBP. Similar to other criminal justice professionals, CCOs must grapple with the implementation of new laws, changes in administrative policies, a complex professional culture, exposure to liability, and the potential for public scrutiny in the wake of sensational cases. They must also be prepared to change with the times. Just as corrections once moved from rehabilitation to punishment, CCOs now must adapt to a new era of corrections responsible for both control and implementing EBP. Evidence-based practice requires CCOs to contemplate how their role may expand within a professional environment increasingly sensitive to what works and how community corrections agencies and officers achieve positive outcomes.

The changes inspired during the get-tough era remain—with a focus on surveillance, monitoring, and offender accountability—but expectations are changing. Researchers in the last 30 years working with corrections professionals in search of what works discovered that implementing programs according to the principles of effective treatment, managing organizations intentionally to change outcomes, and targeting high-risk offenders significantly reduced recidivism (see Chapter 5). These findings, in the context of the overwhelming costs of corrections (both monetary and human) and the recession of 2007–2008, forced policymakers to reconsider punishment as the sole force driving corrections and to invest in practices that are proven to work or are at least promising given their design.

This shift in corrections, like those of the past, is inspired by good intentions, is implemented within the reality of existing operations, and poses opportunities and challenges to CCOs. The coexistence of offender accountability and evidence-based practices provides opportunities for CCOs to fluidly combine law enforcement and social work approaches. Many of the same old challenges, however, remain, such as an overwhelming need to minimize professional risk due to the danger many offenders pose to the community. While multiple opportunities for professional development emerge with EBP, issues such as risk assessments, liability, large caseloads, safety, and managing stress will persist unless significant and relevant changes are made to contemporary community corrections. Innovation and change are challenging in the current political, economic, and social climate, as they have been throughout the history of corrections (McCorkle & Crank, 1996; Pisciotta, 1994; Rothman, 1980).

BALANCING RISK MANAGEMENT WITH EVIDENCE-BASED CORRECTIONS

The advent of the punitive, get-tough era unforgivingly spotlighted the worst of failures in community supervision with little attention paid to its successes (see Gunnison & Helfgott, 2013). The political and public pressure to hold offenders accountable and zero tolerance for failure have led to a hyperfocus on risk management and monitoring of not just offenders but also the work of CCOs in an attempt to regulate risk and avoid public embarrassment to the agency. Contemporary attempts to implement innovative practices and change are constantly bound within this context of risk management. Thus it is important to understand how the management of risk, real and perceived, influences the agency and CCOs in how they conduct the work of supervising offenders. Risk is ever-present and even when managed well can never be completely controlled. Policymakers, administrators, supervisors, CCOs, and the community are certain to be reminded when something goes violently wrong.

Media Sensationalism and Community Corrections

Over 50 years ago, before 24-hour news cycles and immediate Internet access, Ohlin, Piven, and Pappenfort (1956) observed that the media were a powerful force influencing community corrections. Ohlin and his colleagues state,

> The failure of probation and parole are more spectacular than those in most other professions, and newsmen have the occupational motive of "good copy" to encourage them to scrutinize correctional practice and organize critical public opinion around a dramatically destructive episode. Elected judges, legislatures, and other public officials have a vested interest in being on the popular side of a crisis, and occupational groups whose interests are inherently in opposition to client-centered probation and parole supervision are able to use periods of public excitement to further their own purposes. Consequently the administrator is under pressure to anticipate possible criticism and to organize the agency and its policies in self-protection. (p. 218)

Similarly, others have observed that negative public opinion and a general lack of interest or understanding—and sometimes outward hostility—from other agencies toward probation and parole added to CCOs' difficulty in serving offenders in a manner most likely to reduce recidivism (see Takagi, 1973; Weber, 1958). Weber (1958) even went so far as to accuse researchers of being unduly swayed by the extraordinary by writing, "The collection of convenient, exciting or sensational phenomena, while interesting, contributes very little to what is needed" (p. 583). He advocated for science to discover what works and transfer this knowledge to those working in the field.

Although social science research has come a long way to help inform policy and practice, little has changed related to media depictions of sensational cases, which often portray the most heinous of crimes, and the scrutiny administrators and front-line officers have to endure as they defend against the public, political, and legal attacks soon to follow (see DeMichele, 2007; Lynch, 1998; Morgan, Belbot, & Clark, 1997; Surette, 2011). In response to an overwhelming desire by policymakers to be viewed as taking action in response to public outcry, new legislation and administrative policies are often created to control behavior and limit the discretion of the agency and CCOs.

Sensational cases often start local but have the capacity to expand and drive public policy at the state and national level. These policies often result in the adoption of new state laws such as "three strikes" or congressional acts at the federal level that are then expected to be implemented by the states (see Lovrich, Lutze, & Lovrich, 2012). Such laws are commonly named after the victims, as with Megan's Law, the Adam Walsh Act, and the Wetterling Act (Griffin & Stitt, 2010; Harris & Lobanov-Rostovsky, 2010). Although well intended, many of these laws become extremely burdensome to implement and expensive to sustain over time and may not achieve their goal of increasing public safety. Recent examples include the federally legislated Adam Walsh Act, which the majority of states have found expensive and cumbersome to implement, or the state-level "three strikes" legislation in California passed by ballot initiative in the early 1990s and recently repealed through the same process during the 2012 election due to its negative impact on corrections (see Freeman & Sandler, 2010; Harris & Lobanov-Rostovsky, 2010). As one of the community corrections officers in Lynch's (1998) study observed,

> Mostly what you see happen is an incident occurs involving a parolee, there's a public spotlight on it, there's a knee-jerk reaction, but the response is so cumbersome and ridiculous that it just, it's self-defeating. Instead of trying to deal with the issue in a way that can enhance public safety, it ends up being a cover-your-ass kind of thing. (p. 857)

Agencies oftentimes implement policies in an attempt to defend against accusations of negligence by requiring specific practices and mandating documentation of CCO activities for each person on a caseload. For example, policy may dictate the time frame for completing risk and need assessments and developing a supervision plan, the number of home and office visits, and the number of collateral contacts with employers, landlords, treatment providers, family, or neighbors. Policy may also dictate what activities must be completed during contacts with offenders, such as risk and needs assessments, drug tests, and polygraphs. When something goes wrong, the first line of defense is to see whether the CCO adhered to policy through what is recorded in the offender's case management file. Whether the decisions and actions of the CCO were in line with best practices according to professional standards is often secondary.

The potential for an offender on a CCO's caseload to commit a heinous act, although low, is ever-present. CCOs often believe that even when they do everything right, it probably will not be enough to prevent recidivism in general and more specifically a high-profile crime, such as a homicide, kidnapping, or rape, that brings broad media attention and professional consequences (see West & Seiter, 2004). This concern presents itself as a real threat to the well-being of CCOs and the community, as seen in the following quote:

Well, I got up on a Sunday morning, my wife, reading the paper, says, "Hey, you know a [name of offender]." "Yeah, I do." "Well, he just [cites specific violent crime and victim characteristics]." [tears welling up in subject's eyes] I said, "Oh, shit." That right there, you know, is a nightmare. He's on my caseload. What could I have done to prevent that? I just saw the guy in the afternoon and it happened that night. What could I have done to prevent that? Nothing I could have done would have prevented it. But, like anything else, if something happens, someone has to be blamed. Someone's got to be blamed for this. So, who do you think is going to be blamed but the officer? So, yeah, you are constantly under— something is going to blow up that you are going to be held accountable for. You know, we're held accountable. (CCO ---)

He's got "Hail Hitler" across his back…it's a religion to him. He is the chosen race. He is the master plan. This guy, right here [showing a picture], shot his own girlfriend. [graphically describes injury]…Come on man! This guy's going to be on CNN before I know it, and someone's going to ask me, "Have you been doing your job on this guy?" That's the reality. That's a lot of liability. (CCO ---)

The observations of these officers illustrate the concern about outcomes outside of CCOs' control, whether it is an offender who presents obvious indicators of risk or one seemingly benign.

CCOs do not seem totally media adverse. They often see the media as having the power to inform and educate the public about what CCOs do and the importance of their work to the criminal justice system and community. For instance, one CCO observed,

It would be nice, and it had happened in Spokane two or three times in the last couple of years where the media has done a special segment over a week or two period of time involving community corrections officers and the police and community resources as just an informational-type thing on what we do and how we interact with other people and what each agency's role is and that sort of thing….And that's where people get their information, is out of the newspaper and out of the TV stations and stuff like that. (CCO 243)

Therefore, at both the organizational and individual level of operation, there are very legitimate concerns about managing risk. Administrators attempt to manage risk through the implementation of policies to either guide or mandate the actions of CCOs. These policies generally require extensive documentation that results in a significant amount of office work. CCOs attempt to manage risk by meeting face-to-face with offenders and trying to be in the field as much as possible to monitor their behavior and determine whether it may result in a new crime. Although different approaches are taken by administrators and CCOs, both groups tend to embrace a "cover your ass" (CYA) mentality that permeates the profession. Although the media consistently focus on the failure of individual offenders and then direct blame at the organization, researchers have begun to focus first on organizational structure and how this may lead to the success or failure of individuals.

Structuring Agencies to Manage Risk

The ongoing political and public fallout from sensational cases, and their use to promote crime control policies, has created a context and culture within community corrections that emphasizes risk management. As a result, risk prediction has become an important commodity within corrections and how agencies as well as offenders are managed. Many have argued that the scales have tipped from managing offenders based on face-to-face interactions and professional instinct (clinical risk assessment) to scientific-based risk prediction models driven by data (actuarial risk assessment) (see Andrews & Bonta, 2010; Feeley & Simon, 1992; Latessa & Lovins, 2010; Takagi, 1973). Contemporary scholars have argued both the pros and cons of shifting to scientifically informed management and supervision.

The criticism of data-driven approaches is founded on the belief that they abandon human interaction and relationship building with offenders to achieve effective supervision and successful reintegration. Takagi (1973) observed that new management styles emerging after World War II focused on data-driven management and the development of regulations to replace the discretion of corrections workers and to enhance uniformity of CCO activities so their work could be easily monitored. Uniformity and the documentation of each activity as well as the provision of detailed information about offender characteristics allowed administrators to analyze data, be assured CCOs were adhering to policy, and make decisions based on overall patterns versus individual cases. Takagi (1973) argues that this resulted in an "administrative structure in which the worker becomes diverted from the primary task of serving the client in favor of an inordinate concern with the administration of the organization's regulations" (p. 314; also see Gregory, 2010). Takagi proposes that "supervisors and superiors evaluated subordinates on the basis of these standards, and in the process, organizational *efficiency* became confused with organizational *effectiveness*" (emphasis in original quote; p. 314). There is evidence in the contemporary literature to support Takagi's position.

For instance, Lynch (1998) observed in a qualitative study of a California field office that supervisors scrutinized CCOs' case management files, not to determine the quality of their work with parolees but instead to determine whether agents had adequately kept written documentation of required tasks, such as making the mandated number of contacts, collecting urine samples, and completing reports within the required time limits. Management encouraged CCOs to "cover their butts" by completing proper paperwork (Lynch, 1998, p. 850). Recognition and awards were given for successfully meeting record-keeping expectations and not for the quality or outcomes of supervision.

The proponents of data-driven actuarial models of managing risk and informing community supervision practice argue that scientific assessments of risk, anchored in the analysis of organizational data, are more reliable than clinical assessments or CCO intuition (see Andrews & Bonta, 2010; Latessa & Lovins, 2010). In other words, when attempting to predict who is most likely to reoffend, formal risk assessment tools are more accurate than professional perceptions of the offender's likelihood to reoffend. Organizational data can be used to show both the strengths and weaknesses of various approaches to supervision, whether they are punishment or rehabilitation oriented, and inform how programs and practices may be strengthened to improve outcomes (see Cullen & Jonson, 2012).

Efficiency and accuracy are also perceived as benefits of data-driven management approaches to risk control. For instance, community corrections populations have grown extensively in recent years, creating organizational pressure to more efficiently and effectively manage this population to assure community safety. Formal risk assessment tools allow agencies to more reliably classify offenders into low-, moderate-, and high-risk groups than do traditional approaches. This risk classification scheme allows agencies to direct the greatest number of resources toward those most likely to reoffend and minimize time and energy on those at low risk of reoffending. Therefore, risk is managed by requiring CCOs to spend more time with high-risk offenders through a greater number of home and office visits, increased drug and alcohol tests, and more contact with treatment providers.

Actuarial risk and need assessments do more than just classify offenders into groups. They also identify which attitudes, behaviors, and needs should be targeted to effect change (see Andrews & Bonta, 2010). For instance, research shows that risk, need, and responsivity (RNR) are important to changing behavior and improving agency and offender outcomes. Andrews and Bonta's (2010) RNR model, based in psychology and extensively studied in criminal justice, shows that targeting the criminogenic risks (e.g., antisocial attitudes, peers, and personality of offenders with a criminal history) and needs (e.g., familial circumstances, educational or vocational attainment, leisure or recreational activities, and substance abuse problems) significantly reduces recidivism compared to unstructured and vague clinical approaches (see Andrews & Bonta, 2010; Cullen & Jonson, 2012). In short, best practices include using standardized, validated assessment tools to assess risk and identify needs, targeting high-risk offenders for treatment and services, and making referrals or providing treatment to address offender risk and needs (see Andrews & Bonta, 2010; Cullen & Jonson, 2012; Farrell, Young, & Taxman, 2011; Latessa & Lovins, 2010).

Although the importance of risk assessment has been evident in corrections for over 100 years, tension still remains between the organization and officers about how risk should be measured and managed. Even though actuarial models and clinical models are often pitted against each other, it does not mean they are mutually exclusive. Data-driven approaches should inform best practices that are then incorporated into the human relationships inherent to community corrections. The unease between CCOs and the agency seems to surround the balance between the agency supporting CCOs to achieve implementation of risk assessment tools and other evidence-based practices and the required administrative tasks necessary to support data-driven, evidence-based practices. As shown shortly, even though agencies can improve supervision outcomes based on what is learned through data collected by field officers, CCOs often express a need for relief from the burden of clerical work necessary for administrators to justify their practices and for CCOs to defend against a lawsuit. Current managers are under constant pressure to not only protect the agency from outside criticism but also to prove that what they are doing works to change outcomes.

Structuring Agencies to Support Evidence-Based Practice

Recent research has begun to focus on how community corrections agencies are structured to achieve success. For too long, outcome failure has been sheltered within a philosophy that nothing works to reform offenders and therefore all correctional agencies can possibly do is manage risk through rearrest, revocation, and readmission to prison. This philosophy focuses on negative behavior and accepts failure as the status quo, thus skewing outcomes toward short-term failure instead of long-term change and reintegration (see Harris, Gingerich, & Whittaker, 2004; Latessa, Cullen, & Gendreau, 2002; Lynch, 1998). With the advent of evidence-based practices, it has become clear that offender change is possible and can be enhanced through organizational philosophy and structures geared toward achieving successful outcomes (see Farrell et al., 2011). This research has shifted the focus away from the offender and on to the quality and function of the organization to effect change and enhance both agency and offender outcomes.

Several core principles guide the function of effective corrections agencies at the organizational level (Andrews & Bonta, 2010; Latessa et al., 2002). The principles include a strong organizational culture with well-defined goals reinforced through training, a professional staff, and built-in quality assurances to evaluate ongoing effectiveness. Managers select and support programs consistent with the organization's values that are theoretically informed based on a thorough review of the literature. The core correctional practices emphasize anticriminal modeling, problem solving, structural learning and skill building, cognitive-behavioral treatment, and motivational interviewing. Client risk and need assessments are used to accurately predict and target the type and level of intervention necessary to achieve improved outcomes related to accountability, support, and treatment. Interagency communication is used to aggressively refer offenders to services in the community and to advocate on their behalf to assure reasonable access to and receipt of quality, evidence-based treatment.

Organizations demonstrating greater levels of structural integrity through hiring qualified staff, implementing theoretically informed programs, building quality assurances to sustain program integrity, and targeting appropriate populations to receive services achieve significantly greater (up to 30%) reductions in recidivism than those that lack structural integrity. Importantly, those agencies that fail to incorporate the principles of effective interventions may actually increase recidivism (see Andrews & Bonta, 2010; Fulton, Latessa, Stichman, & Travis, 1997; Latessa, 2008; Lowenkamp, Latessa, & Holsinger, 2006; Lowenkamp, Latessa, & Smith, 2006). Many agencies, however, struggle with implementing and sustaining operational integrity over time. For instance, one study assessing the operational integrity of corrections organizations found that 68% were rated as "unsatisfactory," and another 35% were found to be "satisfactory, but needs improvement" (Lowenkamp, Latessa, & Smith, 2006).

The characteristics of organizations are important to the implementation of EBP. Agencies with staff more likely to engage in evidence-based practices have supervisory leadership that is more likely to support service-oriented practices (Farrell et al., 2011; Henderson, Taxman, &

Young, 2007). They also hire and promote administrators who have the educational and professional experience to understand the importance of EBP to organizational and client-oriented outcomes and who are support-ive of rehabilitation (see Henderson, Young, Farrell, & Taxman, 2009). The climate of the agency is also important, with EBP more likely used when staff experience low levels of conflict, clarification of roles, support from others, and minimal exposure to cynicism (see Farrell et al., 2011). Finally, staff from agencies that dedicate resources to training on EBPs and the importance of adhering to the integrity of model interventions are more likely to use EBP in their work (Henderson et al., 2007).

Not surprisingly, research shows that the characteristics of the state and the parent institution to which agencies belong are also important to imple-menting and sustaining EBP (see Henderson et al., 2009). States with fewer barriers between community corrections and health service agencies have more networking relationships among criminal justice agencies, more staff who remain at the executive level for a longer period of time, and adminis-trators who hold positive attitudes toward correctional treatment and are more likely to adopt EBP (Henderson et al., 2009; Lovrich et al., 2012). Within state-level organizations are multiple subunits or agencies, and implementation of EBP may vary based on the jurisdiction. For instance, agencies that develop strong interagency networks and collaborations within their jurisdictions are more likely to implement EBP. Therefore, the use of evidence-based practices is directly affected by whether they are supported by the state and local communities, the administrative leadership, and indi-vidual supervisors responsible for leading and sustaining best practices.

Latessa et al. (2002) argue that a failure of corrections agencies to con-sider and implement interventions proven to reduce recidivism is equivalent to malpractice and would not be tolerated in any other profession where scientific knowledge directs the assessment, interventions, and practice most likely to work (e.g., medicine, engineering). Yet many corrections agencies continue to function as if "nothing works" and ignore the growing body of scientific evidence that shows following the principles of effective interventions, in both supervision and treatment, matters in reducing recid-ivism (Latessa et al., 2002). Contemporary examples are beginning to appear in the literature showing that agencies can no longer ignore what works. For instance, one of the supervisors interviewed by Armstrong (2012) in a study concerning the implementation of EBP related the obser-vations of a corrections professional who was aware of two cases,

> where the probation officer was sued for being negligent. In both cases, the attorneys hired an expert witness... and they wanted to know whether

they knew or should have known what the evidence says they should have done. (p. 444)

This concern was reiterated by a chief probation officer who commented in reference to determining what may happen if agencies fail to achieve the appropriate span of control necessary to manage CCOs in an EBP model.

perhaps another way of looking at this is liability that your jurisdiction may incur—failure to train, direct, supervise, entrust, discipline, and assignment to name but a few. (Armstrong, 2012, p. 444)

In other words, legal professionals are beginning to establish whether the agency and the CCO did what they should have done according to the professional standards established in the field related to best practices and, if not, determining the possibility of negligence.

The shift to include both EBP and offender accountability in supervision strategies is going to require significant change away from business as usual. Implementing EBP requires a significant increase in the supervisor's and CCO's responsibility related to time investment, task complexity, workforce skill level, and the work environment. Armstrong (2012) reports that EBP requires greater involvement of supervisors with front-line officers who are in turn expected to have greater involvement with their clients. EBP requires greater levels of expertise related to effective supervision practices (e.g., administering risk/need assessments, motivational interviewing, graduated sanctions, rewards) and treatment modalities (e.g., substance abuse, mental health, life skills), support services available in the community (e.g., social services, community action centers, shelters), and collaborations with agencies within criminal justice (e.g., police, courts, jails/prisons) as well as external to community corrections (e.g., social services, mental health, education). Armstrong (2012) reports that supervisors and officers found EBP approaches to consume extraordinary amounts of time because of the complexity of tasks, the ability to learn the necessary skills to effectively supervise staff and offenders, and the management of the work environment to be less reactive to crises and more proactive toward managing behavior. Therefore, EBP must be implemented with these factors in mind or the likelihood of effective implementation and the integrity of supervision may be jeopardized (Armstrong, 2012; Schlager, 2008). The current institutional context in which most CCOs work, however, presents the potential to sabotage EBP just as it has historically (see McCorkle & Crank, 1996).

SABOTAGING THE SUCCESS OF
EVIDENCE-BASED PRACTICES

Implementation has been referred to as the "bane of effective correctional programs" (Rhine, Mawhorr, & Parks, 2006, p. 347) because of the historical trail strewn with the wreckage of programs that began with good intentions, a sound theoretical foundation, and scientific evidence they worked, yet the innovation failed miserably due to a failure to adhere to the original model's integrity (Pisciotta, 1994; Rothman, 1980). Even when implemented as intended, programs often drift from model adherence back to business as usual (see Lutze & van Wormer, 2007; McCorkle & Crank, 1996; van Wormer, 2010). Rothman (1980) powerfully argues that the "conscience" of reformers is well-meaning, and they promote change based on good ideas and theoretically sound principles. New ideas and programs, however, must be implemented within existing systems and a workforce often entrenched in traditional ways of conducting business (see Braga, Piehl, & Hureau, 2009; Payne & DeMichele, 2011). Thus, the "convenience" of using existing resources and staff without adequate skills or expertise to implement new programs often undermines the integrity of the new model and leads to failure. Rothman (1980, p. 10) insightfully concludes in his review of the Progressive Era and the implementation of rehabilitation that "in the end, when conscience and convenience met, convenience won. When treatment and coercion met, coercion won." Consequently, it may be expected that as corrections once again shifts away from a predominately punitive approach toward evidence-based practices expected to balance offender accountability with supporting offender needs, an overreliance on convenience and coercion may derail change. The reliance on convenience in response to innovative change may not be blatant obstructionism but instead be driven by the context in which new programs emerge (e.g., overcrowding, available staff, resources) and a failure to plan ahead for their implementation.

For instance, too often innovations are quickly adopted from other jurisdictions without consideration to whether the new approach or program is compatible with the values and existing systems of operation in the new jurisdiction (Henderson & Hanley, 2006; Lovrich et al., 2012). Implementation within the new jurisdiction oftentimes results in altering the program or practice to fit localized conditions and therefore violates the integrity of the model before it has a chance to prove its success (Henderson & Hanely, 2006). These program modifications and adaptions often lead to underperformance or total failure. Jurisdictions that do not prepare the systems, institutions, agencies, and employees responsible for implementing the new practice in advance are destined for failure. Operationalizing the structural integrity of the system before beginning a new program is crucial to success. In other words, places and people need to be prepared for change, especially when traditional practices are fully engrained and percieved to be "not broken" or working well enough.

Barriers to implementation often include a number of practical as well as political characteristics related to staff and administrative policy. For instance, many programs are hampered by an insufficient number of staff, staff turnover, and resistance to change from line staff or supervisors. Organizational challenges also emerge, such as inadequate funding, poor intraagency communication, agency regulations and policies, inadequate training opportunities regarding core goals and program design, and turf battles over funding, jurisdiction, and administration (Lattimore, Visher, Winterfield, Lindquist, & Brumbaugh, 2005). The leaders of corrections organizations need to prepare their agencies for change and invest in strategies that set CCOs up for success and hold staff accountable for implementing approaches that work to reduce recidivism (see Armstrong, 2012; Henderson & Hanley, 2006).

A review of CCOs' concerns about risk assessment, workloads, caseloads, liability, safety, stress, and a lack of positive recognition provides valuable insight into what corrections leaders need to do to prepare their organizations for change and to achieve the intended goals of evidence-based practices. CCOs express concern and frustration about many of the barriers they encounter as they attempt to manage their everyday work. It really is not all that surprising that many CCOs may be resistant to change unless the agency makes tangible efforts to address their concerns. Otherwise, there is no incentive to support innovations because the next administrative change along with the next political election cycle for legislative policymakers will merely alter the rhetoric without ever addressing the root cause of the perceived or actual problem (McCorkle & Crank, 1996). Research, along with the observations of CCOs, shows that the successful implementation of innovative programs in community corrections will be seriously handicapped if attention is not given to risk assessment, caseload and workload size, legal liability, safety, stress and burnout, and job satisfaction.

Implementing Risk Assessment

Much of evidence-based practice is dependent on using reliable and validated risk and need assessment tools. Risk and need assessments are useful for both informing risk management and directing resources to those most likely to reoffend based on past criminal behavior or current needs such as substance abuse or mental health treatment, unemployment, or inadequate living arrangements. These tools have proven to be significantly more accurate than professional judgments in predicting future behavior (see Andrews & Bonta, 2010). Given the concern about managing risk for both the agency and the CCO, it's odd that risk assessment tools are often absent or their importance downplayed by staff (see DeMichele & Payne, 2012; Farrell et al., 2011; Harris et al., 2004; Lynch, 1998; see DeMatteo, Marlowe, Festinger, & Arabia, 2009, for similar findings in drug court).

It appears that CCOs "object to what they perceive as an affront to their professional judgments" (McCorkle & Crank, 1996, p. 17; also see Ferguson, 2002). For instance, Lynch (1998, p. 855) reports that CCOs had little faith in "making judgments based on any kind of scoring system, agents had their own system—one that relied heavily on actual interaction with the parolee—to decide who posed risks." A lack of total confidence in risk assessment tools and possibly over confidence in their personal ability to determine risk is not uncommon (see Ferguson, 2002). For example,

> I don't particularly care for the LSI-R.[1] I think it just takes up more time, and it just tells me something that I already know—a personal questionnaire and just interviewing—which we have to do anyway in the intake—we cover these areas. . . . We're professionals—I'd rather put my name on a dotted line saying, "This is my professional assessment" and justify it similar to a recommendation to the court whether somebody should do jail time or not or go to prison or go to treatment. We have that latitude, but yet, for some reason or other, the department doesn't feel that we are capable of making an appropriate assessment. I do it because we have to, its policy, but I feel its unnecessary. (CCO 104)

> I think ultimately most of the CCOs who have been around for a while continue to go with their gut instinct and you go on hunches and [use] the LSI-R to back that up. I think that for the most part you find that you know your original opinion was correct and your way of supervising won't change a whole lot. You're going to continue to do the same things we've done in the past. We've always had tools and instruments and ways of assessing folks. (CCO 206)

> To be really honest with you, I've never looked at a LSI number. I mean, I punch in the numbers and hit enter and it gives me a number, and that's the last I ever see of it. (CCO 234)

Given that risk assessment tools are now in their fourth generation (see Andrews & Bonta, 2010), this reluctance to acknowledge their importance and to use them in their work is disconcerting. Even recent research has shown that up to 40% of agencies responsible for the supervision of offenders do not use risk assessment tools to classify offenders or to organize and direct their work (Farrell et al., 2011; Taxman, 2004). There appears to be a difference between administrators and line staff, with directors viewing risk assessment tools as significantly more important to supervision than nondirectors (DeMichele & Payne, 2012). Many CCOs, however, appear to seriously grapple with the use of risk assessment tools and how they may help or hinder their approach to supervision (see Ferguson, 2002).

CCOs spontaneously observe many of Rothman's concerns (1980) about conscience and convenience regarding the transition from adopting a research-based tool and adapting its implementation to the current context of the DOC (also see Henderson & Hanley, 2006). Similar concerns were expressed by CCOs, whether they were in favor of, opposed to, or had mixed feelings about the tool. For instance, a CCO who did not believe it was a useful tool expressed,

[laughing] No. The LSI, as far as the way Dr. Bonta wrote it, it's probably useful for assessing offenders, however, there's like a whole gap of offenders that it doesn't even take into consideration. I guess you always have the exception to the rule, and that's my frustration with it. Plus, our agency took it, and we had this wonderful tool that we told the legislature that we were going to use, and then we immediately bastardized it by altering the scores and altering the levels that Dr. Bonta assessed people at to make it fit our legislature and our budget. (CCO 226)

Another, representing a mixed opinion about the usefulness of the tool and how long it would last in its current state of implementation, says with skepticism (also see Ferguson, 2002),

I think it's a tool we could use. Is there something better out there? Yeah.... It's a tool. And knowing this department like I do and knowing how research is based, somewhere down the line, in the next two or three years, they will either come up with a revised, revised, revised LSI, or they're going to come up with something different.[2] (CCO 115)

Yet another CCO, who was in favor of the risk assessment tool, expressed similar concerns.

LSI-R, I think it's very simple. What I don't like about it is that the "R" is because it's revised.... So what he's [Secretary of DOC] done is adjusted the numbers away from the science of it and so that we have enough CCOs to cover the number of offenders that we do. They're like, okay, well if they only score 18 points then they can go to the minimum-management unit. Oh wait, that didn't qualify enough people to go to the minimum-management unit so we're going to bump it up to 23. Now everybody who scores 23 or lower goes to minimum management, not based on what their needs are or their risk is but based on staff. [laughs] (CCO 201)

Therefore, these CCOs observe the value of the assessment tool based on its original design (conscience) but believe the integrity of the tool is corrupted through modifications made by the agency to make it fit its budget, number of staff, and what was promised to the state legislature regarding managing the offender population (convenience).

Concerns did not focus just on the macro level of the agency's adoption of the model to fit the current context of the DOC but also on the CCOs' level of implementation (Ferguson, 2002). These observations tended to focus more on how officers might interpret and apply the tool and how some might purposefully skew the results to meet the officer's needs versus the offender's risk and needs.

This is confidential [laughing]? Yeah, I think it is, I think it's a good idea, you know. An LSI will turn the lowest ones into another unit so we can just focus on the higher-risk offenders. But I would like to see a universal tester be put in, like one person that does all the intakes who scores the LSI because there are so many subjective things that could change the LSI....It's a nice tool, and I think it's put there in a good name, but I think it's pretty subjective. It could change per the interviewer and how the interviewer sees these questions asked. (CCO 107)

I think it's the best thing that we've had. But it still goes off of their risk needs, and if they don't have a condition, you know, for drugs, and we identify that need, we can't do anything about it. So, that's the tough part. But it does do pretty well as long as people stick with what the researchers [planned]....And I don't know how you would get away with not skewing it because they don't want the person to be a maximum. They want them to be a minimum and get rid of them because they don't want to see them. So, I think if you do it right, you grade it fair, I think it is a pretty good tool from what I find. The people that are maximum supervision are the people that are always in and out of jail. For me, it's worked pretty well. (CCO ---)

Although most risk assessment tools are tested for interrater reliability, it is unknown how often CCOs purposefully take advantage of the "subjectivity" within the tool to skew the results upward or downward. Lynch (1998), who served as an intern while completing her research working in a California parole office, reports being trained to rate everyone as a "2" for risk and a "2" for needs on a 3-point scale, with the exception of sex offenders who were always to be rated as a "3." CCOs in her study also undermined paperwork through careless record keeping in order to conduct their work as they always had in the field versus in the office (also see McCleary, 1992).

Ironically, even though the LSI was put into place to reduce subjectivity, CCOs viewed the tool's subjectivity as its greatest weakness due to the inclusion of items that could not be verified and the differences in how CCOs might ask the questions and interpret the offender's responses (see Ferguson, 2002). Once again, whether believing risk assessment was good or not, similar reasons were given for CCOs' like or dislike related to the validity of the instrument and the subjectivity of many of the measures. For instance,

> I know it's...better than what they had before. Of course, it's...the old one that took so much time. This one is a shorter version, kind of more crunched down, and they do highlight areas that, you know, put together in a big picture, you can see whether they are high risk or low risk. The problem with the LSI is that we're basing an awful lot of it on offender report, and...there's still a lot of things you don't know. I mean family relationships....Anybody in your family ever have a criminal history? They say "no." How are we going to find out? Do you get along with your wife? "Yeah."...You know, they may beat the shit out of their partner and we'd never know. I mean, unless they were arrested for it, and then of course, we have the criminal history. So, I mean, so much of it's self-report that you really can't verify, and I think that's the hardest part about it. But then how else are you going to do it? (CCO 102)

A similar concern was also identified by the following CCO.

> Yes and no. I think just the rating system maybe not, but you get some good information out of it....So, it adds some consistency, and it requires us to be a little more thorough during an intake process. So in that sense, it's okay, but I've got a lot of guys that come off as a minimum case, and, you know, after I go and see them in their house a couple of times, there is no way they are a minimum case, or a medium or a

maximum case. Because they are self-reporting, and the smart offenders learn real quick to lie on the LSI, and the dumb offenders tell you the truth. So, there's some problems with it in that sense. It's a self-report—just self-report. (CCO 103)

Conversely, other CCOs expressed that the assessment tool provided a level of uniformity and continuity missing prior to its implementation. These CCOs felt it could provide needed information in situations where an offender moved from one jurisdiction to another and that in general the score matched with the offender according to their in-person observations. For example,

Again, I think it helps when the person in Seattle has done the LSI, and the person has moved to Spokane, and now I pick up that supervision. I can look at the LSI, and I can get a better feel for who's sitting there. The more information I have about the individual, the better off I am, the more apt I am to provide the proper services to them....From what I can tell, the way the questions are worded, the way we score them, it looks to me like...the score usually meets the offender....You need to have continuity for the offender, for their sake, for the public's sake, for our sake. You know, the more continuity you get, the better off you are. The one thing the LSI provides is that continuity. (CCO 105)

Yes, yeah, because it does clearly show if they need help in one or more of these areas....I really do see that it gives us a place to channel our resources...but it's not like we never did that before because it's obvious stuff. (CCO 201)

CCOs directly connected the benefit of having everyone coming closer together in their assessment and judgments about offenders and increasing the likelihood of predicting offenders' potential for success or failure. They appreciated that the tool could also help them, and therefore the department, to direct staff resources toward those most at risk of failure and therefore increase levels of supervision when needed and present the opportunity to target offenders' needs related to their successful reintegration.

Despite CCOs' diverse views about the implementation of the risk assessment tool and whether it was useful to informing how they might supervise individual offenders, they were reluctant to deviate from the assessment in favor of their own judgment regarding offender risk and need. Most CCOs expressed that they only deviated 5% to 10% of the time, usually for signs of violence, mental or cognitive instability, or a "feeling" that something just wasn't right. As one might expect given the aversion to risk, most CCOs deviated upward and rarely downward when coming to a final risk assessment score. For example,

> I override on all my sex offenders because if one of my sex offenders goes out and does something, he's going to be a max. Once that hits the media, it's going to be a max.... I override an offender like if it's a DV case or something like that and they got [in] contact with the victim, I'll shoot them up. I haven't ever gone in the reverse. I've never lowered anybody. (CCO 101)

A few CCOs were very scientific about their reasons for not overriding the risk score, with one expressing concerns about how the assessment tool will protect them from liability and the other being concerned about the ability of the DOC to determine whether the tool actually works.

> Because we're using it as a research-based tool with, I think, 1,700 papers that have been done on it, I would probably deviate maybe 5%. And the reason why is because it becomes a matter of liability for me. If we're dealing with it as research based, and the LSI says this is specifically where the offender should be at for risk level, and if I ever have to go to court, I'm going to use that research to my advantage. So, that's why 5% is a good number. (CCO 115)

> Yeah, definitely under 10%, and I'll tell you the reason I do that is because I think if there's going to be anything close to empirical data out of the LSI-R we're going to have to follow it and not override everybody that we think is kind of a little fishy. "Whoa, you know, he had beady eyes so I think I'm going to override him." And that's what I've seen other officers do because they don't want to let go, they know this person is going to reoffend, and they don't want to let go of the person into a lower level of supervision so they go ahead and override him. I understand that idea, but at the same time how are we going to know if the LSI-R is an effective tool of assessing people if we're always overriding them to some other classification.... So, that's why I don't do it, and how do I sleep at night? [laughter]... I don't think it makes that big of a difference whether they are a medium or maximum. I really don't. (CCO 201)

Some also expressed more practical reasons for not deviating from the original risk assessment score.

> Well, see, to me, it's like once they're scored, they're scored.... You know, unless they came in and said, "Oh, wow, I got a job now," there'd

be no reason to change it. I mean I barely have time to see everybody. I don't race back in there and go do my LSI reassessments. (CCO 226)

CCOs, whether they liked or disliked the risk assessment tool, expressed similar discomfort with both the DOC and individual CCOs adapting the tool. Violating the integrity of the tool for convenience sake did not sit well with many CCOs' "conscience" and the true meaning and usefulness of the tool to their actual work. Also of interest is the notion that even though the DOC implemented the risk assessment tool with the intention to reduce caseload size and relieve CCOs of some of their burden by focusing resources on high-risk and -need offenders, CCOs were skeptical of whether this was happening. Therefore, based on research and the experiences and perception of CCOs, it is clear that if EBP, based on risk and need assessment tools, are to be successfully implemented, DOC administrators and supervisors will need to prepare for implementation by providing adequate training and by adhering to the fidelity of the intended tool (Ferguson, 2002).

Workload and Caseload Issues

The DOC has no control over the number of offenders sentenced to its care and is fiscally limited in adapting its workforce to adjust to demands for services (DeMichele, 2007). The size of caseloads and the overcrowding of corrections supervision, whether institutional or community corrections, has been an ongoing issue since the beginning of prisons, probation, and parole (Pisciotta, 1994). Administrators have had to reconsider how to manage caseloads, the number of offenders supervised by an officer, workloads, and the amount of time committed to tasks related to supervision (DeMichele, 2007; Harlow & Nelson, 1990). Given that the risk and needs of offenders have become more serious over the last four decades, the increase in caseloads and the increased time demands necessary to effectively supervise high-risk offenders has become a serious issue for officers and corrections administrators (DeMichele, 2007; Petersilia, 2003). In addition, movement toward implementing EBP requires more attention to detail and understanding how CCOs' workloads change in relation to the type of caseloads managed. Inattention to workload may therefore defeat the effective implementation of EBP (Armstrong, 2012).

Evidence-based practice requires the proactive management of information and using what is learned to maintain, adapt, or totally change course from current practices, whether regarding resources, staff, or offenders. Many officers express conflict between the time it takes to manage administrative tasks and that spent actually managing offenders (DeMichele & Payne, 2012). A federal probation officer states, "Paperwork can easily be deemed the probation officer's nemesis" (Pierson, 1992, p. 19). This is obviously not news to the community corrections field, as Takagi (1973), nearly 40 years ago, pointed out that CCOs have moved from being field officers to office workers in order to achieve managerial efficiency. CCOs oftentimes express how managing paperwork puts them at risk of not having enough time to manage offenders, but without the paperwork they would be in professional peril if one of their offenders committed a heinous crime (DeMichele, 2007; Drapela & Lutze, 2009). The following quotes express concerns about the stressors and conflict of documentation and CCOs' beliefs about what it takes to do a good job.

> You know, we've got time frames on the LSI-R, when they want them done, and when they want a plan built. You're not letting me investigate to find anything about this person. I am like anybody else, I get to a point, I am like, "Screw this shit, I've got workload issues. I can play by the book. I can have my files lined up, all the i's dotted and the t's crossed and look right on paper and look great on the computer, and have my people going crazy. (CCO 227)

> I'd say about 50 would be a manageable caseload....We've become slaves to the computer. We don't do anything without documenting it into the computer. And when you have 85 people that you're trying to maintain some kind of continuity in supervision.... (CCO 115)

It is still uncertain in community corrections at what point an overburdened workload produces inefficiencies that lead to ineffectiveness and failure to reach organizational goals and increases the likelihood of catastrophic incidents. DeMichele (2007) argues that inefficiencies in community corrections may result in more attention on the eleven o'clock news. Excessive caseloads and workloads result in the inability of CCOs to properly monitor, engage, or record activities according to policy or offender needs. This is too often illustrated when investigations of high-profile incidents reveal that CCOs did not respond according to policy regarding offenders' noncompliance (see DeMichele, 2007). For example, in a case in Detroit involving a probationer involved in a police shootout, the statement given by the CCO was that she "was so overworked that she failed to get an arrest warrant for [the probationer] when he became a fugitive [4 months ago] for missing his monthly probation office appointment" (*The Detroit News* as cited in DeMichele, 2007, p. 20). Another officer released on sick leave reported, "I am currently actively supervising in excess of 156 probationers. . . . I am trying to do the work of two people and find it virtually impossible to perform all duties assigned to me within the time frames set forth and in accordance with departmental policy and procedure" (*The Detroit News* as cited in DeMichele, 2007, p. 20).

It is difficult to determine the appropriate caseload and workload for CCOs because so much depends on the type of offenders being supervised, the resources available within and outside of the agency, and the level of coordination between systems (see DeMichele, 2007). Many argue that the appropriate caseload size for those actively supervising offenders in the community should range from 30 to 50 people, but most caseloads far exceed this range (see DeMichele, 2007; Grattet, Petersilia, Lin, & Beckman, 2009; Kerbs, Jones, & Jolley, 2009; Lutze et al., 2004; Petersilia, 2002; Taxman, 2002; West & Seiter, 2004). As community corrections moves toward an emphasis on evidence-based practice, it is clear from concerns expressed by CCOs related to their experiences that the "convenience" of large caseloads and excessive workloads needs to be more seriously considered by administrators (see DeMichelle & Payne, 2012).

Recall that officers felt large caseloads inhibited their ability to develop meaningful professional relationships with offenders and to be proactive instead of reactive when addressing offenders' risk and needs (see Chapter 2). In addition, CCOs enjoyed working with the community but often felt they did not have the time to engage the community as expected and effectively supervise their large caseloads (see Chapter 3). Thus, it is not surprising that when CCOs were asked what the DOC could do to alleviate stress, the most often cited answer was to reduce workload or caseload size so they could do a better job. For example,

> Lower my dang caseload so I can spend more time in the community. That would make it a lot better. You know, so I don't feel so overwhelmed all the time. (CCO 103)

> Reduce the caseload. If I could change that, then I could focus on doing a better job, focusing on people. Feel like they're not just a number passing through the system, because with so many people, you can hardly remember what their needs are. When they're in and out and, you know, you're dealing with 80 to 90 people—10% you're dealing with full time because they are the problem, then when the other 90% comes up, it's like, "What was your name again?" So, I'd like to lower caseloads if that could ever be done. (CCO 107)

> Just a balance in workload for me...I guess, and you're going to hear
> that probably from everybody, that "workload, workload, workload." It's
> outrageous. I don't know. Management, because they're so top-heavy
> anymore, I think they're walking with their heads like this [gesturing
> upward]. They don't see down below what we are really going through
> and what's needed by us to effectively do our job. (CCO 245)

Many CCOs, one way or another, also connected workload directly
with the work created by ever-changing DOC policies and the burden of
administrative tasks.

> A decrease in workload, a better ability to have more face-to-face contact
> with offenders....I would like to see less continuous change of policies
> and additions of new policies and changes—that just drives everybody
> crazy because as soon as we learn the new system, it becomes the old
> system and a new one is in place. (CCO 217)

> Yes, I wish there was a magical fairy with a wand that would come in and
> touch me on the head and then say, "You now understand the computer
> thoroughly. You are an expert at report writing. You can make all your
> contacts. And you know all the policies." (CCO 110)

Therefore, seen throughout the literature and as reflected within the
comments of CCOs, caseloads and workloads are intertwined and permeated with challenges related to administrative tasks, changing policies, and
a desire to have more meaningful contacts with offenders (DeMichele &
Payne, 2012). Without dealing with the overwhelming nature of caseloads
and the associated workloads, the implementation of EBP will have little
integrity and the supervision of offenders is likely to revert to business as
usual. Excessive workloads, oftentimes due to excessive caseloads, erode
the potential for EBP (conscience) and overemphasize the pressure on the
agency to manage large offender populations with too few staff (convenience). Consequently, even as the image of contemporary community
corrections changes, the actual work may remain consistent with an overreliance on surveillance, monitoring, and sanctions due to the overwhelming caseloads and the amount of paperwork necessary "to satisfy
bureaucratic demands rather than helping CCOs to provide rational crime
control over offenders in their charge" (McCorkle & Crank, 1996, p. 17).
It is not difficult to imagine how overwhelming caseloads result in the
neglect of crucial duties, inadequate supervision, and the fear of liability
(DeMichele, 2007).

Fear of Liability

Holding CCOs accountable for their work transcends professional boundaries when CCOs are held personally liable for negative outcomes, especially when offenders on their caseloads violently reoffend, CCOs can be held both criminally responsible for committing crimes with offenders or abusing individuals on their caseloads and be civilly liable for neglecting to follow policy regarding supervision when a third party is harmed by an offender (Drapela & Lutze, 2009; Jones & del Carmen, 1996; Morgan et al., 1997). Both the agency and the individual CCO may be sued and held responsible for monetary damages. It is not unreasonable for mistakes to occur due to the complex sets of legal and administrative polices guiding the management of offender risks and needs, extensive requirements to document case management activities, large caseloads, and expectations to participate in interagency partnerships and community engagement (see Drapela & Lutze, 2009). Alternatively, it is argued that full engagement in evidence-based practices, risk assessments, partnerships, and community engagement reduces the likelihood of reoffending and theoretically reduces the risk of liability (Latessa et al., 2002).

Some have observed that community corrections is paralyzed or in a constant state of confusion due to fears of legal liability (see Caplan, 2006). The conflicting demands of a punitive public and the reality of offenders' needs creates conflict regarding the most appropriate response to reducing recidivism—short-term punitive sanctions versus long-term treatment strategies (see Caplan, 2006; Ohlin et al., 1956). Innovation then becomes a risky business because of the real possibility of being sued for failure to immediately sanction an offender who has violated the rules of supervision versus taking the risk of following evidence-based practices that support an offender through the process of change (Armstrong, 2012; DeMichele, 2007; Payne & DeMichele, 2011). As Lutze and colleagues argue, "This ongoing tension between accountability and support often results in role conflict, concerns about legal liability, and stress" (Lutze, Johnson, Clear, Latessa, & Slate, 2012). The fear of either the agency or CCO being sued may stifle innovative and progressive approaches to implementing supervision strategies different from the status quo because of uncertainty about how to manage the risk—thus, a sanction of jail can be tangibly justified whereas waiting for a space in a residential treatment center creates professional insecurity and public scrutiny if something goes wrong.

Fear of being sued appears to permeate community corrections. In an analysis of the CCOs in the Spokane study, 85% of CCOs responded that they were afraid of being named in a lawsuit, with the following quote illustrating this common fear.

> I worry that one of my offenders is going to "go off" because I didn't have time to be knocking on his door like I thought I should have. I'm always afraid of being sued. I mean, that's probably my biggest fear. (CCO 102; Drapela & Lutze, 2009, p. 376)

Another CCO captures the conflict of deciding between sanctions and treatment when addressing noncompliance and offender behavior.

> That's the worst part of the job, I think, liability. That's what brings me home with an ulcer every night because I deal with an offender and I deal with sanctions, [and I put him in treatment]…what if that guy walks out of treatment and goes out and does bad things? You know? That was my call and we don't have any immunity like judges or a little parole board—we're open to liability on that. And I don't know who made that call, but it's not a good part of the job, it sucks, but the worst part of being on the job is liability. (CCO 107; Drapela & Lutze, 2009, p. 377)

Similarly, an officer in Lynch's (1998, p. 859) study related,

> If you're lying about this, what the heck else are you doing? I've got people who do really bad things to people. If they're not necessarily honest, I think the worst. I will err on the side of the community each time….I like to sleep at night.

Additional concerns related to whether CCOs believed their agency would back them up and represent them in a lawsuit. Drapela and Lutze (2009) reported that approximately 50% of CCOs in Spokane reported mixed feelings about whether the DOC would support them in a lawsuit, with approximately 25% believing the DOC would not support them if they were sued. These concerns most often revolved around whether they would be perceived as following DOC policy. DOC policies, however, were described as multilayered, complex, and oftentimes vague, making it nearly impossible for CCOs to know whether they are truly following policy. For instance, Washington State's sentencing laws have been changed multiple times since the early 1980s, and the supervision parameters differ based on the law under which the offender was sentenced at the time of conviction. Thus, within a single caseload, multiple sentencing structures need to be adhered to depending on the offender. In addition,

DOC policy has sometimes been adapted so that competing policies may be applicable to the same individual or behavior. This complexity often makes it difficult for CCOs to know whether they are in compliance even when their intent is to abide by policy. The following CCOs capture these concerns (Drapela & Lutze, 2009, p. 378).

> Every supervisor and every manager I've always talked to has always said that if you have acted in good faith, yes, you're fine, blah, blah, blah. But I think if it came down to it and they were looking for a scapegoat, you're hanging out. (CCO 226)

> As long as you follow policy, they'll stand by you. But what if the policy is vague in some areas? What if there's a gray line in which the policy is vague in order for them to get out of it, you know? Just by going by policy may not be good enough. What if my interpretation of policy is not exactly what DOC's interpretation of policy is? And if it's not, are they going to stand by me? Who knows. (CCO 107)

Even when CCOs are following policy and supervising individuals according to the conditions imposed by the court, the DOC may not be immune from responsibility if an offender harms someone. This fear resonated with the following CCO who observed,

> If they're doing some behavior that is not violating their [conditions of] supervision, however, it's dangerous behavior. There was a case not too long ago over in western Washington where an offender killed somebody else in an auto accident. But the CCO had been monitoring the offender for their court-ordered conditions, because that's all that the law allowed them to do. Yet the prosecutors and the judge found the department negligent in that case. So, that's always stressful too, even if I do my job to the best of my ability, that it won't matter, that something will happen because I can't monitor the person 24 hours a day, 7 days a week. They're still going to commit crime, and I can be held liable. (CCO 217)

CCOs are concerned about liability, but few studies have dedicated specific attention to how these fears directly affect the management of the DOC and how officers supervise offenders. Although there are plenty of examples in the literature showing corrections driven by a punitive public, and the work of supervisors and CCOs dominated by "putting out fires" and "risk management," few have directly considered the impact of litigation on the implementation of innovative practices or its potential to skew decisions toward punitive versus evidence-based practices (see Armstrong, 2012; Drapela & Lutze, 2009; Lynch, 1998; Ohlin et al., 1956). It is also unknown how corrections policies across the states differ in their complexity and clarity and whether policies, or a lack thereof, help or hinder CCO approaches to supervision or the agency's vulnerability to lawsuits (see Drapela & Lutze, 2009; Lutze et al., 2012).

It is not surprising then that the political, public, and institutional climate contributes to a hyperfocus on risk management and an aversion to taking chances that may result in failure. It is unknown how attempts to implement EBP will be affected or sabotaged by agency-level and individual CCOs' fears of being sued. EBP may be embraced by administrators as an attempt to reduce liability by relying on science to defend their practices. CCOs, however, may remain cautious of EBP because of their inability to control outcomes and a general distrust of how EBPs are implemented. Given the concerns expressed earlier about implementation of the risk assessment tool and the contextual elements of their work, such as large caseloads, the implementation of EBP according to policy may be inhibited, leaving the DOC and CCOs open to liability (see Armstrong, 2012; Drapela & Lutze, 2009; Payne & DeMichele, 2011).

Safety, Firearms, and EBP

Community corrections populations have become increasingly more serious (Petersilia, 2003; Travis, 2005). The rapid growth in the community corrections population has led to the need to focus limited staff and other resources on those potentially at the greatest risk to reoffend and who have the greatest need. Most states require high-risk offenders to receive more contacts, including field visits, office visits, and collateral contacts with treatment providers, employers, landlords, and family members. For many field officers, this shift in the community corrections population has resulted in having less balanced caseloads related to offenders and risk levels.

Therefore, CCOs' work has intensified as they increasingly manage caseloads dominated by individuals with serious criminal records and those with violent tendencies, such as gang members and sex offenders; more serious treatment needs, such as substance abuse and mental health problems; and serious deficits in education, employment, and basic life skills (Petersilia, 2003; Travis, 2005). Home visits oftentimes require entering dangerous neighborhoods and encountering high-risk people not on supervision but involved in the offender's life or living in the same area (see Clear, 2007). Although CCOs have always had to deal with dangerous and volatile individuals, such offenders tended to be seen as the exception rather than the rule. Thus, working in community supervision has come to be viewed as far less safe than in the past (Lindner & Koehler, 1992; Petersilia, 2003). This lack of safety and the 30-year trend toward more surveillance and law enforcement strategies has led to ongoing pressure to arm CCOs.

The American Probation and Parole Association's (APPA) National Firearm Study (2006) found that 40 states allow CCOs to carry firearms with 14 of these states mandating that those who supervise adult offenders be armed. The remaining states have policies that allow officers to decide whether to carry a gun, and some states only allow CCOs to carry when working with special populations. The APPA has taken a neutral stance:

> The American Probation and Parole Association neither supports nor opposes the carrying of weapons by probation and parole officers; however, should the decision be made by an agency to authorize officers to carry weapons, that decision must be made within the framework of actual need, officer safety demands, and must be consistent with the laws and policies which guide that agency. (APPA, 2006, n.p.)

Although it appears states are still not totally committed to the idea of CCOs carrying firearms, whether CCOs should be armed lends some interesting insight to whether this would contribute to or hamper the implementation of EBP. Insight is provided by CCO as they express their concerns about safety and their perceptions of how officers' role orientations are interwoven into the debate about carrying firearms.

Safety. Concerns about safety have been attributed to changes in how CCOs conduct and experience their work. Studies show that from 39% to 55% of CCOs have been victims of work-related violence, including physical violence and threats (Finn & Kuck, 2005). Approximately one-quarter of these events took place in someone's home, and another quarter took place at the office (Finn & Kuck, 2005). For instance, a majority of officers surveyed in New York State reported feeling unsafe, and CCOs in Pennsylvania reported a range of victimization resulting in physical trauma, fear, avoidance of contact with clients, reduced self-confidence, and reduced trust of and sensitivity to clients (see Linder & Koehler, 1992; Parsonage, 1990). It is easy to imagine how each of these factors may minimize CCOs' willingness to implement EBP as many safety concerns are related to contacting offenders in their homes and working with them to provide structure, support, or treatment services outside of the office or after hours. Linder and Koehler (1992) recommend that corrections administrators address safety issues by restructuring home visits so that there are fewer of them, establishing team visitations so officers are not alone in the field, increasing staff training related to de-escalation and self-defense tactics, improving critical-incident reporting systems to better track the victimization of CCOs, and increasing the use of body armor, body alarms, phones, radios, and firearms (also see Parsonage, 1990). As related shortly, these concerns were reiterated by a number of CCOs.

Safety is an ongoing issue for CCOs because offenders have access to them at work, potentially know where officers live, and can encounter them in the community when they are going about their personal lives. Similar to prior research, in general, CCOs expressed feeling safe but felt most threatened when making arrests, conducting home visits alone, and working with offenders known to be violent. The following comments capture concerns about working with violent offenders.

> I don't feel extremely threatened all the time, but I feel there's always a certain level of hazard to the job. A lot of the offenders are violent individuals who have been convicted of violent crimes, and a lot of them aren't real rational so they tend to pick out individuals within the system and blame them for their problems rather than seeing it as part of the system as a whole or their own actions. (CCO 216)

Working alone while conducting field visits was a prominent concern officers expressed. Their concerns about working alone generally revolved around not always being able to predict what might happen or just being exposed to neighborhoods and places that felt unsafe. For example,

> I think it is probably doing fieldwork alone. And typically I do fieldwork alone. And it's not so much feeling threatened by an offender on my caseload but having to go into certain areas, certain situations, certain environments where you virtually have no control. (CCO 231)

Although direct threats appeared to be fairly rare, they generally increased feelings of being unsafe until resolved.

> Knowing that an individual's in violation and he's had problems with having firearms in his possession. Recently an individual pretty much said, "Fuck you," and, "I'm going to come out and get you." Well, he has a history of following through with this stuff. And yeah, that made me feel kind of threatened, but you know, you just push it to the back of your mind and wait until he gets released and watch his movements for a

while until he calms down. Then you get him into your office, talk to him a little bit. And then you've got a feel if he's going to actually follow through with it or not. And they never have—for me, anyway. (CCO ---)

You know, you're real cognizant of your environment. During the point where I had two folks who [we] actually went to trial on these people. They physically threatened to harm us—to me, specifically. We imposed a personal protection plan, which included the option of being armed, but I already was, so it was a moot point. It says things like, "You will explore the option of taking an alternate route home each night." You can only have so many routes; I don't care where you live. If somebody wants to get you, you're going to be got. End of story. (CCO ---)

Many CCOs adapted their behavior to try to avoid letting offenders know where they lived.

Well, what I do is I take different routes when I go home. And I try not to... like when I was doing MRT [moral recognition therapy], they knew my car and everything. I tried to park someplace else. If I see somebody in the store, I just pretend that I don't know them. Because I'm sure they can find out where you live and all that. And be polite to people. I mean, if somebody comes in here and you're calling him a jerk, then he might be waiting for you outside. It's the way you treat the people. (CCO ---)

Most CCOs were constantly aware of their surroundings and made a point to work with other officers, including law enforcement, when making an arrest or visiting an offender's home when they were uncertain about their safety (see Murphy & Lutze, 2009; Parsonage, 1990).

Many CCOs argue that carrying firearms is also a way to achieve increased levels of safety, whether real or perceived (also see Sigler, 1988; Sigler & McGraw, 1984; Sluder & Shearer, 1991). When asked if CCOs should carry firearms, most CCOs thought it should be an option and individual officers should determine what was best for them (Sluder & Shearer, 1991). Several officers cited safety as a key reason for being armed. For example,

Sure. Yeah, why not? You never know when something is going to happen. It might be a false sense of security, but I would [rather] have a false sense of security than no security at all. (CCO 110)

I think it enhances your safety today because there's a lot of people out there with weapons. Twenty years ago, it wasn't that big a deal. Ten years ago, it wasn't that big of a deal. But, last night, another killing in an apartment complex between two people. We probably have somebody on supervision in that apartment complex, and there's no reason for that shooting last night. So it enhances our safety and it enhances our opportunity for protecting ourselves more than anything else. And it enhances our opportunity to protect the public. (CCO 115)

Not all CCOs felt safer with officers being armed, as evidenced by the following CCO:

I think I'm more at risk now because everybody knew that we were not carrying guns, and I think we were safer, criminals knowing that we don't carry guns. The other thing is that I'd be afraid that some of my own peers would shoot me, because they're not police officers. They haven't had the training. I don't care what you say, they haven't had the training. (CCO 219)

Similarly, female CCOs in Ireland and Berg's (2008) study overwhelmingly emphasized intuition, verbal skills, and communication to ensure safety and not guns, badges, or physical strength (male attributes). When asked if not for safety why carry guns, the female CCOs in Ireland and Berg's (2008) study responded that it was now required, and carrying increased the respect from male parole agents. Women were comfortable with guns but just preferred not to carry them. It is uncertain whether this is true for male officers as well. A male officer in the Spokane study, however, did suggest that this may be true across gender.

I don't [think CCOs should carry guns]. I can think of about three occasions where I might have killed somebody if I had been carrying a firearm. And I was able to handle it, verbally diffuse it, and walk out of it without ANY of us getting hurt. Now I'd like to think I'd have enough judgment not to pull a pistol, but the reality is that unless we're extremely well trained with firearms, and unless we're very comfortable with ourselves, we feel braver if we're carrying a pistol. We also feel more macho when we're carrying a pistol. And the damn testosterone is running a little bit thicker if we're carrying a pistol, which is not a good situation. (CCO ---)

In spite of greater perceptions of danger in community supervision work, there is still controversy about whether CCOs should carry firearms. Although this controversy appears to be related to the role orientation of CCOs (see Chapter 2), there is also ongoing debate between CCOs and corrections administrators about the need for CCOs to carry firearms. A number of complex issues emerge for departments when officers become armed. For instance, agencies transitioning from unarmed to armed need to consider the psychological stability of their workforce to carry and potentially use deadly force. For community corrections, unlike law enforcement, not all officers were hired with the intention to carry a firearm, and therefore they need to be psychologically tested. Field officers also need to be trained, equipped, certified, and requalified on an ongoing basis, creating additional financial obligations for the agency, which is significant given the statewide workforce. Issues regarding safety and securing firearms within the office and on the street must also be addressed. Policies must be developed about when officers may unholster their weapons and when they may use deadly force, such as in self-defense to a direct or perceived threat or as a preemptive act to avoid a threat. In addition, policy needs to be developed regarding whether they may draw their weapons in support of law enforcement officers. Liability also becomes a concern of the department when an officer shoots a person on their caseload or a bystander. Therefore, the use of firearms moves beyond the individual CCO's need for personal safety to administration- and agency-level concerns.

Although it is unknown how other agencies have transitioned to carrying firearms, CCOs in Spokane expressed appreciation for having the choice to carry but were frustrated with the way the policy was implemented. For instance, once officers choose to carry, are trained, and qualify with their weapons, they must be armed and wear their body armor every time they leave the office, but their weapons must be locked in a secure box and inaccessible while in the office. There are also strict rules about how CCOs may use their weapons while in the field that differ significantly from law enforcement's rules. Frustration regarding the firearms policy was evident across officers in support of or against the carrying of firearms.

> [CCOs] should be able to carry firearms. The way that current policies are written, it's a royal pain in the ass to carry a firearm, which is why I am not a carrying officer at this point. But I think it's fair and I think it's just an added level of safety, so yeah. (CCO ---)

> Pretty much our policy is you have to be personally threatened with bodily harm before you can even access your firearm. I think by that time it's too late. We should be able to, maybe not use them as much as the police do,...but somewhere in between there. (CCO 108)

> I don't like the policy surrounding firearms. I think it's ridiculous that they have to take them off when they are in the office and yet we have no metal detectors, so somebody could come in here with a gun, start shooting up the place. Officers who do have guns, if they are even in the office, would have to unlock their safety box, get them ready, by then everybody's dead. So I think that they should be able to carry them all the time if that's their thing, but me personally I don't. I don't want to have that responsibility. It's a huge responsibility. (CCO 201)

> I don't have a problem with people being armed. But it seems like management didn't want us to be armed and they set the policy so rigid that it's not supportive like in a law enforcement agency or a law enforcement way. I think what's kind of misleading is that the police accept or have this idea that if something goes down, we're gonna back them up, and the way our policy's written is that you don't draw your weapon unless you're in the line of fire. I mean the only way we draw a weapon is for self-defense. (CCO 226)

Although CCOs' concerns about liability permeate so much of what they do, only a few officers mentioned concerns about liability in carrying a firearm. One officer stated,

> I know some people feel safer with that weapon. I just don't want to carry a weapon. Part of the reason I don't want to carry a weapon is I'm not convinced, based on everything I told you about policy, following policy, AG [attorney general] defending you, and all that stuff, I'm not convinced the Department of Corrections will be in my best interest if anything came push to shove. And I'm not willing to go there. (CCO 229)

CCOs expressed mixed feeling about carrying a firearm, with most accepting that those who wanted to should have the choice. Most officers, whether carrying or not, viewed the way the policy was implemented as problematic. Clearly, concerns about safety permeated both sides of the issue. The concerns about safety that permeate CCOs' observations about whether they should carry firearms are key to the implementation of EBP. Individuals, both CCOs and offenders, must feel safe and have some level of trust in order to move forward and engage offenders in the process of change.

Role conflict. Some researchers have found that carrying a firearm is a clear indication of CCOs' role orientation and whether they are more likely to embrace surveillance and law enforcement strategies or social work and treatment strategies when conducting their work (Petersilia, 2003; Sigler & McGraw, 1984; Sluder & Shearer, 1991). Sigler (1988) suggests that policies related to carrying guns magnify the potential differences in CCO roles related to law enforcement and social work, causing role conflict between the CCO and the agency. Sigler and McGraw (1984) in a study of Alabama parole officers found officers did not report role conflict because those with a law enforcement orientation supported carrying firearms while those with a treatment orientation viewed qualifying with a weapon as a means to increase one's pay for hazard duty and not as a judgment about their treatment orientation. A replication of Sigler and McGraw's study on federal parole officers found a weak relationship between firearms and role conflict (Sigler, 1988). Sigler (1988) suggests that outsiders see role conflict as a logical issue for CCOs, but it may not actually exist for CCOs working in the field. Yet whether CCOs choose to carry firearms may give an indication of their willingness to either embrace a more law enforcement orientation or a social work orientation, and this distinction may be important as agencies move toward evidence-based treatment.

There is some evidence that those who do not carry firearms are better able to empathize with offenders and the complexity of their situations than those who choose to carry firearms. For instance, in a study of state and federal community corrections officers in Washington State, CCOs with greater social distance from offenders and who carry firearms are more likely to have difficulty understanding the past life experiences of offenders, believe that most offenders choose to commit crime, and think some human beings are born evil (Helfgott & Gunnison, 2008). CCOs with low social distance and who did not carry firearms were likely to believe that most offenders feel sorry for what they have done, to feel sorry for some of the offenders on their caseloads, and to think offenders have the capacity to succeed upon release. Unfortunately, this study did not directly compare CCOs who carried firearms with those who did not. Therefore, differences may be more about the social distance CCOs keep with offenders than the decision to carry a firearm. Nonetheless, research in general tends to show that CCOs who carry firearms are more likely to be law enforcement oriented than those who do not carry (see Sigler & McGraw, 1984; Sluder & Shearer, 1991).

Carrying a firearm may also be purely related to safety or an indication of whether a CCO is more likely to adhere to one philosophy of supervision and be less fluid in interactions with offenders. Some of the CCOs in Spokane spontaneously expressed strong positions about whether CCOs who carry guns are more law enforcement oriented when simply asked "Should CCOs be allowed to carry firearms?" For instance, the following officer did not believe carrying a gun made officers more law enforcement oriented:

> I think it's positive in general; you know, in [another state], we went through this, I think it was a mind-set that it would affect our relationship between the offenders—you know, they would see us [as] more law enforcement oriented, that sort of thing, and historically, that's never been the case. Never happened, and I don't believe ever will. (CCO ---)

Another CCO recognized firearms as being acceptable for self-defense but not for the purposes of determining their style of supervision.

> Truthfully, yes they should if they're carrying the firearm to protect themselves. No, they shouldn't if they think the firearm makes them the CCO. (CCO 101)

Some CCOs believed carrying did alter the atmosphere of the contact and limited the broader use of interpersonal skills to deescalate dangerous situations.

> You know, I think it can, the offender can look at you in a little different light if they know you are carrying a firearm. You know, its back to that, Mr. Cop, law enforcement–only-type officer versus someone that is also kind of a social worker, willing to help, that sort of thing. (CCO 114)

> I did carry one, but I don't carry it anymore. [Interviewer: Why?] I didn't feel the need. I didn't like going to a house where a lot of my clients are family oriented–type people. They have a bunch of kids and things, and I didn't like going in there with guns. I didn't like bringing my gun home with my grandkids around. Some of the clients felt uneasy. I could go there with a gun and with a vest on; they almost felt like they wanted to say, "Whoa, what have you got that gun for, and what have you got the vest on for? You don't trust me or something?" (CCO ---)

> You know, I believe in personal choice. Personally, I'm not at any point in my career that I would feel compelled to do so. I know many people who have done this for many, many years, and they've never carried a firearm—didn't have to. I really believe that our best weapon is our mouth and how we speak with people and how we communicate with people and use our gut.... I think sometimes that carrying those firearms could instill kind of a false sense of security. And I'm not quite sure that

the people who are currently carrying them, quite frankly, are ones that will use their other skills. You know, I know the folks that carry. Some of them I respect; some of them I don't respect as far as how they deal with offenders and their motivation to carry. (CCO 238)

As the discussion about firearms suggests, safety is an important issue and interwoven into how CCOs view their work and what they believe should be emphasized. They grapple with the need to be safe from high-risk offenders and in the communities in which they work and the need to engage offenders in a meaningful way that enhances the potential for positive outcomes. Therefore, a lack of safety may quietly sabotage EBP because it inhibits free-flowing interaction with offenders and the ability to both hold them accountable and connect them to support services capable of addressing their needs. Conversely, it is unknown how offenders' perceptions of safety influence their willingness to engage supervision or EBP opportunities. It is clear that carrying firearms, feelings of safety, large caseloads, and risk management are all interwoven and present the potential to influence stress and job satisfaction.

Stress, Burnout, Job Satisfaction, and EBP

It is easy to imagine the stress caused by the professional responsibility of having to balance the protection of the community with simultaneously addressing the serious and often volatile needs of offenders challenged by substance abuse, mental illness, and antisocial personalities and peers. Underlying the everyday work of managing a caseload is the persistent threat that an offender may act violently, resulting in personal injury or the victimization of someone in the community. In addition, the organization's need to manage risk through a set of complex policies and practices designed to control both CCOs' discretion and offender behavior creates ongoing concerns about balancing the needs of the administration with those of the offender. It is not surprising that community corrections officers have been found to have higher stress levels than the general population (see Slate, Wells, & Johnson, 2003).

Stress in community corrections has been linked to the increased likelihood of job dissatisfaction, burnout, absenteeism, turnover, and also health problems (see Slate et al., 2003; Wells, 2003; Wells, Colbert, & Slate, 2006). Given that the successful implementation of EBP requires greater staff commitment to understanding and implementing what works, it is understandable how each of these stress outcomes may undermine the ability of community corrections to pursue innovative strategies that work for both the organization and community. Burnout, absenteeism, and job turnover are direct threats to continuity in the supervision of offenders and in building relationships with professionals across systems necessary to address offenders' risks and needs. Stress among CCOs has been studied in relationship to individual and organizational characteristics. CCOs' perceptions and experiences related to stress give critical insight about how organizational structure may help or hinder positive outcomes for employees and offenders (Wells, 2003).

Individual characteristics and stress. Much of the research on individual characteristics and stress is mixed, but it appears that in general female, minority, younger, single, or nonreligious officers experience greater levels of work-related stress than do others (see Lee, Joo, & Johnson, 2009; Simmons, Cochran, & Blount, 1997; Slate et al., 2003; Wells et al., 2006 for reviews). Many of the explanations given for these differences are based in speculation and anecdotal evidence.

A review of the literature on female CCOs reveals a shortage of studies focused on their unique professional experiences. Women surveyed in one large study (n = 626), where women were the majority of officers, showed that gender was not significantly related to internal or external stress, job stress, or personal stress (Wells et al., 2006; also see Simmons et al., 1997). Female CCOs, however, were significantly more likely to report higher levels of physical stress. In general, higher levels of recorded stress for women may be due to their greater likelihood to report their stress, whereas men may be less willing or free to do so because of social stigma and the fear of being perceived as weak or vulnerable (see Kilmartin, 2000; Slate et al., 2003). In addition, women's greater stress levels may be related to working within a male-dominated workforce and with a primarily male clientele that may result in a climate conducive to gender and sexual harassment (see Slate et al., 2003; Wells et al., 2006) or a general lack of respect for women's capacity to "physically" supervise male offenders (see Ireland & Berg, 2008).

Not much is written about why racial and ethnic minority CCOs might experience more stress than their colleagues, but it may be due to their token status in many agencies and the diligence necessary to gain legitimacy as a professional working against the stereotypes and overrepresentation of minority offenders in the criminal justice system (Walker, Spohn, & DeLone, 2007). Research indicating higher levels of stress for both minorities and women needs additional study. The professional ramifications for women and minorities in community corrections who suffer from increased stress may result in contextually different professional experiences leading to burnout and job turnover. These additional professional costs may diminish continuity and culturally diverse and competent responses within the profession.

Although few researchers have attempted to explain why single and nonreligious CCOs are more likely to experience stress than married or religious CCOs, these characteristics may be proxies for informal social support, external to the agency, that helps offset the pressures of the job or a perceived lack of support from within the organization (see Wells et al., 2006). It is possible that CCOs who are able to share their concerns with a life partner or friends outside of work or who have a safe place to escape from their professional identity for a while have more opportunities to manage and reduce their work-related stress (see Finn & Kuck, 2005).

There are mixed findings concerning the length of time CCOs work for the agency and stress. Some research shows that those at the beginning and at the end of their careers experience less stress than those in the middle of their careers. Other studies, however, that include physical symptoms of stress show greater levels of stress and burnout the longer a CCO is on the job (Slate et al., 2003). Stress was also found to be significantly greater among officers in managerial or supervisory positions (Wells et al., 2006). Therefore, it appears that stress varies for CCOs based on their individual characteristics in addition to the length of time they have served on the job and the type of position they hold. Even though personal characteristics are related to stress, the primary causes of stress in community corrections are organizational.

Job-related attributes and stress. CCOs have reported that the three most common sources of stress in community corrections are high caseloads, administrative tasks, and deadlines beyond their control that coalesce and produce the frustration of not having enough time to adequately supervise their caseloads (see Finn & Kuck, 2005; Lee et al., 2009; Simmons et al., 1997; Slate et al., 2000, 2003; West & Seiter, 2004; Wells et al., 2006). Stress from being overburdened is often connected to the perception that management could do something about it but chooses not to. For example,

> There's...I guess it's extremely frustrating for field officers to hear that we don't have any money to hire any more CCOs, yet we see management, upper management, growing by leaps and bounds in headquarters. That's really frustrating. But really, [it hurts] morale. (CCO 231)

> It is extremely important to me and the officers that you would talk to because we're living it...our workload is enormous and you're expected

to do it and do it well. But, yet, we're not given, field officers aren't given, the resources, the time, the kudos, the praise, the understanding that they need to do an effective job. Right now, we do a Band-Aid. We've put a Band-Aid on the problem. And management is not willing to... the state of Washington is not willing to do what is necessary to help their officers do a good job. (CCO 235)

Additional stressors identified in prior research include a dislike for supervisors or a disconnect between management and field officers' work (see Finn & Kuck, 2005). These stressors are further illustrated by the following comments. Notice the common theme that engaging with management causes more stress than working with offenders.

...sometimes it's more difficult to work... with people you work with than the offenders you work with. I'm not saying in terms of this unit, I'm just mainly talking about other units I've been in where you have supervisors who are literally oppressive to their employees, to the people they supervise. (CCO 229)

Paperwork. I don't care if I have to go out and arrest a 300-pound offender out there. I don't care if I'm working with sex offenders or whatever. They don't bother me. The pressure the administration applies... we have all these little checks and balances. We have more and more and more and more and more. And so my anxiety on the job is centered almost totally around the administration. Its all internal, within the Department of Corrections. It doesn't come from the offenders. It comes from the department. (CCO 251)

Similar to that reviewed earlier, officers consistently report that too little time and inundation with paperwork prevent them from dedicating the effort necessary to effectively supervise offenders as they believe most fitting to reduce recidivism and support long-term reintegration (see Simmons et al., 1997; Slate et al., 2003; also see Chapters 2 and 3). CCOs associate the lack of time with a failure of the organization to address or even acknowledge workload issues and being overwhelmed with having to learn new policies, comply with existing policies, and manage the internal politics of the organization.

The inability to participate in the decision making that guides the agency and its policies regarding CCOs also leads to increased stress and decreased job satisfaction (Lee et al., 2009; Simmons et al., 1997; Slate et al., 2003). For example, the following observation by a CCO illustrates the frustration and the associated stress of not having input into the policies that ultimately guide CCOs' work.

> I feel, and most officers that I work with, that the DOC management in Olympia [headquarters] has no conception of what the job involves and what we're doing, and they have, kind of, this pie-in-the-sky philosophical ideas on how things ought to be done and they are trying to implement them without really knowing what's going on. That's where 99% of the stress of my job comes from, feeling in conflict with the management of the agency that I am employed by. (CCO 216)

> I at times am very frustrated with my job because a lot of times I think policy is being written and driven by people who have no idea what happens on the streets, and you have these policies that are so out of whack with reality. I wish they would talk to line staff about things like that, but that would make too much sense. (CCO 226)

The first comment also implies concerns about role conflict with "pie-in-the-sky philosophical ideas" without the guidance or support necessary to move forward with organizational changes and the supervision of offenders.

An inability to spend as much time as needed on each case is oftentimes related to role conflict created by the agency's expectations and the individual officer's need to hold offenders accountable or to provide support, whichever is needed by the offender or directed by the agency. Role conflict occurs when "different actors hold different expectations for a role or roles performed by an individual" (Sigler, 1988, p. 122). The greater the difference in expectations, the greater the potential for role conflict. Examples of role conflict in community corrections are often presented as they relate to the emphasis that should be placed on law enforcement and social work strategies to achieve the goals of supervision. Organizational factors, such as the philosophy embraced by the leadership, matter in clarifying what is important to the day-to-day work and what type of activities will be supported by administrators and supervisors. One CCO captured the need for the administration to decide on an organizational philosophy or to at least embrace multiple aspects of the job and allow people to develop an expertise in the approach best suited to their professional style. For instance,

> It depends on what they want us to do when we grow up. Do you want us to be a cop? Do you want us to get into physical confrontations with

offenders? Do you want us to not have such a social worker mentality? Well, what is it that you want? Tell us what you want. If there are people in the department who want more in social work, get them more social work training. I think that's really cool because you've got to have it. There are people who want to be the rough and tumble boys and have their guns, who want to be cops, then you train them for that. That way they can be the best "wannabe" cops in the business. It depends—you shouldn't train everybody the exact same way and think that they are all going to use the exact same tools. You know, find the strengths... it's okay to have two different sides of the same coin. We're not all the same. (CCO 234)

In addition, it appears that in some agencies, being a CCO is a thankless job. CCOs have reported greater stress and burnout due to inadequate salaries, a lack of compliments or praise for their work, boredom, and a dislike for their supervisors (see Finn & Kuck, 2005; Schlager, 2008; Slate et al., 2000, 2003). One CCO captured a couple of these sources of stress, salary and lack of acknowledgment, when responding to a question about how the DOC might improve job satisfaction.

I don't know that there's an answer to that. But money always works [laughing]. Hey, I work for a paycheck and agencies like to try to—"how about a new title? Bigger office?" Give me some money. Money talks, the rest of it walks. So, you know, pay me overtime if I need to do something outside of my regular hours or if my caseload is such that it indicates that. Acknowledge that there is a workload issue there. Acknowledge that I provide something to the community by being out in the field by making the contacts that I do at the time of day that I do them, then pay me. Then I'll do whatever you want. I'll carry out the mission of the state. The other things, the political things, they are what they are. (CCO 227)

A lack of recognition and the perceived lack of logic to the process of annual evaluations also appears to be problematic. For instance, in response to the question "How are you rewarded or recognized for your work?" many CCOs were not impressed with how they were recognized. For example,

"A-plus" and a little happy face. "You did a nice job, you're CCO of the month, CCO of the quarter." I mean, you know, nothing that truly counts. Every time I go in for my yearly evaluation, I'd mark that I always did "far exceeds." My sup. would come back in and give me "exceed," "normal exceed." "Okay, that's cool, if that's what you see, now tell me how can I do better?" They go, "Well, you really can't, but we just can't give 'far exceed' because there is nowhere else to go." I'm like, "Wait a minute here, if I earned an A-plus, don't I get an A-plus?" "Well, then what happens next year if you don't do so well?" [I'm like] "Then grade me down!" But that's not how it works. So when I get that little piece of paper that says "good job," I'm like, "Get bent!" (CCO ---)

You get a little plaque like that every 30 years. That's about what you get for a reward [dryly stated]. (CCO ---)

Verbal, letter of commendation. You saw that the other day. Recognition of the support staff, Officer of the Year, Officer of the Quarter. Things like that. Too bad there's not monetary rewards, but [laughing]. Well, "adda boys" and stuff like that. You know, that happens, that comes with the territory. There could be better ways for rewards, I think. (CCO ---)

One CCO expressed the long-term consequences of not receiving the same recognition as the police even though the CCO's job is as dangerous and as stressful.

Personally, I have to do 42 years with this department in order to get my full retirement and continue to get paid without a gap. Forty-two years! You think I can do this job for 42 years? We deserve 20-year retirement for what we do. Absolutely. My life is in more danger working with the people I work with every day than a police officer's is....I shouldn't have to die in order to retire from this place. I should have some quality of life left after I have put in a long, hard career. God, this job is hard, it is negative, it takes its toll. There is very little about this job that is positive. Especially when you can't gauge change yourself. (CCO ---)

Most positive comments were not in relationship to the DOC overall but instead were connected to the actions of supervisors. It really did not appear to take much to make officers feel good about their work. For example,

[My supervisor] will do stuff like, you know, on a violation report, I mean, simple things like "good report." But that means a lot. You know, people worked their butt off on a report and here's their supervisor acknowledging "good job." Two words can mean a lot. Or, I had surgery on Friday, and he's like, "You know, hey, if you can't come back Monday, you just call me." You know, now, I've had bosses in the past in DOC, "You need to come back right away." You know what I mean? He accepts that the job we're doing is tough, it's stressful, but he treats us like we're human. That's the bottom line. You know, he understands we have other lives going on, we've got kids, we've got this, we've got that. You know, and nobody abuses it with him because he is our supporter, he's always there for us, he lets us do what we've got to do, you know what I mean? And nobody abuses it. Now, some of the other supervisors, there's a couple of the other units, I will not even work there. (CCO ---)

My supervisor is excellent at that. He takes every opportunity to tell us when we do something good. Some supervisors out there are more quick to say something when you don't do so well than they are to let you know when you do well. (CCO ---)

Although some studies have shown CCOs are not very satisfied with their work and do not like their supervisors (see Simmons et al., 1997), a majority of CCOs in Spokane appeared to be satisfied with their work and in general liked their working relationship with their immediate supervisor (80%), although less so with their field administrator (41%, with the same percentage reporting little to no contact; Drapela & Lutze, 2009). Drapela & Lutze (2009) reported that 66% of Spokane CCOs were satisfied with their jobs, followed by 19% who reported mixed feelings, and 15% who reported being dissatisfied. Those who expressed satisfaction often described the variety of experiences their work offered, the challenges, and that what they did was meaningful and important to individuals as well as the community. Job satisfaction was expressed in multiple ways, with some highlighting the boundary-spanning aspects of their work. For example,

I love it. It's crazy. I cannot articulate why. I'm going to tell you. I see myself having a critical role, and I'll tell you, I feel needed. I do not feel expendable. I feel like I make a difference. And I certainly find challenge in it every day. It's the most frustrating piece-of-shit job I've ever had sometimes, but you know what? I love it. I love being the center of the spoke on the wheel of the criminal justice system. I love having cops, judges, treatment providers, attorneys, all these people coming to me and go, "Hey, you know this guy better than anybody else. What can we do to effectively and positively change their life?" (CCO 207)

Others considered positive change over time and the importance of the mission of the DOC and their work.

> Well, I'm 2 years until retirement. So, yes, that will make my job better! I want to retire. But I'm quite honestly...I'm pretty much content with what I see going on in corrections right now. Because when I started, social work and social workers were not welcomed in DOC. NOT, NOT. And DOC was not welcomed in social work, was NOT. So, I see them coming together more now and the social sciences coming more together....And so, yeah, I see us as growing. Because I know when I first started, they asked me, "What's your degree in?" "I went to school in social work." "Well, where are you working?" "Corrections" [whispering, embarrassed]. You know, so I see a big change now. And so I think there are a lot of things that have changed. (CCO ---)

> I think so. Yeah. Because the nice thing about it is that I have a huge challenge that I need to rise to, and it is a very good mission...a mission I believe in. There's so many positions out in the community that don't have quality missions. We have a lot on the line. I like that. So, I like dealing with people to change. (CCO 248)

Other CCOs highlighted that the ability to be proactive, the variety of activities, and the different types of people are what make the job very rewarding.

> I enjoy my job very, very much. And I think that one reason is, is that I've taken an active role in my job in that I have worked a number of different caseloads, a number of different areas, and my approach has always been, "What can I learn from this?" Where I'm at right now, I thoroughly enjoy the programming aspect of the community justice center. I don't know if I will be ready for a change 2 years from now, but I think employees—as CCOs—need to play more of an active role in where they're at in their career versus letting somebody take care of them. (CCO ---)

> I love my job. Even though it's not perfect, it's not a perfect world we live in, it's not a perfect system we work with, they're not perfect people that we work with, offenders are not perfect, it's a challenging job, it's a never-a-dull-moment job. I like that it's not repetitive. I can do 20 different things in a day. It's not like working on an assembly line and plugging something in. And it's working with people. It's working with different personalities. I'm a people person and I just appreciate and love my job. But I have problems with it, you know. (CCO 245)

Given that the majority of CCOs appear to be satisfied with their jobs in spite of the fear of being sued, the excessive caseloads, the constant changes to policy, and the persistent need to manage risks, it seems possible for community corrections agencies to be structured in ways that reduce stress and increase job satisfaction.

Recent studies on stress in community corrections provide several recommendations for reducing stress and increasing job satisfaction. Slate et al. (2003, p. 537) found that "employees who perceive that they have input into workplace decision making are more likely to express higher opinions of their job and are less likely to report physical symptoms of stress, which can translate to greater productivity and morale, with less absenteeism, health care costs, and employee turnover. Thus, participatory management strategies are critical to maximizing the functioning of human capital." (also see Armstrong, 2012; Lee et al., 2009; Simmons et al., 1997; Whitehead & Lindquist, 1992).

In addition to participatory management, Armstrong (2012) suggests that implementing EBP leads to CCOs enjoying more discretion because they are able to use their professional expertise to recommend and implement what is best for the offender and to reach organizational goals. EBP was more likely to result in a balanced approach along a continuum of law enforcement and treatment strategies, depending on the risks and needs posed by the offender. The focus on doing what works instead of reacting to crises may increase meaningful and professional exchanges between supervisors and CCOs to proactively problem-solve cases and thus reduce stress and increase job satisfaction. Administrators need to carefully select supervisors who are going to promote a positive work environment and understand how to assure quality work while giving recognition for achieving management's and CCOs' goals (see Simmons et al., 1997; Slate et al., 2000, 2003).

Reducing stress and increasing job satisfaction may also help reduce high caseloads and workloads. Several studies show that stress is related to job dissatisfaction and being dissatisfied with one's job leads to a greater desire to quit or take days off from work and increased physical health problems. Each of these factors contributes to fewer staff to supervise offenders, thus shifting the workload onto other officers (see Finn & Kuck, 2005). Community corrections agencies are encouraged to develop stress reduction programs that focus on all aspects of stress, including physical and psychological causes. Therefore, agencies seeking a diverse and stable workforce should consider strategies to reduce stress within the organization in order to reduce the potential for negative outcomes such as labor force loss, training costs, and workload displacement due to constant turnover and open positions.

Addressing stress related to larger caseloads and critical incidents is also important to enhancing the working conditions for staff and to assure public safety. When CCOs are stressed they may be distracted, unable to concentrate, and less likely to be able to solve confrontations peacefully (Finn & Kuck, 2005). Turnover often results in a greater number of officers who do not yet possess the skills or experience to identify and avoid dangerous situations, resulting in an increased likelihood of injury to themselves and others (Finn & Kuck, 2005). Stressors related to critical incidents, large caseloads, and adapting work roles to accommodate safety concerns may lead to inefficiency and ineffectiveness (DeMichele, 2007; Finn & Kuck, 2005). Therefore, special attention must be paid to the constant concern about critical incidents and the resulting professional and personal hardships that follow due to media attention and professional scrutiny. Administrators must begin to move from a defensive posture regarding critical incidents and become more proactive in preventing and responding to such incidents.

It is also clear that for community corrections to effectively manage risk and implement EBP, it will have to proactively address many of the challenges confronting CCOs that are certain to undermine successful implementation and outcomes of community corrections. Although these challenges are many, they are not insurmountable. They are within the power of policymakers and administrators to change.

BOUNDARY SPANNERS AND IMPLEMENTING EBP

It is clear from the research and based on the experiences of CCOs that working for the DOC and in community corrections is both challenging and rewarding. The contemporary challenge confronting community corrections is how to effectively implement evidence-based practices within the existing economic, political, and social context. Many have argued that even with growing evidence that many types of supervision and treatment effectively reduce recidivism, nothing will change because of the failure of institutions to prepare systems, people, and places for innovations that work (Henderson & Hanley, 2006; McCorkle & Crank, 1996; Pisciotta, 1994; Rhine et al., 2006; Rothman, 1980). Additionally, in spite of knowing what works, researchers have been remiss to inform policymakers how and why it works (Taxman, 2004). The overwhelming power of excessive caseloads, workloads, risk management administration, media, and liability conspire to pressure organizations and CCOs to conduct business as usual and actively sabotage the implementation of evidence-based practices.

What is learned from the professional experiences and perceptions of CCOs is that they desire to conduct their work in an effective manner that takes advantage of their professional expertise. Administrators and supervisors might only begin to implement evidence-based practices when they also begin to see CCOs as dynamic, professional, street-level boundary spanners who can achieve successful outcomes, long-term reintegration, and public safety, rather than as case managers responsible for processing offenders through the system with revocation, readmission to prison, and reintegration all weighed equally.

Considering CCOs as boundary spanners within an evidence-based model of supervision requires corrections administrators to better prepare their systems and agencies to achieve successful outcomes. Managing risk is extremely important. Actuarial-based, validated, and reliable risk assessment tools need to be vetted and then implemented by corrections administrators to support CCOs in managing risk. CCOs need to embrace such tools to guide their work and use their professional expertise and judgment to structure, support, motivate, and treat those most at risk and in need of CCOs' expertise to work within systems and across agencies to clear the path for offender success. Then, once obstacles have been removed and a plan presented, it is the responsibility of the offender to engage the process of change.

To fully use CCOs as boundary spanners, CCOs must be relieved of a large portion of the secretarial record keeping and administrative tasks that are important but serve as a barrier to time spent in the community collaborating with other professionals and offenders to manage risk and needs. Although workload is often considered by administrators, creatively making the space for CCOs to effectively manage their workloads is often missing. Organizing support staff and CCOs to accommodate administrative tasks and fill the gaps created by turnover and absenteeism allows CCOs to fill their time managing offenders instead of paper and prevents them from taking on the work that should be completed by others in the organization.

Supervisors and CCOs have to adapt to evaluations of their work as it relates to achieving goals and outcomes instead of appraisals based on successfully managing the administrative process. This means supervisors and CCOs need to organize their work based on connecting resources, inclusive of surveillance, monitoring, support, and treatment, to offenders' risks and needs in a way that reduces revocations, readmissions to prison, and recidivism and increases long-term success through reintegration and increased public safety. Therefore, administrators and supervisors must know what works, for whom it is most likely to work, and what resources the agency and community have to achieve success. CCOs, as boundary spanners, must be viewed as professionals with an expertise respected within and outside the criminal justice system as a valuable resource and a much needed role to achieve organizational goals and public safety. This places a huge responsibility on CCOs to move beyond business as usual or adhere to narrow conceptualizations of their work as purely law enforcement or social work. It means they must know what works related to managing risk and addressing the needs of offenders to effect real change.

NOTES

1. The Level of Service Inventory-Revised (LSI-R) refers to the risk assessment tool implemented by the Washington State Department of Corrections at the time of this study.
2. This CCO turned out to be correct. The DOC moved away from the LSI-R and transitioned to the Static Risk Assessment (SRA) in 2008 (Drake, 2011), and it is currently considering a new tool.

WORKS CITED

American Probation and Parole Association. (2006). *American Probation and Parole Association adult and juvenile probation and parole national firearm survey.* Lexington, KY: American Probation and Parole Association.

Andrews, D., & Bonta, J. (2010). *The psychology of criminal conduct* (5th ed.). Cincinnati, OH: Anderson.

Armstrong, G. S. (2012). Factors to consider for optimal span of control in community supervision evidence-based practice environments. *Criminal Justice Policy Review, 23*(4), 427–446.

Braga, A. A., Piehl, M. A., & Hureau, D. (2009). Controlling violent offenders released to the community: An evaluation of the Boston Reentry Initiative. *Journal of Research in Crime and Delinquency, 46*(4), 411–436.

Caplan, J. M. (2006). Parole system anomie: Conflicting models of casework and surveillance. *Federal Probation, 70*(3), 32–36.

Clear, T. R. (2007). *Imprisoning communities: How mass incarceration makes disadvantaged neighborhoods worse.* New York: Oxford University Press.

Cullen, F., & Jonson, C. (2012). *Correctional theory: Context and consequences.* Thousand Oaks, CA: Sage.

DeMatteo, D., Marlowe, D., Festinger, D., & Arabia, P. (2009). Outcome trajectories in drug court: Do all participants have serious drug problems? *Criminal Justice and Behavior, 36*(4), 354–368.

DeMichele, M. T. (2007). *Probation and parole's growing caseloads and workload allocation: Strategies for managerial decision making.* Lexington, KY: The American Probation & Parole Association.

DeMichele, M. T., & Payne, B. K. (2012). Measuring community corrections' officials perceptions of goals, strategies, and workload from a systems perspective: Differences between directors and nondirectors. *The Prison Journal, 92*(3), 388–410.

Drake, E. K. (2011). *"What works" in community supervision: Interim report.* Olympia: Washington State Institute for Public Policy.

Drapela, L. A., & Lutze, F. E. (2009). Innovation in community corrections and probabtion officers' fears of being sued: Implementing neighborhood-based supervision in Spokane, Washington. *Journal of Contemporary Criminal Justice, 25*(1), 364–383.

Farrell, J. L., Young, D. W., & Taxman, F. S. (2011). Effects of organizational factors on use of juvenile supervision practices. *Criminal Justice and Behavior, 38*(6), 565–583.

Feeley, M. M., & Simon, J. (1992). The new penology: Notes on the emerging strategy of corrections and its implications. *Criminology, 30*(4), 449–474.

Ferguson, J. L. (2002). Putting the "what works" research into practice: An organizational perspective. *Criminal Justice and Behavior, 29*(4), 472–492.

Finn, P., & Kuck, S. (2005). *Stress among probation and parole officers and what can be done about it.* National Institute of Justice. Washington, DC: U.S. Department of Justice.

Freeman, N. J., & Sandler, J. C. (2010). The Adam Walsh Act: A false sense of security or an effective public policy initiative? *Criminal Justice Policy Review, 1,* 31–49.

Fulton, B., Latessa, E., Stichman, A., & Travis, L. (1997). The state of ISP: Research and policy implications. *Federal Probation, 61*(4), 65–75.

Grattet, R., Petersilia, J., Lin, J., & Beckman, M. (2009). Parole violations and revocations in California: Analysis and suggestions for action. *Federal Probation, 73*(1), 2–11.

Gregory, M. (2010). Reflection and resistance: Probation practice and the ethic of care. *British Journal of Social Work, 40,* 2274–2290.

Griffin, T., & Stitt, B. G. (2010). Random activities theory: The case for "Black Swan" criminology. *Critical Criminology, 18,* 57–72.

Gunnison, E., & Helfgott, J. B. (2013). *Success on the street: Creating opportunities for offender reentry.* London: Lynne Rienner.

Harlow, N., & Nelson, E. K. (1990). Probation's responses to fiscal constraints. In D. E. Duffee, & E. F. McGarrell (Eds.), *Community corrections: A community field approach* (pp. 165–184). Cincinnati, OH: Anderson.

Harris, A. J., & Lobanov-Rostovsky, C. (2010). Implementing the Adam Walsh Act's sex offender registration and notification provisions: A survey of states. *Criminal Justice Policy Review, 21*(2), 202–222.

Harris, P. M., Gingerich, R., & Whittaker, T. A. (2004). The "effectiveness" of differential supervision. *Crime & Delinquency, 50*(2), 235–271.

Helfgott, J. B., & Gunnison, E. (2008). The influence of social distance on community corrections officer perceptions of offender reentry needs. *Federal Probation, 72*(1), 2–12.

Henderson, C. E., Taxman, F. S., & Young, D. W. (2008). A Rasch model analysis of evidence-based treatment practices used in the criminal justice system. *Drug and Alcohol Dependence, 93,* 163–175.

Henderson, C. E., Young, D. W., Farrell, J., & Taxman, F. S. (2009). Associations among state and local organizations contexts: Use of evidence-based practices in the ciminal justice system. *Drug and Alchohol Dependence, 103S,* S23–S32.

Henderson, M. L., & Hanley, D. (2006). Planning for quality: A strategy for reentry initiatives. *Western Criminology Review, 7*(2), 62–78.

Ireland, C., & Berg, B. (2008). Women in parole: Respect and rapport. *International Journal of Offender Therapy and Comparative Criminology, 52*(4), 474–491.

Jones, M., & del Carmen, R. V. (1996). When do probation and parole officers enjoy the same immunity as judges? In T. Ellsworth (Ed.), *Contemporary community corrections* (2nd ed., pp. 375–386). Prospect Heights, IL: Waveland Press.

Kerbs, J. J., Jones, M., & Jolley, J. M. (2009). Discretionary decision making by probation and parole officers: The role of extralegal variables as predictors of responses to technical violations. *Journal of Contemporary Criminal Justice, 25*(4), 424–441.

Kilmartin, C. T. (2000). *The masculine self* (2nd ed.). Boston: McGraw Hill.

Latessa, E. J. (2008). What science says about designing effective prisoner reentry programs. *Wisconsin Family Impact Seminars No. 26.* Madison, WI: Policy Institute for Family Impact Seminars.

Latessa, E. J., Cullen, F. T., & Gendreau, P. (2002). Beyond correctional quackery: Professionalism and the possiblity of effective treatment. *Federal Probation, 66*(2), 43–49.

Latessa, E. J., & Lovins, B. (2010). The role of offender risk assessment: A policy maker guide. *Victims & Offenders, 5*(3), 203–219.

Lattimore, P. K., Visher, C. A., Winterfield, L., Lindquist, C., & Brumbaugh, S. (2005). Implementation of prisoner reentry programs: Findings from the Serious and Violent Offender Reentry Initiative multi-site evaluation. *Justice Research and Policy, 7*(2), 87–109.

Lee, W.-J., Joo, H.-J., & Johnson, W. W. (2009). The effect of participatory managment on internal stress, overall job satisfaction, and turnover intention among federal probation officers. *Federal Probation, 73*(1), 33–40.

Lindner, C., & Koehler, R. J. (1992). Probation officer victimization: An emerging concern. *Journal of Criminal Justice, 20,* 53–62.

Lovrich, N. P., Lutze, F. E., & Lovrich, N. (2012). Mass incarceration: Rethinking the "war on crime" and the "war on drugs" in the United States. *Journal of Crime Prevention and Corrections, 16,* 23–53.

Lowenkamp, C. T., Latessa, E. J., & Holsinger, A. M. (2006). The risk principle in action: What we learned from 13,676 offenders and 97 correctional programs. *Crime & Delinquency, 52,* 77–93.

Lowenkamp, C. T., Latessa, E. J., & Smith, P. (2006). Does correctional program quality really matter? The impact of adhering to the principles of effective interventions. *Criminology and Public Policy, 5*(3), 575–594.

Lutze, F. E., Johnson, W., Clear, T., Latessa, E., & Slate, R. (2012). The future of community corrections is now: Stop dreaming and take action. *Journal of Contemporary Criminal Justice, 28*(1), 42–49.

Lutze, F. E., Smith, R. P., & Lovrich, N. P. (2004). *A practitioner-initiated research partnership: An evaluation of neighborhood-based supervision in Spokane, Washington (Grant #: 1999-CE-VX-0007).* Washington, DC: National Institute of Justice.

Lutze, F. E., & van Wormer, J. (2007). The nexus between drug and alcohol treatment program integrity and drug court effectiveness: Policy recommendations for pursuing success. *Criminal Justice Policy Review, 18*(3), 226–245.

Lynch, M. (1998). Waste managers? The new penology, crime fighting, and parole agent identity. *Law & Society Review, 32*(4), 839–870.

McCleary, R. (1992). *Dangerous men: The sociology of parole* (2nd ed.). New York: Harrow and Heston.

McCorkle, R., & Crank, J. P. (1996). Meet the new boss: Institutional change and loose coupling in parole and probation. *American Journal of Criminal Justice, 21,* 1–25.

Morgan, K. D., Belbot, B. A., & Clark, J. (1997). Liability issues affecting probation and parole supervision. *Journal of Criminal Justice, 25*(3), 211–222.

Murphy, D., & Lutze, F. (2009). Police-probation partnerships: Professional identity and the sharing of coercive power. *Journal of Criminal Justice, 37*, 65–76.

Ohlin, L. E., Piven, H., & Pappenfort, D. M. (1956). Major dilemmas of the social worker in probation and parole. *National Probation and Parole Association Journal, 2,* 211–225.

Parsonage, W. H. (1990). *Worker safety in probation and parole.* Washington, DC: National Institute of Corrections.

Payne, B. K., & DeMichele, M. (2011). Probation philosophies and workload considerations. *American Journal of Criminal Justice, 36,* 29–43.

Petersilia, J. (2002). Community corrections. In J. Q. Wilson, & J. Petersilia (Eds.), *Crime: Public policies for crime control* (pp. 483–508). Oakland, CA: Institute for Contemporary Studies.

Petersilia, J. (2003). *When prisoners come home: Parole and prisoner reentry.* New York: Oxford University Press.

Pierson, J. E. (1992, December). Enhanced supervision—not necessarily "tail 'em, nail 'em, and jail 'em." *Federal Probation,* 18–19.

Pisciotta, A. (1994). *Benevolent repression: Social control and the American reformatory prison movement.* New York: New York University Press.

Rhine, E. E., Mawhorr, T. L., & Parks, E. C. (2006). Implementation: The bane of effective correctional programs. *Criminology and Public Policy, 5*(2), 347–358.

Rothman, D. (1980). *Conscience and convenience: The asylum and its alternatives in Progressive America.* Boston: Little, Brown and Company.

Schlager, M. D. (2008). An assessment of parole officer and administrator attitudes on organizational culture and parole supervision in a northeastern state. *Journal of Offender Rehabilitation, 47*(3), 271–289.

Sigler, R. T. (1988). Role conflict for adult probation and parole officers: Fact or myth. *Journal of Criminal Justice, 16*, 121–129.

Sigler, R. T., & McGraw, B. (1984). Adult probation and parole officers: Influence of their weapons, role perceptions and role conflict. *Criminal Justice Review, 9*, 28–32.

Simmons, C., Cochran, J. K., & Blount, W. R. (1997). The effects of job-related stress and job satisfaction on probation officers' inclinations to quit. *American Journal of Criminal Justice, 21*(2), 213–229.

Slate, R. N., Wells, T. L., & Johnson, W. W. (2000). Probation officer stress: Is there an organizational solution? *Federal Probation, 64*(1), 56–60.

Slate, R. N., Wells, T. L., & Johnson, W. W. (2003). Opening the manager's door: State probation officer stress and perceptions of participation in workplace decision making. *Crime & Delinquency, 49*(4), 519–541.

Sluder, R. D., & Shearer, R. A. (1991). Probation officers' role percpetions and attitudes toward firearms. *Federal Probation, 55*(3), 3–9.

Surette, R. (2011). *Media, crime and criminal justice: Images, realities, and policies* (4th ed.). Belmont, CA: Wadsworth, Cengage Learning.

Takagi, P. (1973). Administrative and professional conflicts in modern corrections. *The Journal of Criminal Law and Criminology, 64*(3), 313–319.

Taxman, F. S. (2002). Supervision: Exploring the dimensions of effectiveness. *Federal Probation, 66*(2), 14–27.

Taxman, F. S. (2004). Research and relevance: Lessons from the past, thoughts for the future. *Criminology and Public Policy, 3*(2), 169–180.

Travis, J. (2005). *But they all come back: Facing the challenges of prisoner reentry.* Washington, DC: The Urban Institute.

van Wormer, J. (2010). *The operational dynamics of drug court.* (Unpublished dissertation.) Washington State University, Department of Criminal Justice and Criminology. Pullman, Washington:

Walker, S., Spohn, C., & DeLone, M. (2007). *The color of justice: Race, ethnicity, and crime in America* (4th ed.). Belmont, CA: Wadsworth.

Weber, G. H. (1958). Exploration in the similarities, differences and conflicts between probation, parole and institutions. *The Journal of Criminal Law, Criminology, and Police Science, 48*(6), 580–589.

Wells, D. T. (2003). *Reducing stress for officers and their families.* Washington, DC: U.S. Department of Justice.

Wells, T., Colbert, S., & Slate, R. N. (2006). Gender matters: Differences in state probation officer stress. *Journal of Contemporary Criminal Justice, 22*(1), 63–79.

West, A. D., & Seiter, R. P. (2004). Social worker or cop? Measuring the supervision styles of probation and parole officers in Kentucky and Missouri. *Journal of Criminal Justice, 27-57*(2), 27.

Whitehead, J. T., & Lindquist, C. A. (1992). Determinants of probation and parole officers professional orientation. *Journal of Criminal Justice, 20*, 13–24.

FIVE

EXPANDING THE EXPERTISE OF COMMUNITY CORRECTIONS OFFICERS

Embracing Evidence-Based Practice

The multiple problems confronted by offenders supervised in the community clearly demonstrate that oversimplistic approaches will not result in long-term change. Offenders need assistance with educational and skill deficits, mental health problems, substance abuse, housing, employment, and reintegration with family. They also must change their antisocial attitudes and behaviors that increase their risk to recidivate and threaten community safety. In recent decades correctional interventions have emerged that provide a complex array of supervision strategies and treatment options that work to achieve correctional goals. Due to a growing body of knowledge about evidence-based practice (EBP) and evidence-based treatment (EBT), community corrections agencies and CCOs have more options concerning the best approach to supervision and the interventions most likely to reduce risk and meet the needs of offenders and the community. The availability of so many options requires CCOs to hone their professional skills to determine what works and who it is most likely to work for in the immediate context of the offender's life. It also requires CCOs to rely on other agencies to capture the expertise and resources outside of the criminal justice system to fully address offenders' behavior and possibly the needs of offenders' extended network of family and peers.

This chapter identifies what works to manage offender risk and to change the behaviors and conditions most likely to result in recidivism. Attention is given to supervision strategies related to understanding offenders' criminogenic risks and needs. Obviously, in order to manage both risk and need, it is important to know what types of supervision—surveillance, monitoring, support, or treatment—work to change offender behavior in the short and long term. Relatedly, a review of what works in social services and public health gives insight to how CCOs may cross institutional boundaries to improve the lives of offenders as well as their families to help stop the immediate and intergenerational cycling of people through the criminal justice system.

Although a multitude of interventions have been tried over the years with mixed results, recent research is narrowing the scope of what works, why it works, and for whom it works. Possibly the most influential theoretical foundation driving the "what works" movement within corrections is the risk, need, and responsivity (RNR) model developed by Andrews and Bonta (2010). In addition to the RNR model, multiple scholars have investigated how to determine the strategies and interventions that best improve outcomes for correctional populations (Cullen, 2005). This research has produced an impressive and growing body of evidence showing that many interventions significantly reduce recidivism and improve outcomes while others may actually do more harm than good (Cullen & Jonson, 2012). Since a general consensus has emerged among researchers that correctional interventions do work, the movement has begun to shift toward the transfer of knowledge gained from research to effective implementation in real-world settings. Consequently, new emphasis is being placed on researchers and practitioners to responsibly work together to share knowledge and implement best practices to achieve correctional goals (Latessa, Cullen, & Gendreau, 2002; Lipsey & Cullen, 2007; Taxman, 2004; Taxman, Shepardson, & Byrne, 2004).

Evidence-based practice and treatment refers to the implementation of programs proven through rigorous scientific evaluation to increase intended outcomes. Research clearly shows that correctional programs are effective in decreasing recidivism when theoretically informed, targeted toward high-risk and high-need offenders, and implemented with structural integrity according to the model's intended design (Andrews & Bonta, 2010; Cullen & Jonson, 2012; Harris, Gingerich, & Whittaker, 2004; MacKenzie, 2006). Program integrity is a key element to translating EBP from research to practice. Program integrity or fidelity is the extent that program staff organizes and acts within the scope of the program's intended design. As Andrews and Bonta (2010, p. 393) state, it is "the extent to which treatment staff actually do what the program model says they should do." Therefore, program integrity is enhanced when there is a clearly defined theoretical model with written documentation and staff are selected and trained to implement the intervention. Integrity is also enhanced when staff are clinically supervised and the program is delivered with the appropriate intensity (Andrews & Bonta, 2010; Harris et al., 2004). Failing to understand the basic premises of the intervention and how the underlying theory of the model is directly related to professional practice produces disappointing outcomes and may even result in harm to the participant and community (see Andrews & Bonta, 2010; Barnoski, 2004; Harris et al., 2004; Lipsey & Cullen, 2007; Wilson & Davis, 2006, for examples). As mentioned, much of the current research on what works in correctional interventions is driven by Andrews and Bonta's (2010) RNR model. Therefore, before reviewing the different interventions that work it is important to understand the framework that guides successful programs.

UNDERSTANDING RISK, NEED, AND RESPONSIVITY

In the early 1990s, Andrews and Bonta (2010) set out to determine the individual and contextual attributes repeatedly shown to be highly correlated with criminal behavior. Based on an extensive review of theory and research, Andrews and Bonta (2010) outlined four key attributes common to the majority of offenders: antisocial attitudes, antisocial peers, antisocial personality, and a criminal history. They also discovered that familial or marital circumstances, educational or vocational attainment or involvement, gratification in leisure or recreational activities, and substance abuse problems are scientifically relevant to criminal conduct. They argue that programs that do not target these risks and criminogenic needs will fail to change behavior or impact recidivism. Risks, as articulated by Andrews and Bonta (2010, p. 20), are "characteristics of people and their circumstances that are associated with an increased chance of criminal activity." They identify criminogenic needs as those risk factors that are "dynamic," meaning risk factors (e.g., antisocial attitudes, substance abuse) that can be changed through interventions (Andrews & Bonta, 2010, p.21). Responsivity is an approach that considers the "ability and learning style of the offender" in an effort to empower him or her in the rehabilitation process (Andrews & Bonta, 2010, p.49).

Andrews and Bonta (2010) contend that correctional interventions must target high-risk offenders and be capable of intervening directly into the dynamic, and therefore changeable, criminogenic needs of offenders. Interventions must be designed in a way responsive to offenders' learning styles, cognitive abilities, cultural expectations, support networks, and the current context of their lives. Programs that purposefully target offender risks, needs, and responsivity (RNR) have repeatedly been shown to reduce recidivism among high-risk offenders. Several studies have shown that interventions based on the RNR model are effective in reducing recidivism up to 30% while those that fail to include the principles of RNR have resulted in no effect or may even have an iatrogenic effect by increasing recidivism (Andrews & Bonta, 2010; Cullen & Jonson, 2012; Drake, 2011; Lowenkamp, Latessa, & Holsinger, 2006; Lowenkamp, Latessa, & Smith, 2006).

In order to effectively target risk and needs, corrections agencies and treatment providers must have the ability to accurately assess offenders. Thus, risk and need assessment tools serve to move the RNR model from theory and research to practice by helping professionals to reliably identify who among the entire correctional population of offenders possesses the attributes most likely to result in reoffending. Risk assessment tools that generate reliable risk and need scores provide the basis for practitioners to direct resources related to surveillance, control, support, and treatment to those most in need. Risk assessment tools are not just one more administrative task to manage risk but instead allow professionals to target groups of offenders based on their criminogenic needs to reduce recidivism. The power to target the attitudes and behaviors most likely to result in harm to the community increases the likelihood of success for the offender, the CCO, and the system across institutions of criminal justice, social services, public health, and education.

Unfortunately, not all risk assessment tools are created equal. In order for risk assessment to be effectively used, it must be accurate in predicting who is most likely to reoffend. Acceptable risk assessment tools must be both reliable and valid (Latessa & Lovins, 2010). Reliability is a measure of how often different people using the same tool to assess an offender come to the same conclusion. Validity measures the degree to which the instrument is predicting what it is supposed to predict. The most reliable and valid risk assessment tools are able to accurately predict recidivism about 70% of the time (Andrews & Bonta, 2010; Latessa & Lovins, 2010). Risk assessment tools are generally used as screening instruments, comprehensive risk and need assessments, and specialized tools to predict the behavior of specific populations (e.g., substance abusers, sex offenders, mentally ill offenders). Many risk assessment tools measure static risk factors that cannot be changed (e.g., criminal history, demographic characteristics) and dynamic risk factors that can be improved by interventions (e.g., antisocial attitudes, substance abuse, employment, education). Contemporary risk assessment tools are designed to measure both risks and needs and to connect the assessment's findings directly to case planning and the targeting of dynamic risk factors related to offenders' criminogenic needs (Andrews & Bonta, 2010; Latessa & Lovins, 2010).

Once offenders are properly assessed, CCOs can then contemplate, based on their professional EBP expertise, what each individual needs to be successfully reintegrated into the community. Knowing what types of interventions work empowers CCOs to manage risk and to direct offenders to the programs that operate with integrity and are most likely to lead to success.

WHAT WORKS TO ENHANCE SUCCESS IN COMMUNITY CORRECTIONS

Strategies and programs that work address the key concerns expressed by CCOs related to managing risk and increasing public safety. When designed and implemented with integrity, according to the principles of successful interventions or treatment, these strategies work to reduce recidivism and increase prosocial behaviors and are proven to be cost effective. Effective treatment interventions provide intensive cognitive-behavioral learning programs, target high-risk individuals, enforce program contingencies in a firm but fair manner, are of an appropriate duration or dosage to produce the intended effect, and match clients to staff in programs designed to meet their criminogenic needs (Gendreau, 1996).

Although a fluid approach to supervision is the most effective in achieving correctional goals, it is important to note that interventions, whether originating from a law enforcement or social work perspective, are most effective when they address both risk and need. Therefore, CCOs that find themselves adhering to one extreme or the other will need to consider the evidence about what works and incorporate this expertise into their supervision practice to improve outcomes.

Moving From Prison to the Community

The emphases on punitive- and sanction-oriented approaches to supervision are popular strategies to manage risk and increase public safety (see Feeley & Simon, 1992; McCorkle & Crank, 1996; Petersilia, 2003). These approaches generally focus on surveillance, monitoring, and sanctioning of offenders on supervision. These control- and sanction-oriented strategies have led to a significant increase in the use of jail time or revocation to prison as a response to noncompliance (Burke, Gelb, & Horowitz, 2007; Petersilia, 2003).Given the popular use of jail and prison as a primary form of punishment and sanctioning strategy, it is important to consider the effectiveness of confinement on recidivism. Understanding the impact of prison on offender behavior is necessary because community supervision is often held responsible for what may actually be the harmful effects of prison on the potential of many offenders to be successful in the community. Conversely, a failure in community corrections may sabotage gains made by offenders while in prison due to a failure to provide continuity in care upon reentry.

Reviews of the impact of incarceration on recidivism show that jail and prison sentences tend to increase recidivism from 4% to 14% for both juveniles and adults (Lipsey & Cullen, 2007). Boot camp prisons have been shown to have no effect on recidivism for adult offenders and to increase recidivism up to 10% for juvenile offenders.[1] Recent research is beginning to explain why prison often produces such negative outcomes. It appears that many prisons do little to change the factors associated with crime such as antisocial attitudes and behaviors, substance abuse, lack of education and vocational skills, and the long-term effects of trauma due to violence perpetrated in the community and the home (see Johnson, 2002; Lutze & Kigerl, 2013; Petersilia, 2003; Zamble & Porporino, 1988). Prisons also appear to add to the traumatic life experiences and poor coping strategies many offenders experience prior to prison (Haney, 2001; Zamble & Proporino, 1988).

Some argue that adjusting to the physical and psychological pains of imprisonment has serious consequences postrelease (Haney, 2001; Johnson, 2002; Sykes, 1958). The prison environment is oftentimes a violent space void of emotional support and trusting relationships and therefore must be carefully navigated both physically and psychologically. Attributes necessary to survive the prison environment (e.g., distrust, suspicion, alienation, social withdrawal, isolation, emotional "overcontrol," physical aggression) are counterproductive to effectively developing close personal relationships and becoming a prosocial member of the community after release (Haney, 2001; Zamble & Porporino, 1988). Recent research shows that increased coercion by staff and other inmates, experiencing violence while in prison, and increased discomfort resulted in decreased psychological well-being and feelings of hostility after release (Boxer, Middlemass, & Delorenzo, 2009; Hochstetler, DeLisi, & Pratt, 2010; Listwan, Colvin, Hanley, & Flannery, 2010). Conversely, increased levels of social support and safer prison environments increased the chances of successful reentry and overall feelings of well-being (Hochstetler et al., 2010; Listwan et al., 2010). Lutze & Kigerl (2013) conclude that "it is clear that prison context matters to how inmates experience reentry. Harsh prison environments, as intended, may successfully punish criminal offenders and make their lives physically and emotionally miserable, but they do not make for safer communities post release."

Many of the evidence-based practices discussed later as they relate to community supervision are also effective when implemented within prisons (see Aos et al., 2011). The degree to which they reduce recidivism is often smaller than when implemented in the community, but nonetheless they work to improve outcomes. Unfortunately, too few inmates have access to treatment and other programs in prison that could make a significant change in their lives and improve their chances for success postrelease (Petersilia, 2003). Too often, even when inmates participate in programs, they still have to contend with a lack of support in the general prison environment (Johnson, 2002). Some have argued that the effectiveness of programs in prison could be significantly increased if implemented within institutional environments that emphasize safety, structure, support, and emotional feedback (see Johnson, 2002; Lutze, 1998; Toch, 1977). These attributes require both custody and treatment staff to construct institutional environments that promote positive interactions between correctional staff and inmates.

Recent research has begun to focus on corrections staff and the implementation of core correctional practices within prisons. Core correctional practices refer to the skills and competencies correctional professionals should demonstrate whenever they interact with inmates (Andrews & Bonta, 2010; Smith & Schweitzer, 2012). These include anticriminal modeling; reinforcement of positive behavior and disapproval of negative behavior; effective use of authority; and practicing structured learning, skill building, and cognitive restructuring as real problem-solving opportunities arise (see Smith & Schweitzer, 2012). It is time to design and implement prisons that not only safely manage inmates but do so within a therapeutic environment that emphasizes and reinforces positive coping strategies (Johnson, 2002; Lutze, 2006; Lutze & Bell, 2005; Smith & Scheweitzer, 2012; Zamble & Porporino, 1988).

Many prisons have implemented limited versions of therapeutic prisons through special units within the prison such as honor blocks, milieu therapy, and therapeutic communities (TC). Each of these strategies attempts to arrange the prison environment to provide a supportive climate that reinforces prosocial behavior and participation in treatment and other programs. Therapeutic communities generally segregate inmates with substance abuse problems into special units where they are expected to participate in drug treatment and help each other with abstinence and practicing a prosocial lifestyle (Andrews & Bonta, 2010). Staff, through custody and treatment, are expected to reinforce positive behaviors and work with inmates to support and motivate the process of change. Additionally, attempts have been made to implement the concepts of therapeutic communities throughout entire prisons by modeling and reinforcing "right living" principles to improve prison safety for staff and inmates, reduce infractions, and enhance participation in prosocial behavior such as work, education, and treatment that will ultimately reduce recidivism (Heinrich, 2012). These types of programs, including milieu therapy and TCs, reduce recidivism by an average of 24% (Lipsey & Cullen, 2007).

Work to improve prison environments and implement evidence-based practices is important to community corrections because ultimately CCOs have to manage the successes and failures of the prison. Thus, many have been advocating for a continuum of care from the prison to the community. During the 1990s, researchers, practitioners, and policymakers developed reentry initiatives that relied on evidence-based practices coordinated across providers and embedded within a continuum of care (Duwe, 2012; Lattimore, Visher, Winterfield, Lindquist & Brumbaugh, 2005; Taxman et al., 2004; Winterfield, Lattimore, Seffey, Brumbaugh, & Lindquist, 2006). These initiatives were designed to address the high-risk period immediately following release, to bridge the gap between prison and community corrections services, and to coordinate across institutions (e.g., criminal justice, social services, public health) to provide wraparound services to address both risk and need. As Taxman and Bouffard (2000, p. 42) state, "By each organization focusing on the overall process and not simply on its own goals and responsibilities, services can be implemented in a manner that maximizes their overall efficiency and effectiveness." They propose that integrated service models must become "boundaryless organizations" that share goals and develop mutually beneficial practices at key decision points common for both criminal justice and treatment agencies (Taxman & Bouffard, 2000, p. 39).

It became clear that in order to affect the time immediately following release into the community, community corrections needed to start preparing inmates for reentry before their release from prison. Prerelease preparations for inmates within the institution needed to include meeting with a community corrections officer to explain the process and to develop a reentry plan, arranging for the continuation of treatment with a community provider, extending drug prescriptions for physical and mental health, obtaining state identification and a social security card to ease the transition to employment, arranging for safe housing, and beginning the search for employment or the continuation of benefits (Petersilia, 2003).[2] After release, services needed to be coordinated within and between agencies in order to immediately stabilize high-risk offenders and address their criminogenic and basic life needs.

Research shows that coordinated responses to reentry are effective in reducing recidivism. For example, process evaluations of the Serious and Violent Offender Reentry Initiatives (SVORI) show that programs that provide a continuum of care between prison and the community and provide wraparound services significantly increase the number of services used by offenders compared to traditionally supervised parolees (Bouffard & Bergerson, 2006; Lattimore, et al., 2005; Winterfield, et al., 2006). Outcome evaluations of coordinated approaches to reentry also show promise, in that they significantly reduce recidivism and increase many prosocial behaviors such as gaining employment, reducing drug use, increasing medication compliance, and acquiring stable housing (Bouffard & Bergerson, 2006; Braga, Piehl, & Hureau, 2009; Culhane, Metraux, & Hadley, 2002; Duwe, 2012; Lutze, Rosky, & Hamilton, forthcoming; Worcel, Burrus, Finigan, Sanders, & Allen, 2009). These findings reinforce the notion that risks can be managed through multiple approaches that bridge the gap between prison and the community and are inclusive of monitoring, support, and treatment.

Community Supervision Strategies That Work

Community supervision can be implemented in ways that emphasize how CCOs' time is structured and how to best interact with offenders during contacts. Research shows that some forms of supervision are more effective than others (Drake, 2011; Lipsey & Cullen, 2007). In general, punitive approaches are less effective than more balanced approaches that provide monitoring, structure, and support geared toward moving offenders through the process of change. Just as in prison, overly controlling and punitive approaches to community supervision are also challenged to effectively reduce recidivism and increase well-being. Some community supervision approaches show modest improvements in reducing recidivism while some may actually increase recidivism depending on the target population and the program used (see Lipsey & Cullen, 2007). Supervision as an intervention, when compared to no supervision or to regular supervision, shows modest reductions in recidivism ranging from 2% to 8% (Lipsey & Cullen, 2007). Intermediate sanctions designed to increase the severity of supervision show mixed results ranging from reducing recidivism by approximately 8% to increasing recidivism up to 14% (Lipsey & Cullen, 2007).

The initial research on intensive supervision programs (ISP) revealed that increased control of offenders through surveillance, monitoring compliance, and sanctioning does not reduce recidivism but instead increases the detection of technical violations resulting in revocations to prison (Latessa, Travis, Fulton, & Stichman, 1998; Petersilia & Turner, 1993; Taxman, 2002). Yet more recent studies of ISPs also show that their failure may be due to a lack of balance between treatment and surveillance and not the intensity of the program per se. ISPs that significantly reduce recidivism include a balance between law enforcement and social work orientations, provide rewards that outnumber sanctions, and are strength based within organizational environments supportive of rehabilitation (Jalbert, Rhodes, Flygare, & Kane, 2010; Paparozzi & Gendreau, 2005; Wodahl, Garland, Culhane, & McCarty, 2011). Relatedly, recent research on traditional parole supervision by Steiner, Makarios, Travis, & Meade (2012) found that sanctions administered in a swift and certain manner with progressive severity reduced recidivism within the first year of parole. In addition, they found that providing support to parole violators in maintaining residential stability, employment, and participation in appropriate treatment programs also reduced recidivism (Steiner et al., 2012). They conclude that "it is not simply treatment or sanctions that reduce offenders' odd[s] of recidivism, but both types of control, treatment *and* sanctions" (Steiner et al., 2012, p. 247; also see Schaffer, 2011).

A combination of treatment and sanctions may work better because they are more in line with the realities of offenders' lives and the process of change. Get-tough, punitive-oriented strategies tend to approach offenders as capable of stopping their behavior immediately. It is rare, however, that offender change happens all at once as an epiphany. Instead, change is most likely to develop over time with successes and setbacks until stability is achieved. Successful interventions have begun to recognize that offenders are often at different points along a continuum of change and thus may need to be motivated to proactively move forward. The stages of change have been identified as precontemplation, contemplation, preparation, action, and maintenance (see Andrews & Bonta, 2010). In the precontemplation stage, offenders may be experiencing social, legal, and health problems related to their behavior, but they have not yet begun to consider how they may change to avert future difficulties. Individuals in the stage of contemplation may begin to recognize a need to change but are grappling with whether they are ready or how to go about changing their behavior. People often begin to prepare for change long before they finally take action by exploring treatment options (e.g., community, residential, cognitive behavioral training [CBT]), planning to address practical challenges (e.g., child care, transportation, finances), negotiating social support (e.g., eliminating antisocial peer influences, reliance on family), and becoming mentally prepared to embrace the challenges inherent in changing one's attitudes and lifestyle. Finally, action is taken to effect the change by participating in programs, breaking bad habits, and complying with rules and conventional expectations. Long-term change is achieved by actively working to sustain the change over time.

Due to a greater understanding of the process of offender change, many interventions have begun to incorporate the stages of change into the program design, recognizing that momentum may stall during the process and even regress depending on the type and magnitude of the risks and needs confronting clients (e.g., drug addiction, severe mental health problems, social and economic deprivation, antisocial peers). Approaches that prepare offenders for change show promise by improving the interaction between offenders and their CCOs or treatment providers and ideally the connection of offenders to interventions with integrity that promote positive outcomes. To enhance the quality of CCO contacts with offenders, motivational interviewing has become a popular approach to guide the content of conversations that CCOs have with offenders in an attempt to change outcomes.

Motivational interviewing (MI) "is a style of interaction intended to help individuals resolve ambivalence about behavior change. It involves a collaborative partnership between the provider and client, a focus on drawing out internal motivation for change, and a respect for the client's right and capacity to choose what to do about his/her problematic behavior" (Walters, Alexander, & Vader, 2008, p. 67; also see Aos et al., 2011). MI also provides a client-centered counseling technique that emphasizes empathy, optimism, and respect for client choice and builds the counselor's ability to respond to offender needs and motivation for change empathetically (Walters, Vader, Nguyen, Harris, & Eells, 2011). Although MI has been effective in non–criminal justice therapeutic settings by reducing negative behavior and increasing positive outcomes related to drug addiction, smoking cessation, and other behaviors closely associated with offending behavior, the findings related to MI implementation in probation and parole settings are few and mixed (Walters et al., 2011). This may be due to the fact that meetings with offenders under community supervision are inherently different than in other treatment settings. During office visits with offenders, CCOs have a dual role: authority over offenders and counseling them during multifaceted and assessment-oriented meetings (Walters et al., 2008) that are oftentimes brief due to extensive caseload demands (see Bonta, Rugge, Scott, Bourgon, & Yessine, 2008; Grattet, Petersilia, Lin, & Beckman, 2009; Petersilia, 2003; Takagi, 1973; Weber, 1958).

Research is beginning to reveal that the interactions between CCOs and offenders are also important to outcomes (Bonta et al., 2008; Dowden & Andrews, 2004; Taxman, 2002; Trotter, 2000). Additional time spent on offender problems such as antisocial attitudes, relationships, work, and other issues relevant to the offender's ability to cope and problem-solve decreased recidivism compared to time spent on compliance requirements, which tend to increase recidivism (Bonta et al., 2008). As discussed more fully in previous chapters, it is unfortunate that most CCOs are prevented from spending much time helping individuals because of large caseloads and truncated meeting times. For instance, the majority of CCOs have two to four contacts with offenders each month that range in length from 10 to 20 minutes each and include record-keeping tasks as well as therapeutic discussions (Bonta et al., 2008; DeMichele, 2007; Grattet, Petersilia, Lin, & Beckman, 2009).

How community corrections is structured and how CCOs go about their work matters in achieving positive outcomes. Singular approaches to supervision, whether purely rehabilitative or punitive, tend to be less effective than those fluid and responsive to an offender's demonstrated risk and need over time. Overreliance on confinement and punitive strategies is less effective than balanced approaches more likely to be firm, fair, and consistent, resulting in greater levels of compliance and program completion. Considering reintegration as an ongoing process of change supported through a continuum of care that respects the need to manage risk while directly targeting offender needs is likely to produce positive results. Fortunately, research shows many treatment strategies can effectively change the behavior and risks posed by offenders.

Interventions that work to change behavior and attitudes tend to be grouped within two broad categories. One set of interventions includes treatment modalities that directly focus on changing specific criminal behaviors and the thinking errors that sustain them. These include cognitive behavioral treatment, sex offender treatment, substance abuse treatment, and mental health treatment. The other category of interventions focuses on improving the skills and conditions that tend to sabotage successful treatment completion and reentry. These strategies include education, vocational training, employment, housing, and other general forms of support.

Treatment Interventions That Work

Most effective treatment approaches include cognitive and behavioral learning components that tie the participant's thinking errors to problematic behavior. Cognitive behavioral treatment (CBT) is a learning-oriented approach that demands the client engage in the here-and-now in an effort to address problematic thinking and behavioral patterns. Although CBT is sometimes thought of as a single approach, it actually represents a wide range of therapeutic methods (Gideon & Sung, 2011). Thus, CBT interventions can be adapted to the targeted cognitive processes and behaviors that need to be changed, such as antisocial attitudes, substance abuse, anger, and other behaviors highly correlated with criminal behavior.

Several meta-analyses have shown that CBT interventions effectively reduce recidivism when used with offender populations (Andrews & Bonta, 2010; Landenberger & Lipsey, 2005; Lipsey & Cullen, 2007;

Lowenkamp, Hubbard, Makarios & Latessa, 2009; MacKenzie, 2000; Wilson, Bouffard, & MacKenzie, 2005). CBT has been shown to work with both adult and juvenile offenders and achieve reductions in recidivism ranging from a low of 8% to a high of 32% (Lipsey & Cullen, 2007). For example, Wilson et al. (2005) found that moral recognition therapy (MRT) resulted in a 32% reduction in recidivism, and cognitive restructuring or reasoning approaches resulted in a 16% reduction. Landenberger and Lipsey (2005) found that increased dosages of CBT, as measured by the total number of hours per week, reduced recidivism by 25% and that CBT programs using a higher standard for quality implementation had a greater impact on reducing recidivism. Similarly, Lipsey, Chapman, and Landenberger (2011) found that, while overall those offenders who participated in CBT recidivated at approximately one-third the rate of those who did not participate, programs classified as "demonstration" programs were more effective in reducing recidivism (also see Lipsey & Cullen, 2007). Even though demonstration projects implemented by program developers or evaluators tend to be most effective across studies, Lowenkamp and colleagues (2009) have discovered that CBTs can be successfully implemented in "real world" settings. CBTs have also been shown to be cost effective. The benefit-to-cost ratio for prison-based CBT programs is $49.50, and community-based CBT programs return $35.70 for every dollar spent (Aos et al., 2011).[3]

Several types of treatment combine multiple approaches, oftentimes including CBT as one intervention grouped with others, shown to be effective with specific types of offenders such as sex offenders, substance abusers, and those suffering from mental illness. Frequently offenders have specific attributes or conditions that need attention above and beyond traditional approaches to supervision and treatment.

Sex offender treatment. Sex offenders can pose unique challenges to assessing risk and designing effective supervision strategies. Sex offenders often lead conventional and law-abiding lifestyles independent from committing sex crimes and often score low on risk assessments, yet they pose considerable concern to CCOs and the community due to the seriousness of their offenses. Fortunately, several meta-analyses have shown that sex offender treatment programs are effective in reducing recidivism for both juveniles and adults (Lipsey & Cullen, 2007). Decreases in recidivism range from a low of 10% with adult offenders to as high as 36% in reviews of studies that include both adults and juveniles. These are important findings given the unease expressed by CCOs about sex offenders' risk of reoffending and their legitimate concern for wanting to manage risk and protect the public.

Substance abuse treatment. Drug offenders also cause concern about recidivism if their substance abuse is not directly targeted by treatment. Substance abuse and drug addiction have long been connected to poor performance for those supervised in the community. Drug use violates the conditions of supervision and makes it more difficult to sustain a viable place to live, find employment, and refrain from committing new crimes (Petersilia, 2003). Addiction also diminishes one's cognitive abilities to make proper decisions or to consume new information relevant to supervision and treatment success (Lutze & van Wormer, 2007). When considering interventions it is important to distinguish among substance abuse treatment, education, and support programs. Drug treatment programs provide interventions designed to directly change thoughts and behaviors that cause individuals to abuse drugs and alcohol. Drug education programs focus on building awareness about the dangers of substance abuse and how it eventually causes problems related to health, relationships, and economic well-being. Support programs provide a safe place for substance abusers to engage others and to find supportive relationships as they attempt to quit, work through the process of change, or actively sustain their recovery. Education and support programs are not considered treatment; however, they are often combined with treatment programs for obvious reasons.

Therapeutic communities (TC) and drug courts are examples of drug treatment programs that take a holistic approach through the use of treatment, education, and support. Therapeutic communities are structured communities in which participants are surrounded by positive peers and staff to provide a universal approach to achieving and sustaining sobriety. Although TCs are often seen as prison programs (Andrew & Bonta, 2010), they are also provided in the community through group living arrangements or housing programs (Seiter & Kadela, 2003). Therapeutic communities are effective in addressing community reentry, particularly by helping offenders with co-occurring disorders (Deitch, Carleton, Koutsenok, & Marsolais, 2002; MacKenzie, 2006) and creating a group atmosphere that provides support and accountability (Kennard & Roberts, 1983; Prendergast & Burdon, 2002) to reduce recidivism (Seiter & Kadela, 2003).

Drug courts have also become a successful tool often used for substance abusers who are likewise on community supervision. Drug courts combine accountability (e.g., surveillance, monitoring, immediate sanctions) with intensive substance abuse treatment, support, and education to motivate addicted offenders to achieve sobriety and to stop committing crime (Lutze & van Wormer, 2007). Drug courts bring together an interdisciplinary team (judge, defense attorney, prosecutor, treatment provider, case manager, CCOs, law enforcement) to review cases on a weekly basis and to provide incentives, rewards, treatment, or immediate sanctions depending on the participant's conduct (van Wormer & Lutze, forthcoming). Drug courts have been found to reduce recidivism from 8% to 20% for adult offenders and from 14% to 24% in studies that include both juveniles and adults (Lipsey & Cullen, 2007). The most successful of drug courts, however, target appropriate populations, have leverage over participants, set expectations appropriate for the population being served, and have well-qualified and competent staff (Schaffer, 2011). Drug courts have also proven to be cost effective by returning $2.87 for every dollar spent in cost-benefit analyses (Aos et al., 2011).

In general, drug treatment programs have been found to significantly reduce recidivism and increase other prosocial behaviors (Butzin, O'Connell, Martin, & Incairdi, 2006; Lipsey & Cullen, 2007; MacKenzie, 2006; Prendegast & Burdon, 2002; Prendergast, Podus, Chang, & Urada, 2002; Taxman & Bouffard, 2000). Lipsey and Cullen (2007) report that drug and alcohol treatment programs reduce recidivism from 6% for adult offenders up to 14% in studies that include both juveniles and adults. These programs also appear to be cost effective, with a cost-benefit ratio of $3.69 when implemented in prison and $7.35 when used in the community (Aos et al., 2011).

Mental health treatment. Offenders experiencing mental health problems can also pose a greater risk to reoffend if their mental illness is not proactively treated and managed within prison and upon release through treatment and medication (Wolff, Bjerklie, & Maschi, 2005). Approximately 20% of those reentering the community from prison have mental health problems, and an estimated 67% of those have serious mental illness, including schizophrenia, major depression, and bipolar disorder (Wolff et al., 2005). Many people with untreated mental health problems self-medicate with alcohol or illicit drugs. Therefore, mental health issues are often complicated by substance abuse problems resulting in co-occurring disorders needing simultaneous care. Mental health interventions are also cost effective. A return on investment for the dangerously mentally ill is $3.28 and for a mental health court is $4.95 (Aos et al., 2011).

The research on CBT, drug treatment, sex offender treatment, and mental health treatment shows that treatment interventions, combined with the structure and oversight of the offender by the criminal justice system, work to reduce recidivism. Depending on the integrity and context of implementation (prison versus community), outcomes can be diminished or enhanced. Improving the skills and living conditions of offenders can also enhance the effect size of supervision and treatment outcomes.

Improving Individual Skills and Living Conditions

Individual interventions directed toward education, housing, and employment also are effective strategies to reduce recidivism and aid in the successful reintegration of offenders into the community. Many offenders under community supervision live in the same economically depressed and socially disorganized communities they did before prison (Clear, 2007; Kirk, 2009, 2012; Kubrin & Stewart, 2006). Thus, many need help with basic human necessities such as a place to live, personal safety, nourishment, and companionship. While these specific needs are not in and of themselves criminogenic, the pressure they put on offenders can negatively impact their ability to engage in programs necessary to bring about change (see Lutze & Kigerl, 2013). Therefore, the most successful strategies for reentry often focus on changing attitudes and behaviors (RNR and CBT) while at the same time addressing the basic human needs necessary to clear the path toward program engagement and change.

Education and vocational training. Educational performance and functionality are important to offenders' success. Many offenders have low levels of education and are functionally illiterate (Petersilia, 2003). This often prevents individuals from fully engaging in treatment or employment. There is sufficient scientific evidence that educational and vocational programs delivered in prison and in the community reduce recidivism and increase employment opportunities. Reviews of educational, vocational, and work programs show they reduce recidivism from 6% to 20% for adult offenders and are cost effective (Aos et al., 2011; Lipsey & Cullen, 2007). Correctional education and vocational training in prison showed gains of $18.57 and $12.43, respectively, and for work release, $9.97 for every dollar invested. For instance, Wilson, Gallagher, and MacKenzie (2000) in a meta-analysis including educational and vocational programs found that basic education programs were associated with lower recidivism rates (41%) than those programs that did not offer such educational opportunities (50%). The differences in recidivism were even greater for college-level programs (37% vs. 50%) and vocational training (39% vs. 50%) (Lawrence, Mears, Dubin, & Travis, 2002; Wilson et al., 2000). Similarly, work release and vocational training programs are effective in reducing recidivism and improving work-related skills for offenders (Seiter & Kadela, 2003).

Housing stability. There is strong evidence that housing instability often leads to incarceration, and incarceration often leads to housing instability (Geller & Curtis, 2011; Metraux & Culhane, 2004, 2006). Without a stable and safe place to live, individuals must constantly worry about where they will sleep and how they will protect themselves. They also have no place from which to search for work, receive benefits, prepare for treatment, keep their belongings, or take care of their basic human needs (Roman & Travis, 2006). Fortunately, a growing body of research shows that providing housing support, including halfway houses, significantly reduces recidivism for high-risk and -need offenders, substance abusing offenders, and those with serious mental illness (Culhane et al., 2002; Lutze, Rosky, & Hamilton, 2012; Miller & Ngugi, 2009; Worcel et al., 2009; Seiter & Kadela, 2003). For example, Lutze and colleagues (2012) found that providing housing to high-risk offenders who would have been released from prison homeless significantly reduced revocations from supervision, new convictions, and readmission to prison. Homeless offenders were 2 times more likely than those provided housing to experience a revocation from supervision or a new conviction and 2.6 times more likely to be readmitted to prison (Lutze et al., 2012).

Cultural competency. Within these successful interventions, increasing evidence strongly suggests that providers and programs need to be culturally competent and responsive to enhance outcomes across different groups (see Lutze, 2006; Lutze et al., 2012; Lutze & van Wormer, 2007; Sue, Zane, Hall, & Berger, 2009). Justice and social service agencies often require participation in "one-size-fits-all" programs without considering how one's sense of the world is experienced based on race, ethnicity, gender, sexual orientation, religion, socioeconomic status, language, and other characteristics that may influence receptivity or resistance to intervention strategies. Culturally competent staff and programs feature cultural awareness, knowledge, and skills (Sue et al., 2009). *Cultural awareness* refers to the provider's sensitivity to personal values and biases that may influence the interpretation of clients' behavior and affect the professional relationships developed with clients. *Cultural knowledge* refers to awareness and understanding of clients' culture, worldview, and expectations for the relationship. *Cultural skills* refers to the ability to intervene in a culturally sensitive and relevant manner (Sue et al., 2009). Sue and colleagues (2009, p. 541), in a review of the scientific evidence of including cultural competency in psychotherapeutic interventions (including CBT), conclude that "a preponderance of the evidence shows that culturally adapted interventions provide benefit to intervention outcomes" and the added value appears to be greater for adults than for children.

Many correctional interventions have historically been designed to serve adult male populations and then are extrapolated to other groups with the expectation that they will work just as well. It is well known, however, that race, sex, class, and sexual orientation are powerful influences on whether one experiences social inclusion or rejection, experiences privilege or discrimination, or perceives government institutions as helpful or controlling (Newman, 2007). It is well established that interventions are often perceived and experienced differently based on the life experiences of those involved. Understanding people's similarities and differences can broaden responses to include a variety of counseling approaches, create relevant community resources, and make appropriate referrals to achieve greater responsivity.

Unfortunately, the demographic differences in outcomes within successful programs are oftentimes ignored in favor of reporting the overall success of the program. Although it is important to know which programs are most effective in reducing recidivism overall, it is also relevant to know who they do not work for, and why, so that positive outcomes can be shared by all participants. There is evidence that crafting interventions to meet the needs of specific populations can be effective in enhancing outcomes for those groups (Sue et al., 2009). For instance, research on drug treatment programs shows women are more likely to be victims of sexual abuse, be the primary caretakers of their children, lack vocational skills, and relapse if their spouse is abusing drugs than are men (Hser, Huang, Teruya, & Anglin, 2004; Lutze & van Wormer, 2007). African American women released from prison are also more likely to be the caretakers of their extended family members, including children, parents, and siblings, and this may create additional stressors that men are less likely to incur (Leverentz, 2011). Men are also much less likely than women to seek mental or medical health care because of the additional stigma of being perceived as weak if a man asks for help, especially for African American men and Latinos (Kilmartin, 2000). Men and women who return to disadvantaged communities are also more likely to live in close proximity to other felons and have fewer resources to draw on to support their recovery or reintegration (Hipp, Jannetta, Shah, & Turner, 2011).

Therefore, intervention strategies must be developed to address these differences or outcomes will be diminished. For example, programs targeting the needs of women decreased recidivism by 28% (Lipsey & Cullen, 2007). Some drug court studies have shown that African Americans at a high risk of failure were more likely to graduate when the treatment was run by an African American male who implemented culturally sensitive interventions (Dannerbeck, Harris, Sundet, & Lloyd, 2006). As Lutze and van Wormer (2007, p. 234) conclude based on a review of cultural competency in drug courts, "Although we must focus on equality in access to services, giving everyone treatment that is based on a male model of addiction is not equality and may lead to disparity in outcomes." Cultural competency goes beyond merely building awareness about group differences and instead necessitates an understanding about how life experiences differ and influence both perceptions of and engagement in interventions. Poor outcomes may not be because the offender failed to engage in the treatment but because the treatment failed to engage the offender.

To enhance the positive outcomes of treatment interventions, participants need to be prepared for success by being provided educational opportunities, stable housing, and programs responsive to meeting their cultural needs and expectations. Although it is important to consider the success or failure of offenders as individuals, offenders are often intertwined in family and social networks crucial to their success. Families and offenders both help and hinder each other, and therefore these primary relationships also need to be considered when contemplating interventions.

Working With Offenders and Their Families

Offenders, although isolated through incarceration, are not alone in the world. Families provide offenders refuge, emotional support, stability, and loyalty even through the most difficult of times (Shapiro & Schwartz, 2001). Many of the problems offenders experience are also true for many of their family members, friends, and the community. When they return home from prison, offenders are often trying to work through their own problems while having to cope with the ongoing difficulties experienced by their families, such as securing safe housing; gaining meaningful employment; parenting young children; and dealing with substance abuse, mental health, physical health, and other challenges that require a tremendous amount of emotional and physical energy to deal with effectively. Oftentimes the families of offenders are in need of many of the same services as the offender. Therefore, relieving the stress within the offender's social and familial network may assist in supporting and promoting the short- and long-term well-being of the offender (Martinez, 2007; Martinez & Christian, 2009; Shapiro & Schwartz, 2001). Knowing what works outside of traditional correctional services and treatment may be useful to CCOs in stabilizing the lives of offenders within their broader family and community networks.

In addition, offenders' families may be considered "collateral damage" resulting from offenders' behavior and the impact of the criminal justice system on their lives (Comfort, 2007; Foster & Hagan, 2009). Family members also experience the emotional hardship and stress related to the legal process and are expected to pick up the pieces after a conviction or when the offender returns home from prison (see Martinez, 2007; Martinez & Christian, 2009). Law-abiding family members' exposure to the coercive aspects of the criminal justice system, because of their close proximity to the offender, are often invisible or ignored. Family members who live with the offender have to persevere through CCOs and police officers entering their home at all hours and having access to their private lives (see Comfort, 2007; Shapiro & Schwartz, 2001). Although families and CCOs share the desire for offenders' success, they often work at odds with each other due to a mutual lack of respect (Shapiro & Schwartz, 2001). In addition, even though families want their loved ones to be successful, many families are not in a legal, economic, or social position to effectively cope with the complexity of the offender's problems or the offender's ongoing engagement in the criminal justice system (see Comfort, 2007). Family members may be without the social capital to leverage the additional support necessary to help.

Most CCOs are aware of this problem, but they are often focused on the immediacy of managing the offender's supervision rather than considering the offender's family's needs. Although the family's needs are immediate to the offender's likelihood of success, they are not the primary concern of supervision or even within the scope of professional practice for most CCOs; families become third parties that need to be managed versus engaged. Offenders' families and their needs are considered the responsibility of the community or social services and outside the scope of the criminal justice system. The distancing of community corrections from the needs of offenders' families is somewhat ironic given that the criminal justice system, especially corrections, is becoming the primary provider of social, medical, and mental health in many disadvantaged communities (see Comfort, 2007; Dumont, Brockmann, Dickman, Alexander, & Rich, 2012; Wakefield & Uggen, 2010).

CCOs often have a window of opportunity while the offender is under supervision to provide offenders access to resources that may help to stabilize and support the entire family and stop the revolving door into the criminal justice system. Although many CCOs realize the problems that lead to repeatedly cycling through the system often lie beyond corrections, what is effective in social services, public health, and education oftentimes remains a mystery that CCOs do not have time to solve. Social services in particular often remains an abstract entity or one not readily accessible for CCOs' collaboration on behalf of offenders or their families (see Chapter 6). Additional barriers are presented by the many civil penalties attached to a felony conviction that bar offenders from participation in state and federally sponsored programs (Mele & Miller, 2005). In addition, social service caseworkers are oftentimes similar to CCOs in having to manage large caseloads with limited resources to meet all of the needs of their clients, let alone embracing the additional burden of working with high-risk felons.

Viewing offenders as part of a broader network, instead of as isolated individuals, expands the possibilities related to managing risk and addressing offender needs. It also shares some of the responsibility of reintegration with other professionals and institutions. There are many programs within social services, education, and public health that significantly improve the well-being of families and the communities in which they live. The ability to motivate offenders and to connect their families with effective services designed to prevent the overuse of the criminal justice system, shelters, hospitals, and other public services in the future is likely to directly help the offender, improve the overall well-being of the community, and increase public safety (Shapiro & Schwartz, 2001).

As CCOs learn from offenders about the challenges confronting their families, they should strongly consider connecting the offender with programs that work in child welfare, education, mental health, public health, and housing. These areas have evidence-based programs that CCOs should be aware of and use when working with offenders and their families. Child welfare is an important resource that could be more fully used by CCOs to assist offenders with their children.

Many incarcerated offenders, approximately 74% of women and 49% of men, are the parents of minor children, whom they lived with prior to prison (Comfort, 2007). An estimated 3 million children in the United States have an incarcerated or recently released parent (Foster & Hagan, 2009). Many of these parents expect to return to their families and to provide some level of care for their children once released from prison and while on community supervision (Foster & Hagan, 2009). Depending on the age of the children, it may be difficult for offenders to reestablish their parenting role, and they may be uncertain about how to parent or provide care for their children. In addition, offenders' children may pose additional challenges, such as emotional, psychological, and learning difficulties, due to offenders' ongoing dysfunction related to incarceration, impoverishment, substance abuse, or mental illness (see Comfort, 2007). It is well known that the children of convicted and incarcerated parents often experience additional hardships related to social stigma, increased poverty, problems in school, and the increased likelihood of encountering the juvenile justice system and, later in life, being incarcerated (see Foster & Hagan, 2009; Wakefield & Uggen, 2010).The stress of parenting for someone recently released from prison or who is going through treatment may contribute to family violence, abandonment, a failure to pay child support, or a general withdrawal due to an inability to cope. Assisting offenders and their families by directing them toward programs that work independent of the criminal justice system may help offender parents to be more compliant with supervision and improve the life chances of their children.

Many child welfare programs are effective in providing support to children and their families and lead to immediate relief for stressed parents and provide long-term benefits for children over their lifetime by increasing prosocial behaviors and possibly saving them from a life of crime (Cullen & Jonson, 2012). Successful child welfare programs target specific groups of people most likely to benefit from a program, provide intensive services (high level of service hours and participant engagement), focus on behavioral-based treatments, include both parents and children, and adhere to the integrity of the program model (Lee, Aos, & Miller, 2008). Child welfare programs that work fall into two primary categories: prevention and intervention (Lee et al., 2008). Prevention programs provide services to young parents and children to avert immediate and future cases of abuse, neglect, quitting school, and juvenile delinquency. Intervention programs target families already involved in the child welfare system and attempt to successfully intervene in crisis situations to reduce the likelihood of abuse, neglect, or out-of-home placement for the child.

Prevention strategies often include early intervention programs for at-risk parents and children. They provide targeted services to address specific situations and behaviors for long-term success. Prevention programs include approaches such as school-based centers that provide educational and family support for parents and their elementary-aged children living in high-poverty neighborhoods; intensive visitation with at-risk pregnant mothers by a nurse or paraprofessional to provide prenatal care and practice parenting skills; programs that attempt to restructure parent-child relationships and improve secure attachment to the parent; and parent-teacher home visitation with the goal of having children ready to learn when they begin school (Cullen & Jonson, 2012; Lee et al., 2008). For example, nursing programs offering intensive visitation with at-risk pregnant mothers reduce the likelihood of low–birth weight babies, babies testing positive for drugs at birth, emergency room services, and child protective services contacts (Lee et al., 2008). These programs also decrease the long-term consequences of neglectful childhoods by increasing school completion and decreasing contacts with the juvenile and adult criminal justice system (Cullen & Jonson, 2012). Child welfare programs that target specific risks and needs of parents and their children are also cost effective by returning a range of savings from $2.73 to $7.50 for every dollar invested (Aos et al., 2011).

Child welfare intervention programs have also proven to be effective by targeting services to families in crisis or who are already involved in the child welfare system. Intervention programs include approaches such as family treatment drug courts that intensively monitor and engage parents with substance abuse problems who may lose custody of their children through the dependency process if they do not become clean and sober; intensive family preservation service programs that provide 24-hour, intensive, home-based crisis intervention services for up to 6 weeks to improve family functioning and prevent removal of the child from the home; family therapy programs to improve communication and problem-solving skills to resolve conflict; and self-sufficiency programs that target women who need additional assistance in moving from welfare to work (Lee et al., 2008). These programs are effective in significantly reducing child abuse and neglect, out-of-home placements, and instability for parents and children (Lee et al., 2008). Child welfare intervention programs are also cost effective, realizing savings ranging from $0.88 to $10.32 for every dollar invested (Aos et al., 2011). Several effective intervention programs focus on children's mental health, including cognitive behavioral treatment for anxiety, depression, disruptive behaviors, attention deficit disorders, and emotional disturbances (Aos et al., 2011). These programs have also shown positive cost-benefit ratios ranging from $1.16 to $18.21 for every dollar invested (Aos et al., 2011).

In addition to reuniting with children, offenders often are reuniting with intimate partners or living with other family members such as parents or adult siblings who have agreed to assist them during their transition back to the community (Leverentz, 2011; Martinez, 2007; Martinez & Christian, 2009). Although many studies show that reunification with family can be a positive experience, it can also result in the offender having to deal with ongoing family dysfunction and challenges above and beyond the offender's return to the home. These stressors often include general chaos, domestic violence, drug use, criminal activity, mental health disorders, and histories of sexual abuse and other trauma (Franklin & Lutze, 2007; Leverentz, 2011; Lutze & Kigerl, 2013). CCOs may be a conduit for educating offenders about how to best help their families to get mental health care, medical care, or substance abuse treatment and how to not become so overwhelmed by their family's problems that they increase their risk of relapse or a return to crime. Fortunately, many mental health interventions, especially cognitive behavioral therapies, are successful in addressing anxiety disorders, depression, and other mental health illnesses or disorders (see Aos et al., 2011). Unfortunately, accessing such treatment is difficult and often is delayed through long waiting periods to get approval for benefits or an available treatment slot.

The effects of concentrated disadvantage related to housing, employment, and unsafe neighborhoods also present ongoing stress for offenders and their families. Although living in disadvantaged neighborhoods increases the likelihood of failure for offenders, the ongoing impact of living with the burden of poverty and how this affects the offender's entire family is often forgotten (see Cunningham, Scott, Hall, & Stanczyk, 2010; Rank, 2004). CCOs may once again serve as a means to support offenders and their families to move to less disadvantaged neighborhoods and closer to employment opportunities, improved schools, supermarkets, parks, and open spaces. Although this may once again be difficult due to civil penalties related to the exclusion of certain types of felons (primarily drug and sex offenders) from state and federally sponsored housing, it may be possible for many offenders through the use of housing vouchers and other programs supported through housing and urban policy initiatives to move their families into safer neighborhoods that translate into improved wellbeing (Cunningham et al., 2010; Hamilton, Kigerl, & Hayes, in press). This may also make it easier for offenders to escape the same environment and peer network that led to prison in the beginning (Dhondt, 2012; Kirk, 2009, 2012; Kubrin & Stewart, 2006).

BOUNDARY SPANNING AND EVIDENCE-BASED PRACTICE

The evidence is clear that supervision strategies that balance control and treatment work to reduce recidivism. There is also no longer a question about "what works" in correctional treatment because of evidence that a full array of treatment programs work to change antisocial attitudes and behavior; enhance skill levels; and provide support to improve the lives of offenders, their families, and the community. Evidence-based practices exist within criminal justice as well as social services, child welfare, public health, and education. Importantly, EBP addresses two key concerns expressed repeatedly by community correction administrators and CCOs: managing risk and enhancing public safety. It is crucial that community corrections agencies structure their supervision practices to incorporate EBP and EBT that allows CCOs to expand their expertise to fully engage the resources necessary to give offenders every chance possible to be successful.

Research on community corrections officers (CCO) clearly shows that supervision is a dynamic process whether applied through a social work or law enforcement perspective or a fluid combination of both. Narrow and static definitions of community supervision stymy innovation and minimize the importance of the complex role community corrections officers serve in managing offender change (Lutze, Johnson et al., 2012; Taxman, 2002). Offenders possess both risk and needs and, depending on the situation, require a multifaceted approach to influence their behavior. Unlike other actors in the criminal justice or social service systems, CCOs have the power to leverage both support and coercion to influence outcomes by knowing where offenders are in the process of change (Lutze, Johnson, et al., 2012). Working with offenders over time in the community is a powerful and important position.

To effectively use evidence-based treatment, CCOs must be willing to take a holistic approach to supervision and view themselves as active agents of change who have multiple tools at their disposal, some coercive and some supportive, that in combination have the potential to make a difference. Few professionals, whether police, social workers, psychologists, or medical doctors, have the power or authority to work with the entirety of the individuals whom they serve to address negative behaviors and inspire positive change. Yet many community corrections agencies and CCOs fail to take advantage of their position and their power by limiting their responses to surveillance, monitoring, and sanctions. Ironically, these measures are advocated as the primary means to control risk, yet the scientific evidence is very weak or modest at best that these strategies alone reduce recidivism or increase public safety (Cullen & Jonson, 2012; Lipsey & Cullen, 2007).

Understanding what works and how other institutions may assist lays the foundation for CCOs to become effective boundary spanners. What works to reduce recidivism and increase prosocial behaviors is for CCOs to network with other professionals in criminal justice, social services, child welfare, public health, mental health, and education to be successful. Collaboration outside of the criminal justice system should not be considered a one-way relationship due to the number of offenders and their families shared across systems.

Open communication flowing back and forth across disciplines may lead to strategies that strengthen responses to offenders and more efficiently problem-solve issues that can divert offenders from returning to prison or being expelled from programs likely to reduce recidism. Collaborations and partnerships, however, must be based on professional respect and trust that others have the expertise and willingness to work together to create change. This means CCOs have to be willing to rely on institutions other than law enforcement, the jail, or institutional corrections and be willing to rely equally on social services and treatment providers in response to offenders' behavioral needs. Likewise, social services and treatment providers cannot rebuff community corrections officers who view them as crucial to the success of their offenders but who cannot get access due to turf protection or ongoing distrust. The next chapter addresses the promise and perils of interagency collaboration and its importance to successful outcomes for CCOs and for the criminal justice system as a whole.

NOTES

1. It is also important to note that Scared Straight, prison visitation, and boot camps have all been shown to significantly increase recidivism for juvenile offenders by rates ranging from 2% to 26%. Clearly, the relevance and use of these programs have to be reevaluated by administrators and policymakers.

2. Traditionally, many departments of corrections released inmates with a small amount of cash ($50–$100), a bus ticket to their jurisdiction of conviction, and an order to report to their community corrections officer within 24 hours of release (McCleary, 1992).

3. Aos et al. (2011) base cost-benefit ratios on 2010 dollars.

WORKS CITED

Andrews, D., & Bonta, J. (2010). *The psychology of criminal conduct* (5th ed.). Cincinnati, OH: Anderson.

Aos, S., Lee, S., Drake, E., Pennucci, A., Klima, T., Miller, M., et al. (2011). *Return on investment: Evidence-based options to improve statewide outcomes.* Olympia: Washington State Institute for Public Policy.

Barnoski, R. (2004). *Outcome evaluation of Washington State's research-based programs for juvenile offenders.* Olympia: Washington State Institute for Public Policy.

Bonta, J., Rugge, T., Scott, T.-L., Bourgon, G., & Yessine, A. K. (2008). Exploring the black box of community supervision. *Journal of Offender Rehabilitation, 47*(3), 248–270.

Bouffard, J. A., & Bergerson, L. E. (2006). Reentry works: The implementation and effectiveness of a serious and violent offender reentry initiative. *Journal of Offender Rehabilitation, 44*(2/3), 1–129.

Braga, A. A., Piehl, M. A., & Hureau, D. (2009). Controlling violent offenders released to the community: An evaluation of the Boston Reentry Initiative. *Journal of Research in Crime and Delinquency, 46*(4), 411–436.

Boxer, P., Middlemass, K., & Delorenzo, T. (2009). Exposure to violent crime during incarceration: Effects on psychological adjustment following release. *Criminal Justice and Behavior, 36*(8), 793–807.

Burke, P., Gelb, A., & Horowitz, J. (2007). *When offenders break the rules: Smart responses to parole and probation violations.* Washington, DC: The PEW Center on the States.

Butzin, C. A., O'Connell, D. J., Martin, S. S., & Incairdi, J. A. (2006). Effect of drug treatment during work release on new arrest and incarcerations. *Journal of Criminal Justice, 34,* 557–565.

Clear, T. R. (2007). *Imprisoning communities: How mass incarceration makes disadvantaged neighborhoods worse.* New York: Oxford University Press.

Comfort, M. (2007). Punishment beyond the legal offender. *Annual Review of Law and Social Science, 3,* 271–296.

Culhane, D. P., Metraux, S., & Hadley, T. (2002). Public service reductions associated with placement of homeless persons with severe mental illness in supportive housing. *Housing Policy Debate, 13*(1), 107–163.

Cullen, F., & Jonson, C. (2012). *Correctional theory: Context and consequences.* Thousand Oaks, CA: Sage.

Cullen, F. T. (2005). The twelve people who saved rehabilitation: How the science of criminology made a difference—The American Society of Criminology 2004 presidential address. *Criminology, 43,* 1–42.

Cunningham, M., Scott, M. N., Hall, S., & Stanczyk, A. (2010). *Improving neighborhood location outcomes in the housing choice voucher program: A scan of mobility assistance programs.* What Works Collaborative: Building Knowledge & Sharing Solutions for Housing and Urban Poverty.

Dannerbeck, A., Harris, G., Sundet, P., & Lloyd, K. (2006). Understanding and responding to racial differences in drug court outcomes. *Journal of Ethnicity in Substance Abuse, 5*(2), 1–22.

Deitch, D., Carleton, S., Koutsenok, I. B., & Marsolais, K. (2002). Therapeutic community treatment in prison. In C. Leukenfeld, F. Tims, & D. Farabee (Eds.), *Treatment of Drug Offenders: Policies and Issues* (pp. 127–148). New York: Springer.

DeMichele, M. T. (2007). *Probation and parole's growing caseloads and workload allocation: Strategies for managerial decision making.* Lexington, KY: The American Probation & Parole Association.

Dhondt, G. (2012). The bluntness of incarceration: Crime and punishment in Tallahassee neighborhoods, 1995–2002. *Crime, Law and Social Change, 57*(5), 521–538.

Dowden, C., & Andrews, D. A. (2004). The importance of staff practice in delivering effective correctional treatment: A meta-analytic review. *International Journal of Offender Therapy and Comparative Criminology, 48*(2), 203–214.

Drake, E. K. (2011). *"What works" in community supervision: Interim report.* Olympia: Washington State Institute for Public Policy.

Dumont, D. M., Brockmann, B., Dickman, S., Alexander, N., & Rich, J. D. (2012). Public health and the epidemic of incarceration. *Annual Review of Public Health, 33,* 325–329.

Duwe, G. (2012). Evaluating the Minnesota Comprehensive Offender Reentry Plan (MCORP): Results from a randomized experiment. *Justice Quarterly, 29*(3), 347–383.

Feeley, M. M., & Simon, J. (1992). The new penology: Notes on the emerging strategy of corrections and its implications. *Criminology, 30*(4), 449–474.

Foster, H., & Hagan, J. (2009). The mass incarcertion of parents in America: Issues of race/ethnicity, collateral damage to children, and prisoner reentry. *The ANNALS of the American Academy of Political Science, 623*, 179–194.

Franklin, C., & Lutze, F. (2007). Home confinement and intensive supervision as unsafe havens: The unintended consequences for women. In R. Muraskin (Ed.), *It's a crime: Women and justice* (4th ed.). Upper River Saddle, NJ: Prentice Hall.

Geller, A., & Curtis, M. A. (2011). A sort of homecoming: Incarceration and the housing security of urban men. *Social Science Research, 40*, 1196–1213.

Gendreau, P. (1996). The principles of effective intervention with offenders. In A. Harland (Ed.), *What works in community corrections* (pp. 117–130). Thousand Oaks, CA: Sage.

Gideon, L., & Sung, H. (2011). *Rethinking corrections: Rehabilitation, reentry, and reintegration.* Thousand Oaks, CA: Sage.

Grattet, R., Petersilia, J., Lin, J., & Beckman, M. (2009). Parole violations and revocations in California: Analysis and suggestions for action. *Federal Probation, 73*(1), 2–11.

Hamilton, Z., Kigerl, A., & Hays, Z. (in press). Removing release impediments and reducing correctional costs: Evaluation of Washington State's housing voucher program. *Justice Quarterly.*

Haney, C. (2001). The psychological impact of incarceration: Implications for post-prison adjustment. *From prison to home: The effect of incarceration and reentry on children, families and communities* (pp. 1–18). National Policy Conference.

Harris, P. M., Gingerich, R., & Whittaker, T. A. (2004). The "effectiveness" of differential supervision. *Crime & Delinquency, 50*(2), 235–271.

Heinrich, K. (2012). The "Right Living" Program at Airway Heights Correctional Center in Washington State. (F. Lutze, Interviewer) Pullman, WA.

Hipp, J. R., Jannetta, J., Shah, R., & Turner, S. (2011). Parolees' physical closeness to services: A study of California parolees. *Crime & Delinquency, 77*(1), 102–129.

Hochstetler, A., DeLisi, M., & Pratt, T. C. (2010). Social support and feelings of hostility among released inmates. *Crime and Delinquency, 56*(4), 588–607.

Hser, Y., Huang, Y., Teruya, C., & Anglin, M. (2004). Gender differences in treatment outcomes over a three-year period: A path model analysis. *Journal of Drug Issues, 34*(2), 419–440.

Jalbert, S. K., Rhodes, W., Flygare, C., & Kane, M. (2010). Testing probation outcomes in an evidence-based practice setting: Reduced caseload size and intensive supervision effectiveness. *Journal of Offender Rehabilitation, 49*, 233–253.

Johnson, R. (2002). *Hard time: Understanding and reforming the prison* (3rd ed.). Belmont, CA: Wadsworth.

Kennard, D., & Roberts, J. (1983). *An introduction to therapeutic communities.* Boston: Routledge and Kegan Paul.

Kilmartin, C. T. (2000). *The masculine self* (2nd ed.). Boston: McGraw Hill.

Kirk, D. S. (2009). A natural experiment on residential change and recidivism: Lessons from Hurricane Katrina. *American Sociological Review, 74*(3), 484–505.

Kirk, D. S. (2012). Residential change as a turning point in the life course of crime: Disistance or temporary cessation? *Criminology, 50*(2), 329–358.

Kubrin, C. E., & Stewart, E. A. (2006). Predicting who reoffends: The neglected role of neighborhood context in recidivism studies. *Criminology, 44*, 165–197.

Landenberger, N. A., & Lipsey, M. W. (2005). The positive effects of cognitive-behavioral programs for offenders: A meta-analysis of factors associated with effective treatment. *Journal of Experimental Criminology, 1*(4), 451–477.

Latessa, E. J., Cullen, F. T., & Gendreau, P. (2002). Beyond correctional quackery: Professionalism and the possiblity of effective treatment. *Federal Probation, 66*(2), 43–49.

Latessa, E. J., & Lovins, B. (2010). The role of offender risk assessment: A policy maker guide. *Victims & Offenders, 5*(3), 203–219.

Latessa, E. J., Travis, L., Fulton, B., & Stichman, A. (1998). *Evaluating the prototypical ISP.* Final report submitted to the National Institute of Justice, Washington, DC. Washington, DC: U.S. Department of Justice.

Lattimore, P. K., Visher, C. A., Winterfield, L., Lindquist, C., & Brumbaugh, S. (2005). Implementation of prisoner reentry programs: Findings from the Serious and Violent Offender Reentry Initiative multi-site evaluation. *Justice Research and Policy, 7*(2), 87–109.

Lawrence, S., Mears, D. P., Dubin, G., & Travis, J. (2002). *The practice and promise of prison programming.* Washington, DC: Urban Institute, Justice Policy Center.

Lee, S., Aos, S., & Miller, M. (2008). *Evidence-based programs to prevent children from entering and remaining in the child welfare system: Benefits and costs for Washington.* Olympia: Washington State Institute for Public Policy.

Leverentz, A. (2011). Being a good daughter and sister: Families of origin in the reentry of African American female ex-prisoners. *Feminist Criminology, 6*(4), 239–267.

Lipsey, M. W., Chapman, G. L., & Landenberger, N. A. (2011). Cognitive-behavioral programs for offenders. *Annals of the American Academy of Political and Social Science, 578*, 144–157.

Lipsey, M. W., & Cullen, F. T. (2007). The effectiveness of correctional rehabilitation: A review of systematic reviews. *Annual Review of Law and Society, 3*, 297–320.

Listwan, S. J., Colvin, M., Hanley, D., & Flannery, D. (2010). Victimization, social support, and psychological well-being: A study of recently released prisoners. *Criminal Justice and Behavior, 37*(10), 1140–1159.

Lowenkamp, C. T., Hubbard, D., Makarios, M. D., & Latessa, E. J. (2009). A quasi-experimental evaluation of thinking for a change: A "real world" application. *Criminal Justice and Behavior, 36*(2), 137–146.

Lowenkamp, C. T., Latessa, E. J., & Holsinger, A. M. (2006). The risk principle in action: What we learned from 13,676 offenders and 97 correctional programs. *Crime & Delinquency, 52,* 77–93.

Lowenkamp, C. T., Latessa, E. J., & Smith, P. (2006). Does correctional program quality really matter? The impact of adhering to the principles of effective interventions. *Criminology and Public Policy, 5*(3), 575–594.

Lutze, F. E. (1998). Are shock incarceration programs more rehabilitative than traditional prison? A survey of inmates. *Justice Quarterly, 15*(2), 547–563.

Lutze, F. E. (2006). Boot camp prisons and corrections policy: Moving from militarism to an ethic of care. *Journal of Criminology and Public Policy, 5*(2), 389–400.

Lutze, F. E., & Bell, C. (2005). Boot camp prisons as masculine organizations: Rethinking recidivism and program design. *Journal of Offender Rehabilitation, 40*(3/4), 133–152.

Lutze, F. E., Johnson, W., Clear, T., Latessa, E., & Slate, R. (2012). The future of community corrections is now: Stop dreaming and take action. *Journal of Contemporary Criminal Justice, 28*(1), 42–49.

Lutze, F. E., & Kigerl, A. (2013). The psychology of reentry. In J. Helfgott, *Criminal psychology* (Vols. 1–4). Westport, CT: Praeger.

Lutze, F. E., Rosky, J., & Hamilton, Z. (forthcoming). Homelessness and reentry: A multisite outcome evaluation of Washington State's reentry housing program for high risk offenders. *Criminal Justice and Behavior.*

Lutze, F. E., & van Wormer, J. (2007). The nexus between drug and alcohol treatment program integrity and drug court effectiveness: Policy recommendations for pursuing success. *Criminal Justice Policy Review, 18*(3), 226–245.

MacKenzie, D. L. (2000). Evidence-based corrections: Identifying what works. *Crime and Delinquency, 46*(6), 457–471.

MacKenzie, D. L. (2006). *What works in corrections: Reducing the criminal activities of offenders and delinquents.* New York: Cambridge University Press.

Martinez, D. J. (2007). Informal helping mechanisms. *Journal of Offender Rehabilitation, 44*(1), 23–37.

Martinez, D. J., & Christian, J. (2009). The familial relationships of former prisoners: Examining the link between residence and informal support mechanisms. *Journal of Contemporary Ethnography, 38*(2), 201–224.

McCleary, R. (1992). *Dangerous men: The sociology of parole* (2nd ed.). New York: Harrow and Heston.

McCorkle, R., & Crank, J. P. (1996). Meet the new boss: Institutional change and loose coupling in parole and probation. *American Journal of Criminal Justice, 21*(1), 1–25.

Mele, C., & Miller, T. A. (2005). *Civil penalties, social consequences.* (Eds.) New York: Routledge.

Metraux, S., & Culhane, D. P. (2004). Homeless shelter use and reincarceration following prison release. *Criminology and Public Policy, 3*(2), 139–160.

Metraux, S., & Culhane, D. P. (2006). Recent incarceration history among a sheltered homeless population. *Crime & Delinquency, 52*(3), 504–517.

Miller, M., & Ngugi, I. (2009). *Impacts of housing supports: Persons with mental illness and ex-offenders.* Olympia, WA: Washington State Institute for Public Policy.

Newman, D. M. (2007). *Indentities & inequalities: Exporing the intersections of race, class, gender, and sexuality.* Boston: McGraw Hill.

Paparozzi, M. A., & Gendreau, P. (2005). An intensive supervision program that worked: Service delivery, professional orientation, and organizational supportiveness. *The Prison Journal, 85*(4), 445–466.

Petersilia, J. (2003). *When prisoners come home: Parole and prisoner reentry.* New York: Oxford University Press.

Petersilia, J., & Turner, S. (1993). Intensive probation and parole. *Crime and Justice, 17,* 281–335.

Prendergast, M. L., & Burdon, W. M. (2002). Integrated systems of care for substance-abusing offenders. In C. Leukenfeld, F. Tims, & D. Farabee (Eds.), *Treatment of Drug Offenders: Policies and Issues* (pp. 111–162). New York: Springer.

Prendergast, M. L., Podus, D., Chang, E., & Urada, D. (2002). The effectiveness of drug abuse treatment: A meta-analysis of comparison group studies. *Drug and Alcohol Dependence, 67,* 53–72.

Rank, M. R. (2004). *One nation, underprivileged: Why American poverty affects us all.* New York: Oxford University Press.

Roman, C. G., & Travis, J. (2006). Where will I sleep tomorrow? Housing, homelessness, and the returning prisoner. *Housing Policy Debate, 17*(2), 389–418.

Schaffer, D. K. (2011). Looking inside the black box of drug courts: A meta-analytic review. *Justice Quarterly, 28*(3), 493–521.

Seiter, R. P., & Kadela, K. R. (2003). Prisoner reentry: What works, what does not, and what is promising. *Crime & Delinquency, 49*(3), 360–388.

Shapiro, C., & Schwartz, M. (2001). Coming home: Building on family connections. *Corrections Management Quarterly, 5*(3), 52–61.

Smith, P., & Schweitzer, M. (2012). The therapeutic prison. *Journal of Contemporary Criminal Justice, 28*(1), 7–22.

Steiner, B., Makarios, M. D., Travis, L. F., III, & Meade, B. (2012). Examining the effects of community-based sanctions on offender recidivism. *Justice Quarterly, 29*(2), 229–257.

Sue, S., Zane, N., Hall, N. G., & Berger, L. K. (2009). The case for cultural competency in psychotherapeutic interventions. *Annual Review of Psychology, 60*, 525–548.

Sykes, G. M. (1958). *The society of captives: A study of a maximum security prison.* Princeton, NJ: Princeton University Press.

Takagi, P. (1973). Administrative and professional conflicts in modern corrections. *The Journal of Criminal Law and Criminology, 64*(3), 313–319.

Taxman, F. S. (2002). Supervision: Exploring the dimensions of effectiveness. *Federal Probation, 66*(2), 14–27.

Taxman, F. S. (2004). Research and relevance: Lessons from the past, thoughts for the future. *Criminology and Public Policy, 3*(2), 169–180.

Taxman, F. S., & Bouffard, J. A. (2000). The importance of systems in improving offender outcomes: New frontiers in treatment integrity. *Justice Research and Policy, 2*(2), 37–58.

Taxman, F. S., Shepardson, E. S., & Byrne, J. M. (2004). *Tools of the trade: A guide to incorporating science into practice.* Washington, DC: National Institute of Corrections.

Toch, H. (1977). *Living in prison: The ecology of survival.* New York: Macmillan.

Trotter, C. (2000). Social work education, pro-social orientation and effective probation practice. *Probation Journal, 47*, 256–261.

van Wormer, J. G., & Lutze, F. E. (forthcoming). The great and powerful drug court team: A look behind the curtain. In D. Shaffer (Ed.), *Drug Courts in America.*

Wakefield, S., & Uggen, C. (2010). Incarceration and stratification. *Annual Review of Sociology, 36*, 387–406.

Walters, S. T., Alexander, M., & Vader, A. M. (2008). The officer responses questionnaire: A procedure for measuring reflective listening in probation and parole settings. *Federal Probation, 72*(2), 67–70.

Walters, S. T., Vader, A. M., Nguyen, N., Harris, T. R., & Eells, J. (2011). Motivational interviewing as a supervision strategy in probation: A randomized effectiveness trial. *Journal of Offender Rehabilitation, 49*, 309–323.

Weber, G. H. (1958). Exploration in the similarities, differences and conflicts between probation, parole and institutions. *The Journal of Criminal Law, Criminology, and Police Science, 48*(6), 580–589.

Wilson, D. B., Bouffard, L. A., & MacKenzie, D. L. (2005). A quantitative review of structured, group-oriented, cognitive-behavioral programs for offenders. *Criminal Justice and Behavior, 32*(2), 172–204.

Wilson, D. B., Gallagher, C. A., & MacKenzie, D. L. (2000). A meta-analysis of corrections-based education, vocation, and work programs for adult offenders. *Journal of Research in Crime and Delinquency, 37*(4), 346–368.

Wilson, J. A., & Davis, R. C. (2006). Good intentions meet hard realities: An evaluation of the Project Greenlight Reentry Program. *Criminology and Public Policy, 5*(2), 303–338.

Winterfield, L., Lattimore, P. K., Seffey, D. M., Brumbaugh, S., & Lindquist, C. (2006). The Serious and Violent Reentry Initiative: Measuring the effects on service delivery. *Western Criminology Review, 7*(2), 3–19.

Wodahl, E. J., Garland, B., Culhane, S. E., & McCarty, W. P. (2011). Utilizing behavioral interventions to improve supervision outcomes in community-based corrections. *Criminal Justice and Behavior, 38*(4), 386–405.

Wolff, N., Bjerklie, J. R., & Maschi, T. (2005). Reentry planning for mentally disordered inmates: A social investment perspective. *Journal of Offender Rehabilitation, 42*(2), 21–42.

Worcel, S. D., Burrus, S. W., Finigan, M. W., Sanders, M. B., & Allen, T. L. (2009). *A study of substance-free transitional housing and community corrections in Washington County, Oregon.* Portland: NPC Research.

Zamble, E., & Porporino, F. (1988). *Coping, behavior, and adaptation in prison inmates.* New York: Springer-Verlag.

⊩ SIX ⊩

COMMUNITY CORRECTIONS OFFICERS AND INTERAGENCY COLLABORATION

"The key is to first recognize that correctional professionals in and of themselves, no matter how hard they work, cannot do it alone. The ownership of both defining the problem and the solutions associated with the release of increasing numbers of offenders to communities must be a collaborative venture."[1]

The discovery of so many evidence-based practices successful in reducing recidivism and increasing community safety has led to consideration about how best to deliver what works in a coordinated manner to enhance overall outcomes. Research consistently shows that most offenders fail within the first 90 days of reentry due primarily to technical violations, and an estimated 65% fail within 3 years (see Hamilton & Campbell, in press; Petersilia, 2003). Attempts to address the multiple needs of offenders through different service providers and across large bureaucratic systems often result in fractured responses to offenders' risks and needs. Not surprising, offenders are oftentimes overwhelmed trying to navigate multiple systems to access services and abide by competing sets of expectations (Lutze & van Wormer, 2007, 2008; Pettus & Severson, 2006). In addition, actions taken within one system may inadvertently sabotage the work being done in another system serving the same client (Henderson & Hanley, 2006; Lutze & van Wormer, 2007; Taxman & Bouffard, 2000). Managing the complex web of services across systems is important to assuring offenders are given the support they need to be successful.

This chapter reviews how community corrections officers partner with other professionals or rely on collaborative efforts to supervise offenders.

187

With most of the emphasis on reentry placed on offenders, often ignored are the experiences of CCOs and their perceptions of working with and navigating multiple systems on behalf of community corrections agencies to achieve positive outcomes. Recent trends in state and federal initiatives to solve large-scale problems shows increasing emphasis placed on developing partnerships or collaborations with those who have the resources and expertise necessary to prevent or respond to recidivism. Little attention has been given to how CCOs perceive or use partnerships and collaborations in their work with police, social service and treatment providers, employers, and other community stakeholders important to successful reentry.

PROMISE AND PERILS OF COLLABORATION

Interagency collaboration has become a popular call to action in response to reentry challenges. Many federal, state, and private foundation initiatives require agencies within systems (*intra*system: police, prosecutors, jails, courts, prisons, community corrections) and between systems (*inter*-system: criminal justice, social services, public health, education) to work together (Lattimore, Visher, Winterfield, Lindquist, & Brumbaugh, 2005; Nissen, 2010; Taxman & Bouffard, 2000; Taxman, Young, Byrne, Holsinger, & Anspach, 2001). Collaboration is generally defined as "a partnership formation that denotes a durable and pervasive relationship and that is characterized by mutual benefits, interdependence, and a formal commitment of working together for specific purposes and outcomes" [references from original removed](Walter & Petr, 2000, p. 495). Collaborations can take place at the service level by providing managerial support for frontline staff or at the administrative level by reframing the structures and functions of the agencies involved (Walter & Petr, 2000). The intent of collaboration is to achieve or enhance outcomes that could not be accomplished independently.

Partnership levels between agencies include cooperation, coordination, collaboration, and integration (Walter & Petr, 2000; also see Fletcher et al., 2009). Cooperation is based on informal exchanges and a "friendly coexistence" in which participants communicate between agencies as often as needed to solve problems or issues on a case-by-case basis. Coordination involves some formal interactions between agencies and an expectation that staff will meet regularly to share ideas and organize activities to solve common problems, but each agency "retains its own set of goals, structure, and responsibilities" and is not held accountable to the other (Walter & Petr, 2000, p. 495). Collaboration requires administrative support for interagency agreements that structure how agency resources such as staff, services, and materials are used to serve the relationship and hold each agency accountable to one another to engage the collaborative and achieve shared goals. Integration requires a change in agency structures and the pooling of resources.

Collaboration varies from informal staff exchanges to highly formal and integrated functions in which agencies are held accountable to each other to achieve a shared mission and outcomes. Most "collaborations" in criminal justice, and specifically community corrections, are actually based on informal "cooperation" between staff from different agencies or mid-level, jurisdiction-based efforts to "coordinate" services for commonly shared clients (Fletcher et al., 2009; Kim, Gerber, & Beto, 2010). In general, agencies that "collaborate" in criminal justice are not held accountable to each other. The distinction between the various levels of collaboration is important to conceptualizing CCOs as street-level boundary spanners. Through the case management of offenders they must develop professional relationships across agencies and systems to be responsive to the individual risks and needs of offenders. Success, if defined as achieving long-term reintegration, is based on their professional savvy to increase their collective capacity by cooperating and coordinating laterally across agencies and systems to work with other professionals. Through the sharing of interdisciplinary expertise and resources, CCOs can share the responsibility of addressing offenders' risk and needs and increase the likelihood of achieving long-term reintegration and public safety.

Conceptualizing the need for CCOs to act as purposeful and planned boundary spanners is even clearer when one considers the context in which collaboration is most likely necessary. Collaboration is most often needed in contexts where "multiple providers carry out highly interdependent tasks under conditions of uncertainty and time constraints" (Bond & Gittell, 2010, p. 120). Offenders' transition from prison to the community creates a great deal of uncertainty due to offenders' individual risks and needs, level of family support, and the conditions of the communities to which they return. CCOs are under tight time constraints to assess offenders, establish contact and conduct routine monitoring, provide services or make referrals, and stabilize individuals as quickly as possible to prevent recidivism. The success or failure of any one system to respond to offenders' risks and needs may mean success or failure for those serving the same person in another system; therefore CCOs' work, although oftentimes isolated within their own agency, is interdependent on the work of others (e.g., housing providers, employers, treatment providers, jails/prisons) (see Pettus & Severson, 2006; Taxman & Bouffard, 2000). For instance, the inability of a CCO to access a social service provider with the capacity to secure difficult-to-acquire housing or treatment for an offender may affect compliance with supervision, participation in treatment, job obtainment, or avoidance of antisocial peers. Similarly, if CCOs use jail as a sanction instead of other less restrictive options for noncompliance, they may sabotage the work of social service providers when the offender is evicted from the housing or treatment program due to a jail stay. This wastes the time of the social service worker who then has to start over in helping to achieve stability for the offender or may have to abandon the case.

Collaboration for those involved in the partnership is expected to improve quality and efficiency of service delivery, resource sharing, stakeholder empowerment, knowledge exchange, and social capital to leverage the resources necessary to affect outcomes (Bonds & Gittell, 2010). It is expected that organizations' collective capacity will improve their response to adversity, problem-solving capacity, and outcomes (Nissen, 2010). For collaborations to work on all levels, they must be based on strong relationships that include trust, mutual respect, and shared core values (Bond & Gittell, 2010; Nissen, 2010; Steadman, 1992; Walters & Petr, 2000).

Although the criminal justice system, social services, and public health agencies may share the core value of supporting healthy and safe communities, their strategies, missions, and goals may significantly differ, thus creating conflict and leading to a mutual lack of trust and respect held by those working in different systems. A lack of trust is fueled by criminal justice, social service, and public health agencies traditionally being pitted against one another in competition for state and local resources and then working in isolation to serve populations that are treated as separate but are often interwoven and share common problems (Bond & Gittell, 2010; Nissen, 2010; Pettus & Severson, 2006). For instance, 36% of clients referred to publicly funded drug treatment originated from the criminal justice system. Twenty percent of those leaving prison have an assessed mental illness, 10% will become homeless and use shelter care, over half are parents, and far too many will return to poor communities and struggle with attaining the education and vocational skills necessary to escape poverty (Clear, 2007; Comfort, 2007; Fletcher et al., 2009; Petersilia, 2003; Roman & Travis, 2006; Wolff, Bjerklie, & Maschi, 2005).

Although the problems each institution confronts are similar, their strategies differ. Social services' mission is to serve primarily poor families with children. Social workers attempt to create change by providing support, connecting clients to resources, and teaching the life skills necessary to successfully manage their lives and raise children free from abuse and neglect. The criminal justice system's mission is to serve and protect the community from crime by processing offenders through the justice system and managing their risk to the community upon conviction and sentencing. Criminal justice professionals attempt to create change through more coercive and controlling measures such as surveillance, monitoring, sanctions, and mandatory participation in programs and treatment to manage risk. Public health agencies' mission is all-inclusive by reducing mortality rates through the prevention and control of infectious diseases and the prevention of injury and death. Public health agencies attempt to create change through health initiatives that prevent the spread of infectious diseases and reduce critical injuries by assuring people have access to safe food, water, and shelter; designing community interventions to deal with substance abuse, mental illness, and medical treatments; and working to reduce or prevent conditions that lead to serious injury or death, such as gun violence, domestic violence, child abuse, and suicide.

Each institution clearly shares values and tries to improve the conditions of individuals, families, and the community. Clearly, their strategies differ dramatically, but they do not need to be mutually exclusive. Each system shares mutual clients, and each could benefit from the other where their clients' risks and needs overlap (Castellano, 2011; Nissen, 2010). For example, the criminal justice system may help to manage risk and provide the structure and motivation necessary for clients on supervision to complete programs and treatment regimens and to reintegrate into their families as productive members. Social services can provide the much needed social support mechanisms to stabilize offenders' lives related to family, child care, housing, food, transportation, and employment. Public health agencies can provide much-needed health care related to infectious diseases, substance abuse, domestic violence, and mental illnesses that undermine offenders' success and often lead to the victimization of others. Thus, collaboration allows for cross-system communication and education regarding shared clients and the challenges and successes experienced through evidence-based practices within each discipline that may be successful if shared and reinforced across systems (see Nissen, 2010).

The potential to bring about change is great when the power of each institution is brought together through coordinated or collaborative efforts to provide structure, accountability, support, and treatment to offenders. Although there is agreement that collaborative efforts are powerful mechanisms for change, coordinating efforts and developing collaborations are easier said than done. Many challenges to collaboration center on relational issues such as conflicting beliefs or goals, confidentiality concerns, territoriality, lack of trust, differences in perceived status, and dissimilarities in decision-making styles (Lattimore et al., 2005; Pettus & Severson, 2006). Practical challenges also arise, such as time constraints, large caseloads, staff turnover, and limited funding, that cause instability and untimely responses to problems (Pettus & Severson, 2006). These challenges may be why approximately one-third of corrections agencies do not collaborate with treatment providers or judicial agencies at all, and those that do collaborate only at lower levels and informally (Fletcher et al., 2009). When agencies do collaborate across systems, collaboration tends to be primarily limited to the sharing of information.

When successful collaborations do occur, they most often result from the work of effective boundary spanners (Lattimore et al., 2005; Nissen, 2010; Pettus & Severson, 2006; Steadman, 1992). Remember, boundary spanners are individuals who "attempt to understand human behavior in the context of the systemic structures, operations, and barriers that exist within and between communities and prisons, seek to bridge communication, understanding, and service gaps and translate the working of one entity into the language of another" (Pettus & Severson, 2006, p. 208; also see Bonds & Gittell, 2010; Nissen, 2010; Steadman, 1992; Taxman et al., 2001). Boundary spanners help to bring the power of multiple institutions together to overcome the challenges posed by working with different systems and to effect system-level changes in policy and practice that support shared values and accomplish goals (see Nissen, 2010; Steadman, 1992). CCOs, as case managers responsible for developing and implementing case plans for offenders with multiple needs, are positioned well to serve as street-level boundary spanners within the criminal justice system and between criminal justice and service providers.

COLLABORATIONS WITHIN CRIMINAL JUSTICE

Although it is important to bridge the gap between systems, isolation also occurs within systems where clients are passed from one agency to another with minimal interaction or understanding about the context or capacity of the other agencies participating in the process. Agencies in criminal justice, law enforcement, courts, and corrections compete for resources, function within separate budgets, and undertake initiatives within their independent agencies that then have an effect on others in the system. Although each agency is concerned with achieving justice and public safety, they often implement different strategies to achieve these goals. For example, mandatory arrest practices implemented by the police for crimes such as domestic violence may create challenges for prosecutors and the courts to then effectively process cases and bring perpetrators to justice (see Lutze & Symons, 2003). The police often attempt to create safe communities by removing violent and persistent offenders via arrest while CCOs attempt to achieve the same goal by keeping offenders in the community through social support, treatment, and monitoring (see Murphy & Lutze, 2009). Without working together, challenges easily arise that may defeat the potential of innovative practices in one agency because of the constraints or traditions of another.

Consequently, criminal justice agencies may share the same core values, but they often work in isolation from one another. For instance, many of the collaborative efforts in corrections have focused on creating a "seamless system of care" from institutional corrections to the community that includes prerelease planning to assure that community supervision, treatment providers, and social support networks are in place before the inmate is released from prison or jail (Taxman & Bouffard, 2000; Taxman et al., 2001). The motivation is for agencies to work together at each decision point of case management, replicating the natural and realistic flow of cases through the system. This provides consistency and continuity in care within and across systems and connects offenders to EBT to achieve long-term reintegration (Taxman & Bouffard, 2000). Taxman and Bouffard (2000) advocate for "boundaryless organizations" that focus on supporting offenders' change across systems versus traditional practices that focus on offenders' control within the criminal justice system.

"Seamless systems of care" make sense so that agencies working toward the same goal do not inadvertently sabotage the work of their colleagues working in other agencies. For community corrections, collaboration within the criminal justice system generally means working with the court, county jail, county and federal probation, and police. Each agency is well positioned to help the other, but intersystem administrative collaborations appear to be surprisingly rare while midlevel coordinated and cooperative arrangements with other agencies are fairly common (Bond & Gittell, 2010; Fletcher et al., 2009). Many CCOs in Spokane expressed the importance of all agencies working together because of the overlap serving a shared population that poses challenges across the criminal justice system as well as other systems such as social services and public health. The need to share information appears to be key to any attempts to achieve a seamless system of care. As the following CCOs stated,

> It's a network, like a web. The more that we can know about someone through other agencies, the better off we will be, the better equipped we will be to protect you as community members. (CCO 235)

> I think it's a sharing of information. I think everybody can do their job a lot better if we communicate and share information. And I look at sharing information...between states, sharing information between the city

level, county level, state level, and federal level.... So, you know, just
sharing that information at different levels of bureaucracy would make
all of our jobs a lot easier. (CCO 231)

Also important to the discussion of intra- and intersystem collaboration is that overwhelmingly CCOs appear to enjoy collaborating with other
professionals across the criminal justice system, social services, and public
health agencies and are very aware of the promise and perils of such relationships. This makes the potential to achieve "seamless systems of care"
and "continuums of care" a realistic goal for community corrections by
building on the work of existing street-level boundary spanners. The following sections explore the contexts and importance of collaborations of
CCOs with other criminal justice agencies.

Police-Corrections Partnerships

Community corrections and police agencies share the goal of enhancing public safety. They may work together to prevent crime, solve neighborhood problems, and increase their effectiveness with high-risk repeat
offenders by sharing information and responding rapidly to potential
threats (see Janetta & Lachman, 2011; Kim et al., 2010; Murphy & Lutze,
2009; Murphy & Worrall, 2007; Travis, Davis, & Lawrence, 2012). Open
communication and the sharing of resources can be of mutual benefit,
espeically where the professional roles of police and CCOs overlap with
law enforcement–oriented responsibilities to manage offender risk, such as
increasing surveillance, identifying offenders still active in crime (e.g.,
gangs, drugs, sex, prostitution, property), delivering warrants, tracking
absconders, conducting searches, and making arrests (Kim et al., 2010;
Murphy & Lutze, 2009). In addition, police may also assist CCOs in their
social work capacity by having a clearer understanding of the challenges
confronting offenders upon reentry. They can alert CCOs when offenders
are observed experiencing or participating in behaviors that may put them
at risk of recidivating but are not necessarily criminal, such as associating
with antisocial peers, frequenting known crime "hot spots," being homeless, or displaying signs of mental illness (Alarid, Sims, & Ruiz, 2011).
Similarly, CCOs may provide police with broader responses than arrest to
address offenders' behavior by enforcing noncompliance with supervision
through intermediate reponses such as curfews, admission to residential
mental or drug treatment, community service, and other activities that hold
offenders accountable, provide support, and redirect their behavior without
a formal arrest (see Murphy & Lutze, 2009).

There are several types of police-corrections partnerships. Parent and Snyder (1999, as cited in Kim et al., 2010) identified five types of partnerships: (1) enhanced supervision, (2) fugitive apprehension, (3) information sharing, (4) specialized enforcement, and (5) interagency problem-solving partnerships. Kim et al. (2010), in a study of police agencies in Texas, found that 70% of agencies had some form of partnership with corrections and that the majority of collaborations were informal. Seventy-two percent of police agencies surveyed reported participating in information-sharing partnerships, followed by specialized enforcment (63%), interagency problem solving (52%), fugitive apprehension (41%), and enhanced supervision (41%). Of those agencies that partnered with corrections, 52% were considered "high partnership" agencies that had greater than average levels of participation in all five types of partnerships. Although very few police agencies had developed formal partnerships with corrections, when they did it was most likely to be specialized enforcement (10%) and information-sharing partnerships (6%). Most of the partnerships focused on enhanced law enforcement roles and objectives, with the possible exception of interagency problem-solving collaborations, and not the broader roles of community supervision. It is unknown which agency, police or corrections, generally initiated the police-corrections partnership, or why, so it may be that corrections only partnered with the police to take collaborative advantage of their law enforcement capacity and reserved collaborations with social work agencies to enhance the reintegration of offenders.

Planned police-corrections partnerships. Both the police and CCOs appear to recognize the benefit of partnering to improve community safety through the sharing of information and participation in joint interventions to prevent or respond to criminal behavior. In general, those participating in police-corrections partnerships felt the partnership improved their ability to engage offenders from their respective roles and improved their image in the community (see Alarid et al., 2011; Kim et al., 2010; Murphy & Lutze, 2009).

For instance, in a study on police-probation partnerships by Murphy and Lutze (2009, p. 72), a police officer appreciated the ability to broaden his responses to offenders and the community beyond his usual role of responding to crisis and relying soley on arrest to solve problems.

> Now that I am working with DOC, we can say, "Hey, you need to straighten up, or—." You have more avenues to go out there and fix problems instead of just, "Well, I can book them or I can't." (Police Officer 503)

Likewise, CCOs, known as neighborhood-based supervision (NBS) officers (NBS) in the Spokane partenrship, appreciated the capacity to more effectively execute an arrest and the added safety police officers brought to the scene.

> On the positive side, you could make an argument about CCO safety. Having a police officer who's trained and consistently trains in arrest and self-defense, and some of those kinds of things. (CCO 103)

In addition, one NBS officer captured the full continuum of working with police officers to achieve both law enforcement and social work goals depending on the situation.

> The more people who have different knowledge and that are helping out for the general cause, you know, a lot of law enforcement want these people to be helped and a lot of them want to be, you know, caught—and if we catch them we have the authority to put them into counseling. So, they help us out a lot and it's all for the general good of the community and helping the offender....So I don't think there can be a negative part of it—it just increases your team—your force trying to help people out. (CCO 107)

Thus, some police and CCOs viewed the partnership as inclusive of law enforcement and social work along a continuum of sharing options that may be more punitive or supportive depending on the situation. Many of the police and NBS officers viewed the partnership as a way to expand their coercive power (Murphy & Lutze, 2009; Murphy & Worrall, 2007). For example, a police officer in Murphy & Lutze's (2009, p. 71) study observed,

> The benefits of partnering with DOC officers are, I think, just being able to access who their offenders are and what their restrictions are. And then having them as a tool to get into houses that we wouldn't otherwise be able to access for people. (Police Officer 504)

Partnerships are also viewed as an opportunity for both parties to improve their image and working relationship with the community. For example, in a study by Alarid and colleagues (2011) of a police and juvenile probation officer partnership in Pennsylvania, a couple of police officers noted,

> In the 15–20 or so times I've been on these ride-alongs, the program better acquaints juveniles with us [police]; it also helps us serve as a role model in the community and leads to quicker resolution of problems.

> ONL [Operation Night Light] improves police/community relations and acquaints kids with the police as helpers. I think juveniles see a different side of us.... We are getting good feedback from the parents and the kids on issues such as school, social life, and neighborhood problems. We are also getting information on other juvenile activity.... This is something that juvenile probation should have been doing all along (p. 86).

NBS officers in the Spokane study revealed that being affiliated with the police in public improved their image as being proactive in solving problems and responding to persistent offenders. For example,

> It increases our visibility. We're out there more and people know that we're making an attempt to solve problems. I think that working with law enforcement just increases our force, so they know that we're out there making a difference. Them seeing us work together, it's like whenever they see a police officer, they may think that, you know, we're working with them or they may be trying to find one of our folks, so they know there's a partnership going on, which increases their confidence. (CCO 107)

> I think it's improved our image because they see us out there more. We drive around in unmarked cars, we don't have DOC marked on them, but we're going around with the police and they see we are working in that capacity. (CCO 112)

NBS officers in Spokane did not think the partnership improved the image of police because the police were already viewed by the public as actively fighting crime, and partnering with CCOs was merely a natural extension of their law enforcement duties.

Information sharing is an important part of collaboration in general, and this was also true for police and corrections partnerships (see Alarid et al., 2011; Kim et al., 2010; Murphy & Lutze, 2009). In Kim and colleagues' study (2010), both the police and CCOs expressed how valuable ongoing and open communication was to the partnership and to achieving their goals. Information sharing appears to include general information about the community and where criminal behavior tends to ocurr as well as specific information about offenders. For example, the following NBS, probation, and police officers comment about the value of learning more about the community.

> The information that they provide is just great. You know, a lot of times, they have contact with people—even if its not one of our

people—numerous times they'll come in, "You know so and so?" Or, "Can you look them up and see if he's DOC active?" We'll look him up and he's on some other CCO's caseload. Then we let them know. "This is what your guy's doing." So it just filters out all over. Yeah, its really cool. (CCO 101)

We now have increased supervision of delinquents and information sharing. We established a database to improve police-probation and family-children outreach. The relationships between police and probation have been extremely successful based on comments that I've received. (Probation officer: Alarid et al., 2011, p. 87)

There has been more information sharing. I've gotten to know more probation officers...I get to meet juveniles I have not met before. Kids from the area are recognized and identification can be made. (Police officer: Alarid et al., 2011, p. 88)

An important part of collaboration is building trusting relationships and getting to know others across agencies who may be relied on to help when necessary. Being colocated, whether in a building or riding around together in a police car, appears to enhance the working relationships of CCOs with the police (see Alarid et al., 2011; Murphy & Lutze, 2009). Enhanced relationships allowed CCOs and police to get to know each other personally and practically, better understand the other's job, and have the opportunity to clear up misunderstandings. The following quotes describe getting to know each other personally and how this helps with increased responsiveness when needed.

Oh, it's been great....You get to know them as friends, get to know their jobs, you know, the stresses and difficulties of their job, and they get to know the stresses and difficulties of our job, and it kind of builds a bond. And so we are working together more. Before, it was more of a separation. (CCO 107)

Again, it's got us in a closer relationship. Where before we might work with a bunch of police officers because you're working with the whole of Spokane. Working out of a COPS Shop, you're working with a few. You get more intimate relationships. You get to know each other better. (CCO 110)

Others highlighted how they got to know more about the responsibilities and the job requirements of the others in the partnerships that they really had not thought much about prior to working together.

A lot of officers stop by, getting to know the NRO [neighborhood resource officer], getting a better feel for where they're at, head-wise. Getting to know different attitudes of street officers and spending some time talking about how we do our jobs and what we do and why so and so doesn't get locked up....Again, when you are working in a main office, you are working with officers from all different sectors, nobody really knows who you are or what it is you do. Very limited contact with law enforcement, so, in that sense, it's really improved everything. (CCO 103)

I have really begun to appreciate what a tough job they have and what they have to do. You know, we don't have many incidents we have to break up, but they have to break up nasty incidents on a regular basis and their training requires them to resolve the incident...we don't have any obligation. I can see why, if you're a police officer 20, 25 years, that's about it. You can't do it too much longer than that unless you move up into management—you have just dealt with too many negative things. So, I have a great appreciation and admiration for what they have to put up with. (CCO 112)

Probation officers in Alarid and colleagues' (2011) study made similar observations.

It's better than it used to be. The police's perception has changed from negative to more well-rounded, more understanding. Probation looks at kids from a treatment standpoint while police come from a law enforcement background.

I never perceived that there was a bad relationship to begin with. But what ONL has done is allow both parties to have a better understanding of what both sides do. Getting to know each other better...creating some connections between the two...beginning to trickle down to the clients and their families. This is really a collaborative effort and is now less intrusive. (p. 89)

Others highlighted the immediate exchange of information and the ability to explain why some things, even very serious events, happen as they do and how the responsibility assigned by the media is not always accurate.

> So, from a police standpoint, I think we are bringing a lot of credibility. I'm not saying DOC was in the dumps, but I'm just saying, you know, it's a big agency, and a lot of times, we take a lot of hits. Especially when one of our guys kills a police officer, we're the shits. And maybe rightfully so. But when I say, "This did happen because of blah, blah blah, you know the guy walked back from Mexico, there's not a lot we can do about it. We probably should have had a warrant out, but that would not have prevented this guy from doing what he did." They still may not go out and hug us, but they are starting to realize that the media may have portrayed it, "If DOC had done their job, an officer wouldn't be dead." Well, that's not the case. (CCO 105)

Therefore, developing relationships was very important and viewed as the foundation for understanding each other's roles and reponsibilities and the challenges confronting the shared goal of enhanced public safety. CCOs recognized the importance of partnering with the police related to shared information, increased surveillance of offenders in the community, enhanced coercive power to assist with arrests and pursue recalcitrant offenders, and public recognition and improved image as active problem solvers who work with the police.

Yet tensions are also evident in police-corrections partnerships (Murphy & Lutze, 2009; Travis et al., 2012). CCOs in Spokane shared concerns about the unequal contribution of resources to the partnership, an absence of formal and lateral leadership positions in each agency, conflicting strategies about how to solve problems, and the use of coercive power that may distort the mission of CCOs to be more like law enforcement (see Drapela & Lutze, 2009; Murphy & Lutze, 2009). Many of these concerns were not evident in other studies (Alarid et al., 2011; Kim et al., 2010)

An important attribute of interagency collaborations is the sharing of resources to bring about advantages that would not exist without the partnerships. CCOs in Spokane were about equally divided concerning whether or not each agency contributed equitably to the COPS Shops. Even those who felt the relationship was good observed that some improvements could be made related to resources and the failure of both the DOC and the police department to contribute basic supplies or adequate personnel. One CCO, although serious, used humor to express the lack of dedicated resources of the DOC to the COPS Shop.

> Yeah, I mean, just the COPS Shop stuff. I mean, we just have to scavenge for supplies and stuff like that. And, you know, we can only steal so much

paper [laughing] from the main field offices and stuff. We do. I'm serious. Toilet paper [laughing]. [Interviewer: Is there a different level of
support?] Well, SPD has a director who's in charge of the COPS Shops.
I mean, we do, but it's [our supervisor], you know what I mean, he's
doing a regular supervisor job as well. We don't have like just a "director" of the COPS Shops....[Interviewer: The resources to keep the thing
running?] Yeah [laughing]. Have you ever run out of toilet paper? Then
you know what I'm talking about [laughing]! (CCO ---)

Yeah, it's not mutual. I think that the SPD puts a lot more resources into
the shop and into this neighborhood than DOC. (CCO ---)

Other CCOs were concerned about the lack of resources provided by
the police department and the lack of understanding about how much time
the CCOs spent taking care of complaints that should have been handled
by the NRO. But the CCOs did not view it as "intentional" and felt it was
mostly a lack of understanding.

I don't think its an intentional thing; I think its just an availability thing.
We wish we had an officer here all day long available to us. Its like,
"Gee, I got this call, you know, it would be nice for [the NRO] to go out
with us." But obviously they can't do that. I mean, they can't be at our
beck and call every day [laughing]. So that conflict would just be on
them just not being available as often as we would like. We could get
one, we can make a phone call, and then we're waiting, and so sometimes that's kind of hard. (CCO ---)

I really don't believe that at some level, the upper echelons of the police
department—chief and them—understand what we do down here. That
is that we deal with, in my opinion, a lot of their job quite a bit of the
time....[The NRO has] got two COPS Shops and frequently is not here.
So, we get the people in the community that'll walk in....We're spending hours doing that. Could be a lot of things. It could be a runaway, a
car is trashed up there, suspect drug house....Now, the easy thing for us
to do would be to say, "You know what? Let law enforcement fill out a
complaint form or you can go down here to the public safety building."
But instead, we're kind of doing referral, assistance, that kind of thing.
(CCO ---)

Possibly the biggest concern that arose about working so closely with
the police in COPS Shops was the use of coercive power and overemphasis on a law enforcement orientation that threatened to highjack the broader
mission of CCOs to provide both surveillance of and support to offenders

to achieve reintegration (Murphy & Lutze, 2009; Murphy & Worrall, 2007). One issue was the ability of CCOs to access offenders' homes without a warrant and the desire of some police officers to take advantage of this power. Both police and CCOs recognized the importance of this boundary and the possibility of it being exploited if both parties were not conscientious (Murphy & Lutze, 2009; Murphy & Worrall, 2007). For example, a CCO observed,

> There are some things that we can do that the police can't do, and I think sometimes some of those boundaries can get crossed...if you have that constant police presence....[W]e don't need warrants to search our offenders [or their] residence. The police do....[I]f they go with us— they act as our agent of protection basically. But they are not allowed to do any actual searching, per se. There's a possibility, if that education piece isn't done—and even if it is—there could be some boundaries they could cross there—the police doing some things that they shouldn't be doing. (CCO 114; Murphy & Lutze, 2009, p. 71)

Similarly, a police officer shared,

> I just try to stay within the parameters of what I know the laws....They have different powers than I do [search and seizure], so you kind of have to blend it together but stay within the realm of what police officers' powers are versus what Department of Corrections officers' powers are....[W]hen you get up to the point where you're at that fine line, you have to let them take over and let them do what they need to do and [you cannot] step over that line and say, "Now I'm a Department of Corrections officer even if I'm using a police uniform." You can't do that. You have to let them do their end of the partnership. You can learn to know each other to make it work. Otherwise you're butting heads with each other trying to figure out, "Well, I can't do this, and you can't do this, and where can we meet in the middle out here?" So, you have to be careful on that. (Police Officer 509; Murphy & Lutze, 2009, p. 71)

Some CCOs also expressed concerns about role conflict and becoming too oriented toward law enforcement if they were not careful. They, unlike the police, felt a need to maintain a broad philosophical orientation.

> I think the [probation officers] can—they tend to get too law enforcement oriented in their thinking. That's my personal opinion, and I've seen that happen. Because we're not cops.We can play a cop role when we need

to, but that's not our main role at all, and I can see that as being a negative. There are some boundary issues that have a tendency to get crossed
if, you know, you are constantly working with the police. Just little things
like that—you become too much of a cop if you are with a cop all day
[laughing]. (CCO 114; Murphy & Lutze, 2009, p. 71)

Well, as management would say, "Look, we're not law enforcement." To
a certain extent, we are—I guess we would be viewed as more of a policing agency, just arresting people—and you can kind of get that way if you
are dealing with the police department. "That guy's a dirtbag!" You know.
"He doesn't deserve any breaks—I've contacted him five times in the last
month—arrest him!" Sometimes it does turn to that. So, I think you still
need to deal with these people when they get back out again, so we can't
be the asshole every time we show up to their doorstep. We have to try and
attempt to work with the offender—so that would be the only downfall
[about the partnership]. (CCO 108; Murphy & Lutze, 2009, p. 71)

[We have] two different processes, two different...goals....[O]ur
[police officer] here, is a "kill them all, let God sort them out" kind of
guy—"arrest that son of a bitch." Well, I can't just arrest him for being
an idiot. You know, I don't have anything to arrest the guy for. Crooks
and law enforcement officers obviously have a different kind of relationship than community corrections officers should have with an offender.
So, no, I don't think [we] should [work together]. (CCO 103; Murphy &
Lutze, 2009, p. 71)

Murphy and Lutze (2009) suggest that CCOs tend to be much more fluid
in their professional orienation because of the need to work with offenders
over time and the opportunity to see both the positive and negative aspects
of their progress while police officers are often limited to negative interactions with offenders defined by periodic crises driven by specific events.
Police officers are able to identify the complex needs of the community but
not necessarily the needs of offenders and therefore tend to narrowly focus
on removing offenders from the community. Police view offenders as a problem in the community versus as members of the community who have problems but also the potential to become law-abiding, productive citizens
(Murphy & Lutze, 2009). Given the more fluid and expansive role of CCOs,
it seems much eaiser for CCOs to embrace and respect the role of police
officers than for police to fully embrace the role of CCOs.

Yet others have found that neither probation officers nor police officers experience mission distortion or role conflict. Alarid and colleagues

(2011) found that juvenile probation officers did not experience role conflict or mission distortion and maintained their leadership role when accompanied by the police while visiting juvenile probationers and their families. Kim and colleagues (2010) found that police officers in agencies with high levels of partnerships experience less role conflict than others, possibly due to the partnership being viewed as merely an extension of community policing activities. They also suggest that the lack of role conflict for police may be because the partnerships tend to be centered on control and surveillance, which are traditionally associated more with the role of policing.

Given community corrections' concern about managing risk, it is interesting that most police-corrections partnerships appear to be informal with few written interagency agreements to guide the collaboration or formal training within and across agencies to help officers understand the legal and ethical parameters of their work together and who is ultimately responsible if something goes wrong (see Drapela & Lutze, 2009; Kim et al., 2010; Murphy & Lutze, 2009; Murphy & Worrall, 2007). Although grassroots initiatives allow for creative innovation and freedom for relationships to germinate into effective and shared strategies, it is unknown at what point these "new" partnerships should become institutionalized as written policies to guide the work of those who join the partnership after it has been established (see Drapela & Lutze, 2009; Murphy & Worrall, 2007). Without a written set of institutional procedures to guide practice, the original purpose and motivation of the partnership may drift into practices counter to the original purpose (see Murphy & Worrall, 2007; van Wormer, 2010). Institutional drift differs from necessary growth or adaptation in that it is not purposeful for the sake of improving the partnership or outcomes but most likely due to a return to "business as usual" or serving the dominance of one partner over the other (see Murphy & Lutze, 2009). Guidelines or policy for collaboration of all types, formal or informal, may assist those to span boundaries informed by evidence-based practice instead of by happenstance (see Janetta & Lachman, 2011; Murphy & Worrall, 2007).

Informal police-corrrections interactions. Not all interactions between CCOs and the police occur within purposeful partnerships. The majority of interactions are initiated during the day-to-day business of working with offenders in the community and enforcing the conditions of supervision. Not much is written about the impressions of CCOs working with the police outside of formal partnerships. CCOs working in Spokane revealed that those who were not colocated with the police in COPS Shops but worked in centralized state offices also worked with the police, but their interactions appeared more limited and less relationship based. Although more limited in their relationships, the majority of CCOs held a positive impression of the police and appreciated their assistance. They also shared a similar set of pros and cons as those who worked in more formal partnerships with the police. CCOs in general expressed the benefits of sharing information and the additional surveillance of offenders, and they fully appreciated the added safety of working with the police. They too expressed concerns about becoming too law enforcement oriented and making sure they remained within the law when asserting their authority when partnering with the police.

The added safety that police provided was a priority. The police's authority to control threatening "third parties," those not under supervision but who may be involved with the offender, such as family members, roommates, or friends, was viewed as a valuable asset.

> Well, I like working with the police because I know that they know how to handle a situation. I mean, they have much better training, they're much more skilled in dealing with people [that] I can't deal with like a third party, but the police can if the third party gets out of hand. All I can do is say, "Please don't hurt me, I'm trying to leave," but the police can…actually just arrest them based on their threatening behavior or something. We don't have those powers, so from a safety point of view I like working with the police. (CCO 201)

Traditional CCOs also appreciated the exchange of information and the additional surveillance the police provide due to their constant presence in the community, often when CCOs are not available.

> Well, the police officers have a lot of contact with our offenders. A lot of times, more than we do. So they are real valuable to us in providing us with information, and then we can likewise provide them with information, and then if our offenders are in violation [or] have warrants out, then the police apprehend them. (CCO 216)

One CCO pointed out a benefit of working with the police was that police could see offenders in a context other than the negative ones in which they normally encounter offenders.

> Well, we educate the police in terms of what exactly our roles are. We give them more intel. We help them to see the other side of the offender

because the police only see people during their worst times. Police don't come to your house when everything is hunky-dory. Okay? They don't go arrest people, and they are always out there on the curb waiting for them, "Come on, take me!" You know, it's the worst of it. And so, we get to put the faces on them. (CCO 234)

Therefore, CCOs in general appear to hold a positive view of working with the police and appreciate their expertise in scene safety, information sharing, and surveillance capabilities in the community regarding offenders on supervision.

Similar to those CCOs working in planned partnerships with the police, traditional CCOs also expressed concerns about becoming too much like the police in their style of supervision or overreaching their authority to help the police gain access to offenders they otherwise would not have. They also expressed concerns about the roles and professional expectations held by police and said that, although collaboration was generally a good thing, there were times when it was better for CCOs to work independently with offenders on supervision.

I think that the police need to remember our role and we need to remember their role. I think sometimes those lines can become blurred. You know, where if the police want you to go in and search a house just because you can get in there without a warrant and they can't....I mean, I've heard of those things happening [and] that's not right. I mean, we still have to uphold the law, and that's just kind of a way around it. I think there's also, could be, concern with armed DOC officers being a bit lax in remembering when they can and can't use their firearms. But I think that the positives outweigh the negatives on it. (CCO 226)

Similarly, the following CCOs were concerned about the police having undue influence and dominating interactions between CCOs and offenders or CCOs attempting to assert their power just to impress the police.

Possibly overinserting your authority [and] some grandstanding...I think that if you get too tight it can create problems. Like I said, there's some jurisdiction that the local law enforcement doesn't have, and you could possibly arrest somebody that didn't need to be arrested at that point. So that's what I meant by overinserting your authority, but I think that the good far outweighs the negative aspects of that, you know, a lot of these folks have been around for a lot of years and create a lot of problems in the community, and you know working together we can kinda curtail that type of behavior. (CCO 206)

Well, the negative outcomes of the relationship would be if you team up with someone and the probation and parole officer is either not strong enough, psychologically, to not be bowled over by unethical police officers who would abuse that. But I can tell you from my experience, most police officers aren't interested in doing that. For one, they've already had enough experience with getting caught in those legal things. If it's bad, they don't want to deal with it. Its too much time and paperwork and trouble. (CCO 227)

Some CCOs view police officers as holding very narrow views about offenders but acknowledged that the police often came to understand that some offenders are also victims or the power of their addictions was too great for traditional law enforcement strategies to be effective at creating meaningful change.

Cops are cops, and they view the world a different way. It's very black and white. They view it differently than, I think, most probation and parole officers....At the same time, the longer I think that they are into it, being a police officer, things become more gray for them and they see. When you lock the same person up over and over and over and over for drug crimes...and you finally come to the last time, you see them over the course of their history being a vibrant young person to a withered-away 40-year-old in an 80-year-old body....And there are those cops out there who look at these things and go, "God, I remember the first time I arrested her for the possession of heroin, blah, blah, blah." What can they do? You've got cops that work with the needle exchange program, that support the needle lady....Cops will tell you, "The war on drugs isn't worth it." (CCO 226)

Another CCO viewed the relationship between community corrections and law enforcement as too one-sided and lacking direction for CCOs to effectively work with the police.

. . . due to the fact that there's no communication. I mean, the only communication that we have is line staff to line staff. You know, POs and CCOs have different philosophies. Some [CCOs] are...a little more conservative, some are a little more social worker related, but you've got policies and guidelines that pretty much dictate what you have to do and when you have to do it, so it's really not a problem. What the problem is, is that you have no training and no protocol on how to deal with law enforcement. The only one we have is if you need them, call them, they're supposed to be there. When they get there, you dump it on them and they put them away....We expect them to help us when we call them. But when they call us, we're told NOT to a lot of times....When we make them lead and dump stuff on them, I don't think it's mutual. (CCO 241)

CCO 241 is one of the few officers who specifically mentioned the lack of training and protocols to guide CCOs' work with police and how most discussions regarding their working relationship with police are "line staff to line staff." It is unkown to what extent this is an issue for CCOs in general (see Drapela & Lutze, 2009).

CCOs also believed the police did not fully understand the extent or limitations of their power to sanction offenders. There was a sense that the police generally respected them but that their respect was limited because of the apparent disconnect between a CCO's limited authority related to court-ordered conditions and their expansive authority to enter offenders' homes and to conduct searches, in which the police had no authority without a warrant. Thus, pereceptions about whether the police respected CCOs and their professional role was mixed, with a tendency to believe they are tentatively respected.

I think there will always be some officers who really don't understand what we are doing. Particularly new officers who haven't been around and have a lot of experience, but I think in general, they respect what we are doing. (CCO 216)

I have no idea [and] the stories I've heard is that [laughs]—well I don't even want to go there because that's all very fourthhand information. No officer has ever come up to me and told me any type of opinion about what they think of CCOs or DOC. (CCO 201)

I think that the police in general don't know what my role as a community corrections officer is. I think that a lot of them think I have more authority than what I have. [I] think one of the biggest things for them is, I mean, they look at you like you're kidding when you have an offender on supervision and they don't have a condition that says "obey all laws." So, its like, okay, this guy's on probation for burglary, and he can go out and break any new laws he wants and I can't touch him. And, I mean, if you think about it, its ridiculous. (CCO 226)

Although tenuous, it appears CCOs believe the police respect their role in the criminal justice system and the importance of their work with offenders but are somewhat confused about where CCOs' power and authority begins and ends.

Ultimately, it appears that police-corrections partnerships bring added benefit to both the police and corrections. CCOs tend to fully appreciate the greater surveillance, information sharing, assistance with arrests, and the general safety police officers provide when needed. The research results are mixed, however, when it comes to the overlap where the police and CCOs' roles end and CCOs' role to build relationships and provide support to offenders begins. Some studies show this is where CCOs begin to have concerns about the partnership because the police's role appears too narrow, inflexible, and impatient in understanding what offenders need for long-term success (Murphy & Lutze, 2009), while other studies do not report concerns about role conflict (Alarid et al., 2011; Kim et al., 2010). For CCOs who work closely with police, it is the sharing of coercive power that most needs to be managed and negotiated for partnerships to be more than just supporting the police mission to remove offenders from the community. Only then can there be a greater understanding about how to work together to meet the goals of both agencies (Murphy & Lutze, 2009).

Working With the Courts

Community corrections work with offenders is highly influenced by the courts and the conditions imposed on offenders at sentencing. The conditions that judges impose are generally dictated by statute and must be related to the crime of conviction or the conditions that may have contributed to the crime. Judges may mandate treatment (e.g., mental health, substance abuse, anger management), prohibit certain behaviors (e.g., consumption of alcohol or drugs, driving), and restrict where offenders may travel (e.g., staying within a certain jurisdiction) and the types of people from whom they must stay away (e.g., felons). CCOs must enforce only the conditions ordered by the court unless they can justify the need to add or subtract conditions based on new information or the offender's behavior.

CCOs interface with the courts at numerous important decision points in the criminal justice process. In some jurisdictions, community corrections officers are responsible for completing presentence investigations to help inform judges about whether a defendant should be retained in jail to await trial, to help inform an appropriate sentence, or to determine the conditions of supervision. Federal probation officers serve under the jurisdiction of the federal courts and not the Bureau of Prisons, whereas in many state jurisdictions, community corrections is within the jurisdiction of the DOC. The development of problem-solving courts and their inter-disciplinary, collaborative approach to interventions helps CCOs interact directly with the court to supervise offenders. Therefore, it is important that CCOs have good working relations with the courts to implement effective supervision.

There are few, if any, studies that focus on the role of CCOs and their interaction with the courts in spite of their responsibility to monitor and enforce the conditions imposed by the court. Most courts consist of "court-room workgroups" where the key participants (judges, defense attorneys, prosecutors, county clerks, and police) work together to efficiently process large numbers of cases (Eisenstein & Jacob, 1991). CCOs must be able to work with defense attorneys, prosecutors, and judges in order to effec-tively adjust conditions of supervision, revoke offenders from supervision to prison, and support the prosecution of offenders who commit new crimes while on supervision. When specifically asked about working with other agencies in the criminal justice system, the courts were noticeably absent from the spontaneous observations made by CCOs in Spokane. CCOs were most likely to refer to working with the police, jail, and other probation or parole agencies at the county or federal level. Although some expressed frustration in how the court was oftentimes disconnected from the reality of offenders' lives and their ability to complete various aspects of supervision (e.g., community service, employment), they rarely spoke of partnering with the court to make their jobs easier or more efficient. With the exception of a few, when they did mention the court, it tended to regard the sharing of information and challenges of getting accurate infor-mation about some of their offenders.

One CCO relayed an experience with the courtroom workgroup and expressed what court research has shown to be true for other professionals who work within the court (see Eisenstein & Jacob, 1991). Eisenstein & Jacob (1991) discovered that if one is out of sync with the courtroom culture and norms of the workgroup, then it may be difficult to efficiently use the process and achieve the tasks necessary to effectively complete one's work. For example,

I mean, we've had some formal training touching on that [the judicial system], but mostly it's my experience working hand-in-hand with the prosecutor's office, defense attorneys, working with various judges and going back in their chambers and talking to them face-to-face, nose to nose, not necessarily agreeing. I've been threatened to pack my tooth-brush several times, and some of them come unglued and "where the hell do you get off doing that?" you know. It's all part of the job, it's all part of the game, and you stand your ground and they respect that. They may not agree with you, but they respect that—you stand your ground and say, "This is why I did that. This is why I recommend that." And you become highly respected in the court system, and you've got to have a good reputation or you're lost. And that's one of the first things you do as a police officer, well especially as a probation/parole officer—gain that respect within the court system that you work in. Then they don't question—they know you know what you're talking about. But they'll definitely test you in the beginning, so if you lose out in the beginning, you're lost for your career. And there again that's something you learn from the job. (CCO 104)

Most other comments about the court were very similar to those about working with other agencies regarding the sharing of information important to the efficient supervision of offenders. These observations reveal communication gaps within the criminal justice system that have the potential to increase risk and sabotage the work of others in the system working toward the same goals. Some of the comments express an understanding of how overburdened the criminal justice system has become for everyone while others reflect unnecessary inefficiencies related to an unwillingness to give priority over the general public to other agencies requesting information. For example, the following comments relate to the inefficiencies.

Communication, I guess, could be better with different agencies that we deal with. A few years ago or probably longer than that ago, it seemed like it was easy to make contact with somebody. You know, a police officer, or somebody at the prosecutor's office or public defender's office. Over the years, every agency had gotten busier and busier, and it takes you longer and its more cumbersome to get information and to make contact and to get a hold of a prosecutor.... So, over the last 5 or 10 years it takes longer to do your job because of other agencies being overloaded too and not as accessible as they used to be. (CCO ---)

Another CCO expressed concern about spending more time than necessary because, even as a member of another criminal justice agency, he often had to go through the same process as a member of the general public.

We had a situation last week where one of our officer's offenders was arrested for statutory rape, and we wanted to get a police report from pretrial services over at the county, and their chief wouldn't let her make a copy of it and let our officer just go pick it up. So, that meant that he would have to spend more time going over there, waiting in line, waiting for them to copy it, at the regular records area, when she already had it right there. She could have just faxed it. But I don't know. (CCO 205)

Another CCO expressed a need to be more conscientious about making sure everyone is working well together and serving the practical and professional needs of others working across criminal justice agencies.

Yeah, I think we need to do a better job. It kind of comes back to the quality control issue. Say, if the judges, the prosecutor's office, the PD— we were in a private enterprise together—let's call them our customers. I want to keep them happy. I want to know how to adjust my inventory or to make modifications to the services I provide those customers. I'd rather be checking with them periodically to make sure that they are happy, to have an environment where they feel comfortable to be honest with me and give us feedback about what we're doing well, what we need to improve. And when it's just pure junk, then we don't do that well here. I've talked to these people, and probably the number one unhappy client is the prosecutor's office. Because I deal with them all the time, and they're honest about how we do a disservice to them, and that could be resolved by cordially sitting down and saying, "Hey, what's going on?" Usually that doesn't happen until there's a crisis—and that's very preventable. (CCO 210)

Accountability between agencies participating in coordinated services is important in establishing effective collaborations. Several states have implemented reentry courts to coordinate services and to establish continuity between the court, prison, community supervision, and social services.

Reentry courts are a recent innovation designed to provide structure, evidence-based treatment, coordinated supervision, rigorous monitoring to hold both collaborating agencies and offenders to a higher level of accountability, and use the power of the judge to be an influential change agent (Hamilton, 2011; Wolf, 2011). These programs establish close working relationships among CCOs, the court, and other providers and provide a weekly forum through the court to work across systems to proactively manage the risk and needs of offenders released from prison. Reentry court team meetings involving the judge, case manager, probation or parole officers, and social service providers allow for the proactive removal of barriers between systems and individualized case plans to meet offenders' needs (Wolf, 2011). Preliminary findings suggest that these programs are effective in significantly reducing recidivism and trend toward reducing rearrest, but they result in higher rates and revocation for noncompliance (Hamilton, 2011; Wolf, 2011). Reentry courts have the potential to increase information sharing and to build awareness of everyone's professional role to implement evidence-based practices across agencies and systems.

Working Among Corrections Agencies: Federal, State, and County

Community corrections is directly tied to institutional corrections by the flow of offenders out of prison and into the community. Many reentry initiatives have attempted to improve the continuity of care from the prison to the community (see Lattimore et al., 2005; Taxman & Bouffard, 2000). CCOs in Spokane did not speak much about institutional corrections, with the exception of specific institutions such as work release programs where offenders reside in prison but work in the community before being transferred to community supervision full time. They were more likely to speak about the county jail and their counterparts working for county and federal probation. Once again, they revealed concerns about information sharing between agencies and gaps in communication directly related to either the sharing of supervision or the management of risk.

Several CCOs spoke about not knowing whether offenders on their caseloads were under supervision in another jurisdiction such as district court (county) or federal probation. This lack of information sharing across agencies prevented CCOs from determining how supervision may be duplicating services, whether offenders were compliant with state supervision or vice versa, and the responsibility for reintegration success or failure. For example,

> I think again it comes back to the sharing of information. The feds will have someone on supervision, and they will never contact us and we will not contact them. The same is true for county, . . . and then I'll get in touch with the other officers. Initially when I started to do that . . . they thought it was really odd that I was even calling them, and to me it only made perfect sense, you're supervising this person, I'm supervising this person, different cases, we should be talking, but then because you have so many people on your caseloads, . . . (CCO 201)

> Oh yeah. There's a lot of duplication with us and district court, and you know, county, city probation. What's kind of interesting is the offender thinks that I know everything going on with him at district court, you know, what his district court or city probation officer is telling him to do.

He thinks that I know every time he gets stopped by the police. You know, and there's just not that communication there. (CCO 226)

One CCO was frustrated with a general lack of respect from other criminal justice agencies at all levels, including other community corrections agencies, and how this made sharing information awkward instead of a free-flowing and natural part of thorough supervision.

People's individual cases are so complex sometimes that it's hard—you know, I'll call a meeting with the feds. That would be helpful because there's often times people on federal probation that are in jail on holds, or whatever, that we have. Now, sometimes they'll report and sometimes they won't. I think that could be refined, somehow. A lot of time it's been when they say, "Oh, you're with DOC? Oh." They'll discount. And I don't know why. Not the feds, just in general.... I'm just saying that a lot of times, even law enforcement, county, city, whatever, they'll think, "Oh, you're with DOC?" (CCO 229)

Similarly, CCOs expressed frustration, laced with feelings of disrespect, by the previous sheriff's tendency to block access to the jail even when an offender on supervision was considered to be an immediate threat to the community. This problem appeared to be solved with the election of a new sheriff and more open communication between the county jail and state community corrections.

We had an issue here in town when we had the other sheriff [name], and, for whatever reason, he had given rules on who could be incarcerated in Spokane County Jail. And, pretty much, it was very seldom, if we had an offender that was totally out of control and he was on a drug high and terrorizing the neighborhood and so on and so forth, hey, there's no room for him in the jail. Our supervisor couldn't [even] get the jail to take the person. You know, you're a DOC supervisor, you should have some influence over that jail. (CCO 112)

The county jail was also viewed as an important source of information and a means to manage risk by both confining out-of-control offenders, as the previous CCO observed, or by knowing when offenders were returning to the community and back to active supervision. For example, the jail was considered key to providing information in a timely manner that would enhance supervision.

Jail, probably, and some with DSHS. I see a need for better communications, you know. We've got, just in the last year, what they call an RMS computer, like a management system where you can run people up to see if they're in jail.... So, it would be nice if we could get computer access to DSHS information and more police information and records and jail information. It gets confusing here where we're moving people from the jail due to overcrowding and then move them out to Geiger work release. So you don't know if the guy's out driving or down at the jail. (CCO 243)

A lot of the emphasis on information sharing was related to very basic professional needs of knowing where offenders are, who has control and influence over them (e.g., police, county and federal probation officers, jail), and how to minimize the risk involved with a lapse or gap in the sharing of information.

Often interwoven within the practical importance of sharing information for the sake of enhanced supervision was the notion that information was key to achieving any sense of continuity in the care of offenders and the ability to get agencies, and sometimes systems, to work together to achieve greater understanding of the other and to improve outcomes for all involved. This is where the role of institutional corrections, prisons and work release programs, was highlighted as important to the success of offenders and community corrections. Possibly the best summary of this is represented by the following observation that includes multiple criminal justice agencies from juvenile through the adult system.

The police department, the prosecutor, the public defender, federal probation and parole, city and county districts. I mean, all of that. And juvenile, cause [unclear] they, graduate and the next thing you know we've got them. We're just now figuring out the continuity within our own setting. It's taken us a long time to figure out that, you know, duh, the person goes from prison to prerelease, to work release to the field, and they're still the same person when they get out here and when they started out in prison. Gee whiz, maybe we should have shared some information about what happened along the way. You know, we'll get there, we're just slow. (CCO 236)

When discussing a need for collaboration, many CCOs also pointed out examples of how the system sometimes sabotages itself. The following quote presents an interesting example of how a failure to work across agencies and between county- and state-level jurisdictions often leads to wasted resources and immediate failure for offenders—not due to current behavior but because of unresolved legal issues related to past behavior. Thus, because agencies do not work well across jurisdictions to solve problems within the criminal justice system, a common set of failures results in spite of attempting to do everything right in terms of addressing offenders' risk and needs. The following CCO presents a valuable lesson in how the criminal justice system often sabotages its own success by interrupting continuity in care and diminishing the potential of success for many offenders. When asked about collaborating with other criminal justice agencies, the following example was given.

> Yes. I think that we should with county probation because their people and our people are the same people. And so, and I don't want to get off on a tangent with this, so I want to see if I can pull this together. For one thing, a real problem I have right now, I have this Hispanic male, he's 25 years old. He's a gang-banger. He comes from California. He's been a banger since he was 9 years old....He tells me, "I'll be a banger 'til I die." He had a good heart. He's not a mean man. He's not a mean person. And his skills are, he's been a migrant farm worker forever, and he comes in here and he has, [in another city], four misdemeanor warrants. So, I can set him up with a job, he can go to [the other city], the minute he hits the street, he's going to get arrested. So, why couldn't DOC work with the court system when a man or a woman goes to prison [to clear] all those warrants? I wouldn't say that domestic violence, those serious ones, but all those warrants that they have, why couldn't they get those warrants taken care of there, at that time? Because that would save so much time for continuity of treatment and continuity of supervision. If we're going to work with them from cradle to grave, why wouldn't we do that? Why would we get them in the Department of Corrections and work with them and they go through all these programs that we have and they do all these things and they come out and they all go to jail. Why wouldn't we work there? Why wouldn't we work with county corrections because they have hundreds and hundreds of people that they're supervising. (CCO ---)

This CCO's observation presents the need to further develop "boundaryless organizations" within criminal justice that, while individual agencies are managing their organizational responsibilities, are proactively working with other organizations to manage the process and natural flow of the offender's case for a smooth transition forward (see Taxman & Bouffard, 2000). The offender should enter the community or the next phase of transition from a position of strength versus a position of weakness and without the burden of unresolved legal processes due to past behavior.

Relatedly, another CCO gave a more proactive and positive example of recognizing that most women in prison have children involved with Child Protective Services (CPS). This means CCOs must proactively, from within the institution, work with women, their children, and CPS to remove barriers in order to achieve a smooth transition to the community.

> It was great. We worked really well with CPS. And I think CPS was pleasantly surprised when they came to work with us. "Come to Eleanor Chase [DOC women's work release facility]. Come and see what we're doing." They have a child visitation program and they have the mother-baby program. Child visitation is where the child, from birth up to 12 years old, can come and stay three days and three nights with the mom. They have a mother-baby where the baby can stay from birth up to 3 years old, live with the mom. Okay? That's for the bonding. Okay. So, most all of our women had CPS issues, so CPS [says], "I'm going to allow a child to go into a correctional facility and stay? I don't think so." But, to go in and explain the program, bring them in, and give them a tour and talk about what the program was about. They were very receptive. [goes on to discuss programs related to child support, drug treatment] (CCO ---)

This CCO recognized that the programs developed within the institution addressed issues relevant to a smooth transition from the institution to the community and bridged the gap between women and their children and mothers and CPS. The programs provided for continuity of care within supervision as well as across primary relationships with other systems with the power to directly intervene in offenders' lives.

The review of how community corrections officers seek out partnerships and cooperative professional relationships with those in other criminal justice agencies reveals a clear understanding that community corrections cannot accomplish credible supervision through surveillance and social work alone. Just as offenders cross organizational boundaries, so must the working relationships of CCOs. Important to community corrections is the recognition that CCOs are best positioned to know the entirety of the offender across criminal justice agencies and are best positioned to work with offenders across systems.

Working With Social Services and Public Health Systems

In order to address offenders' needs, CCOs must work across systems to garner the expertise and resources necessary to provide offenders with social support, practical skills, employment, and treatment. This means tapping into systems of care outside of criminal justice that often bridge the needs of offenders with those of their families and the community. The importance of these systems of care traditionally viewed as working outside of the criminal justice system is that they may continue to provide continuity beyond the term of an offender's community supervision sentence and therefore serve as conduits to long-term reintegration beyond the work of CCOs. Although spanning boundaries within systems presents challenges related to trust, respect, and sharing of common values, working between systems often poses even greater challenges. When successful however, working between systems is likely to provide much greater success for all involved in achieving shared goals (Matz, Wicklund, Douglas, & May, 2012).

CCOs made some interesting observations about whether social services and community corrections shared the same goals, especially since the agencies take different approaches. The following CCO observed the difficulty in bringing people with diverse perspectives together.

> Make no mistake, COPS Shops are good, probation is good, SRA,[2] the OAA, working with DSHS and CPS, and the police—all of these things are absolutely tremendous ideas WHEN they have the common goal. There is no common goal. That's where it starts to fade.... The Department of Corrections is here to help,... You can read and see where they are driving. You want to explain that to a hard-nosed law enforcement type who thinks these guys should be run out of town?... We are mandated to try and help. Explain that to them. You know, you can't. You want to take a guy off the street, but CPS wants him to come home and work. Explain that to them. There are great ideas, it's that the goals change almost daily depending on who you are with and what their expectations [are]. (CCO 234)

While the previous CCOs identified the futility of getting professionals with conflicting goals to work effectively together, the following CCOs observed the overlapping goal of getting people to be productive members of the community.

> I don't think it could hurt. I mean, you want to be in good graces, you want to have good professional working relationships with as many agencies as you can because those are the people that you're relying on to give you the straight scoop and to tell you what's going on with your offenders. You have other state agencies—DSHS, CPS, I mean, even the

local law enforcement and everything else that you deal with—and the big thing is, do you want to have a good working relationship with all these people? Because it's the same person you're dealing with. And I think the goal is the same, which is for us not to have to deal with them anymore. (CCO 239)

Because a lot of our people are involved in those social service agencies, and I think that if we could get together, I think the goal of all of these agencies is to get these people to be productive members of the community. And we can throw them in jail all we want, but if they've got these mental health issues that are not being addressed and maybe these issues with CPS that are causing stressors, which are, you know, causing them to continue to use drugs and all of that stuff—I just think that if we had all these people working together, hopefully we could maybe not see these people coming through the revolving door all the time. (CCO 245)

Similar themes are woven throughout the observations of CCOs and their work with social service agencies and treatment providers. Whether expressing appreciation and respect for the support provided by social services or absolute frustration, the value of working across systems to manage and treat offenders was readily acknowledged, and there was a clear desire to solve conflicts to the advantage of both systems.

The need to work with agencies outside of the traditional criminal justice system was acknowledged by a majority of Spokane CCOs, and most did work directly with social services and treatment providers. Most working relationships with social services appeared to be based on personal contacts made between individual CCOs and social workers instead of planned, coordinated partnerships. Most CCOs found their interactions with their counterpart in social service agencies to be very helpful in solving problems and assisting offenders. For example,

Real good. I mean, I kind of pride myself for maintaining those contacts and working with them. I don't see it as a burden. You'll get stuff in the mail and say, "Oh, I don't know, I need to know what's going on with this or that person." So, yeah, I really welcome it and just try to keep it up. (CCO 210)

Like working with the police, CCOs working closely with social service providers also felt they learned valuable lessons from each other about how they conduct their work and what they have to offer offenders.

Similarly, they learned about each other's boundaries and the extent of their respective workloads.

> I mean, you know, I guess the people that I'm working with and that I'm working mental health and developmental disabilities on some people, and, you know, it seems to be a real open...and in the meantime it's kind of interesting because I think they are learning about DOC as I am learning about DDD and mental health and stuff like that. (CCO 226)

> I have a good one. Everybody's overworked, but anybody that I've ever contacted for information, they've been very cooperative. And I understand their regulations; if they need information, then I accommodate them. If I want the information, I need to do what I have to do to get it. I can deal with whining about it another time, but, you know, they're cooperative given their boundaries. (CCO 229)

Some CCOs and social workers conduct home visits together and some officers, working in COPS Shops and in traditional community supervision offices, advocated a closer working relationship by colocating a CPS worker with CCOs and others at the neighborhood level.

> Pretty good. I go on field calls with them sometimes, or they'll go with me at my request. (CCO 233)

> One thing we've tried to do is—it doesn't seem to work—is connect more on a community level with CPS because a lot of the cases we have have kids, and we're mandatory reporters by statute, and if we see something that appears to put the kids at risk or neglect, we have to notify CPS—and we do that....So, what we've tried to do is get them to kind of partner with us and almost take up kind of a geographic assignment of CPS cases in this community, but I don't know that that's ever going to happen, because they don't assign cases on a geographic basis. (CCO 111)

> I think it would be nice so we have a common plan, CPS and us. I think it would be better if we had more contact. [If] we go out more together to the homes, you know, that kind of thing. I think that would enhance our supervision and theirs too as far as they need to do with CPS. I think a close relationship could help the offenders and their families. (CCO 102)

Nearly all CCOs spoke of the importance of sharing information across systems to better enhance the work of each agency and to provide direct assistance to offenders that community corrections cannot achieve on its own.

> Oh, I have an excellent rapport with them. I was the lead of the sex unit, and I worked with high-risk offenders for so long prior to the implementation of the OAA [Offender Accountability Act]. And I had to develop, need is the best teacher if it comes to that, and I had to develop my own approaches to supervise the group of offenders that I had. I realized that I couldn't do it alone. So I started communicating with these people. That was taken to a new level with OAA. It's mandatory now. So I feel pretty good about it. (CCO ---)

Again, child protective services (CPS) was often mentioned as an agency that CCOs worked closely with due to the fact that CCOs are mandated reporters of child abuse and neglect and many of the offenders on supervision have children and are also involved with CPS. CPS was viewed both as a resource to provide services to offenders and their children as well as a mechanism to enhance the monitoring and surveillance capacity of supervision. Both CPS and community corrections have coercive powers that can benefit each other. The following are examples of how each agency uses its power to assist the other.

> It would vary from officer to officer. We like the people with CPS because we're finding that we have a responsibility in reporting, as being mandatory reporters, that situation like I told you about with this gun [CCO discovered a loaded gun hidden under a child's bed]. They're in agreement. They have a tough time finding delinquent dads on child support, on this and that....I may not be able to find somebody, they may have been wanted for a long time, law enforcement never happens to come across them, but I guarantee you that guy's girlfriend's getting her food stamps, and I can go there and I can go look, here's the deal...we need to put this guy into custody. Can you help us? Can we work collectively together? And God, they're there, all the time, you know. It's a good deal. (CCO 207)

> We do have involvement with CPS. I've gone to court for them, usually taking kids away from parents that really shouldn't have kids. DSHS refers to us all the time. That's probably the majority.... [Interviewer: Are these contacts generally positive?] Most of them are. CPS ones are usually [about] taking the kid away from this person—I'm rarely against it. I'm probably never against it. To that point, then yeah....Most of its positive. (CCO 108)

In the next example, CPS used the conditions of supervision and the power of the CCO to make sure an offender parent trying to reunite with his children is not continuing to use drugs.

> I think that I have a good working relationship with them. CPS, I have a guy right now whose family member, he and his wife went to prison and they lost all six of their children, and they are in the process of getting their children back. And one of the ways to reintegrate the family is to have them go down and do visits down in [city name] where his children [are living]. She [CPS worker] asked me to do a UA, and I'm going to be happy to do a UA for her when he comes back to make sure that he's not using. So, I can call them and get information from them if I need. (CCO 245)

While many CCOs appeared to have a good working relationship with social services and other treatment providers, many CCOs expressed frustration in their attempts to partner with social services. They often identified challenges in getting social service providers to share information and to become actively involved in DOC initiatives. Some CCOs expressed an understanding of the historical distrust between the two systems while others expressed a general lack of respect from both sides.

> I think, because historically, DOC projected themselves as a macho, egotistical entity, not working with anybody, we're having to overcome that right now. There is some resistance out there for very, very good reasons. But, quite honestly, I've had good, good working relationships with folks. (CCO 231)

Another CCO expressed similar views and added that distrust can be overcome by developing personal relationships by "people working with people instead of agencies working with agencies."

> I get a feeling they don't trust us. We're heavy-handed. We come marching in with a court order in our hip pocket and a badge on our pajamas, so they don't trust us so much. If you go in and get to know them and let them know you, then you can accomplish everything in the world working with them. But again, that's people working with people instead of agencies working with agencies. People have to work together before the agency can work together, you know. The other thing is we also have to acknowledge the fact that we have to share responsibility. (CCO 251)

In spite of understanding the need to work together and a general desire to do so, many CCOs were quick to point out the challenges related to a lack of resources, information sharing, and respect and a general distrust of social services from CCOs. Social services, much like community corrections, was generally viewed as having large caseloads and lacking resources to respond to some of the CCOs' needs related to helping offenders. This was often mixed with the perception that due to so many regulations and issues concerning confidentiality, social services was not very responsive to the needs of CCOs or offenders who badly needed their services. The following CCO succinctly captured the gist of it by stating,

> I think they're all bogged down. It's real hard. If someone isn't in crisis at that second, good luck. That's how I see it. (CCO 235)

Other CCOs tended to be much more explicit in their feelings of frustration and the tension in the relationship. Information sharing was often a point of contention based on the belief that the DOC freely shared information with DSHS but that the relationship was not reciprocated. For example,

> Yeah, you know, it would be nice if we worked a little closer with CPS because a lot of times we are dealing with the same people. It seems like if you have to make a phone call with CPS, there's this veil of secrecy that is such that it's not even worth your hassle calling them. Everybody's close-mouthed about everything and/or they will say, "Well the person you need to talk to is so and so, who just happens to be gone for a week and a half." Hey, I am just looking for the information; give me somebody who can do that. If CPS had a better flow of information to us, maybe even DSHS, because a lot of people are on either assistance or something. I wish there was more of an information flow availability. It just seems like everybody is in their own, you know, so I wish we worked a little closer with them, yeah. (CCO 105)

> But I had another experience with DSHS last week where I went up and I wanted to know if one of my offenders had made an appointment. And this was someone that I had hand carried in there to make sure we got the process rolling. And she said, "I can't talk to you without a release!" And I was just like, "You know? I've got a release, but it [is] in the file." I'm sure the offender had a release there, but because it wasn't in front of this lady, we had to play [the] whole release game thing and I said, "It's not worth my time." And I understand people who need to be protective, but I think that within some of these agencies, yeah, there should be a free flow of information. (CCO 205)

Another CCO expressed the same frustration but felt that showing up in person was the best strategy to get results.

> Like a roller coaster. There's up days and down days. It depends a lot on the caseworkers that you're working with, you know. What I've found is the quickest way for me to get response out of another social service agency is to go to their desk. You're like, "Here I am." That seems to be the quickest way. Cause I think, like any other agency, they are probably inundated with what they're doing, and the squeaky wheel gets the grease. So if I've got somebody who I am really concerned about or who I really think needs to be hooked up with services or that I can't clarify information about what's happening with them, I just go there. (CCO 236)

Another CCO captured the essence of concerns about one-sided information sharing and how it may be resolved.

> It's good but it's limited, you know. I think our department, we're making progress, but it still lags in the computer connectedness. I get calls from DSHS workers a week or two after somebody's released from prison. They are aware that they are released from prison, their crimes, where they went to live, and this sort of thing. I think, "Well, how did they get that information because they really aren't sent any notice by DOC." They had some way of pulling that up on the computer and tracking it. It seems that we should have access to pulling up some of their records that would help us in our jobs, you know. (CCO 243)

Similarly, another CCO related how the sharing of information would make everyone's job easier by removing the duplication of services.

> Well, I could see what they're doing with some of my clients to see how they're working with them. Sometimes I'm unaware that they're doing the same thing that I'm doing. I might be referring them to TASC and they're referring them to TASC at the same time. No need for us both to refer them. Sometimes they're working with a client that I can't find. They know where the person is and I don't. Sometimes I know where a person is that they're trying to locate. (CCO 233)

A few CCOs were much more explicit in what they perceived as a general lack of responsiveness and, even when social services did respond, a lack of preparedness.

> Yes! [leaning into microphone]. [Interviewer: Which ones?] CPS, mental health, because, right now, if you have a sex offender who's mentally ill,

nobody will take them. Okay? So, you've got a court order that says he's supposed to be in treatment, nobody will take him because he's a sex offender. Mental health, we went to a gal's place, one of [my partner's] girls, she hadn't eaten in two weeks, she was psychotic. We called mental health. [They said], "We don't have anybody to send down right now." We put her in the car, we hauled her down there ourselves, dropped her off! [laughing] You know what I mean? Like CPS, they'll come to a call—we'll call them—they don't bring their cameras, they don't bring their telephones. You know what I mean? One time I went down to [the grocery store] to get one of those throwaway cameras for the CPS lady to take pictures of the place, because I was like, "These kids need to be out of here." (CCO ---)

The following CCO bluntly depicts the barriers to accessing other systems to address the complexity of offenders with co-occurring disorders (e.g., substance abuse and mental health) as well as other problems and the system's lack of flexibility in providing care to high-risk offenders.

. . . as long as we are going to continue to incarcerate people for being users, then we need to find a way to break them of that cycle. Break the cycle of addiction. We have to team up with DASA, Department of Alcohol and Substance Abuse, because they, the mental health system is, quite frankly, is fucked up. Excuse my lack of professionalism here, but I can't describe it any better way. In the community, it's just screwed up. It takes an act of God to get somebody in. If you have somebody that is dual diagnosis and that, most of my people that have a mental illness also have a dual diagnosis of substance abuse somewhere. So, they've got to be clean and sober, well, god, they're not going to be, maybe EVER! How do I still deal with their schizophrenia; how am I going to deal with their depression; how do I deal with their bipolar disorder? I need some help from you people over there. "Well, not until you get this." It's such a maze to get into the system; if you don't know how to get in, you can't access it. There needs to be some work toward breaking those down. (CCO 227)

As in any relationship, there are two sides to every story, so interviews with social service providers may have revealed similar pros and cons about working with community corrections, and it is unknown to what extent the positive working relationships developed between CCOs and social workers outweigh the negatives. An important insight based on these interviews, however, is that CCOs want to work with social service providers and clearly see their expertise and resources as necessary to their offenders' success in the community. They understand how working with social services and treatment providers reduces risk of failure for their client and ultimately reduces the risk to public safety (Matz et al., 2012).

The examples given by CCOs concerning their inability to gain information and get results from their contacts with social services, sometimes even during a crisis, are noteworthy given CCOs' position and power. If CCOs, as criminal justice professionals, cannot make inroads and easily understand the complex systems and rules governing social services and mental health, then how are offenders going to be successful interacting across systems when struggling with problems and often in the most powerless position of their lives? It is this concern that has led to sincere attempts to create interagency, cross-system collaborations in response to reentry.

COORDINATED RESPONSES TO REENTRY AND A CONTINUUM OF CARE

The importance of coordinating across multiple disciplines, some not normally associated with reentry, is highlighted by the United States Attorney General's Office, Council on Reentry (see Justice Center, n.d.). The Federal Interagency Reentry Council includes agencies one would expect to be involved in reentry initiatives, such as the U.S. departments of justice, labor, health and human services, housing and urban development, and education and the White House Office of Faith-Based and Neighborhood Partnerships. It also includes agencies such as the U.S. departments of interior and agriculture, Veterans Affairs, the Social Security Administration, the Internal Revenue Service, and other government agencies related to personnel, business management, and trade. This comprehensive approach attempts to recognize that prisoner reentry affects all aspects of society's social, political, and economic well-being and requires agencies to work together to coordinate effective responses. As U.S. Attorney General Eric Holder states, "Reentry provides a major opportunity to reduce recidivism, save taxpayer dollars, and make our communities safer" (Justice Center, 2013).

As may be expected, even though coordinated responses are proven to be effective, they can also be complicated. Many of the same barriers to implementing evidence-based practices described in the previous chapter appear in attempts to coordinate services and collaborate across systems. The inclusion of agencies from systems generally not thought of as related to offender reentry illustrates the potential resources necessary to effectively manage reentry and the necessity to coordinate their use. Research shows serious and violent offender reentry initiatives (SVORI) leaders recognized the importance of using boundary spanners to successfully coordinate integrated responses to reentry during the 1990s. For instance, over 90% of SVORI programs employed a boundary spanner to build relationships with community agencies, ensure availability of services to offenders (85%), educate community services providers regarding offender needs (80%), and encourage providers to prioritize services for offenders (73%) (Lattimore et al., 2005).

A few of the CCOs in Spokane were directly involved in bringing together an integrated system of service delivery to offenders on supervision. Some of these attempts were informal and some were formally supported through the development of day-reporting centers or community justice centers. These were conceptualized and later implemented as one-stop shops for supervision, assessment, support, employment resources, basic education, treatment, and other services such as child care or domestic violence counseling. CCOs and service providers appeared to embrace the idea of colocating and working together to address the risk and needs of offenders and believed it would be efficient and instrumental to achieving successful outcomes.

A collaborative approach to reentry appears obvious when one considers the challenges confronting offenders attempting to get help through the traditional processes of each independent system. When speaking of the need for coordinated and colocated services, one CCO depicted the complexity of working with each bureaucracy and the time it demanded, stripping offenders of their motivation for change, whether it was sustaining employment or getting substance abuse treatment.

> Okay, I'll do an intake and the guy's way behind on child support, and before he went to jail, he was making 15 bucks an hour. Now, he lost that job, and there aren't many $15-an-hour jobs in Spokane, so now he's making $6. Well, child support is still set at that $15 range, and so the guy's getting garnished for 50% of his wages. So, I've got to send the guy over to... talk to a support enforcement officer to try to get his child support lowered so he can afford to live. Well, maybe he makes it over there, maybe he doesn't, and he's so pissed off about his garnishment that he quits his job. Now he's not employed, they're not getting anything, and I've got a guy that's unemployed that's going to go out and burglarize somebody's house because he's got to live. Substance abuse treatment is the same way. By the time a guy goes from here, goes to DSHS to get... qualified, if he is... that takes a few weeks to figure out whether he's eligible. Then he has to go to the health department for an eval, which is another couple of weeks down the road, and then, they may or

may not have immediate openings in an intensive outpatient pro-gram,...or he's definitely going to have to wait a few weeks before he can get into treatment. So, we've got a guy who's losing. Maybe he is motivated to go to treatment at the moment, but where's the motivation 6 months or 6 or 8 weeks down the road when he's just dealing with bureaucracy after bureaucracy after bureaucracy. That's the thing. That's the hassle. (CCO 103)

Coordinated responses to reentry attempt to simplify the process in order to reduce the likelihood of losing offenders along the way. As another CCO put it, explaining why day-reporting centers are needed,

The day-reporting unit is to bring those providers into one location so you're not sending your offender out to 17 different places....What hap-pens is you tire these folks out and say, "Well you need to go here, then you need to go here, then you need to go here, then you need to go here, then you come back and see me." It's overwhelming, especially if they just spent 8 years in prison. Society changes a lot in 8 years, and they get out and they're overwhelmed, and it becomes easier for them to go back to prison than it does to try [to] stay out. (CCO 206)

Many of the implementation barriers discovered in other research, such as insufficient staff, inadequate funding, poor interagency communi-cation, and turf battles were also identified as challenges by CCOs (see Lattimore et al., 2005). For example, one CCO observed after working across systems with various representatives to establish a day-reporting center,

Yes. But when it comes down to the social service agencies part of things, everybody is real territorial, everybody's overworked, everybody doesn't have enough money in their budget kind of thing....[lists agen-cies involved: job resource services, employment security, support enforcement, CPS, mental health, substance abuse providers]. Nobody, none of those other agencies—everybody said, "Oh yeah, great idea! We need to do this, we need to do this! But, no, we can't give you bodies. Give us some money and we'll put bodies in your shop." So, that was real frustrating. (CCO ---)

CCOs differed on the level of partnerships needed to improve inter-agency collaboration. For instance, the CCO just quoted suggests that interagency collaborations that colocate experts across systems should be formed by administrators who have the power to provide resources and direct or assign staff to the collaborative effort.

> Yeah, it needs to continue to be pursued, but again, it's territorial stuff and it's budget stuff. [The secretary of the DOC] and whoever the director is at DSHS are the ones that need to say, "No, no, no. I don't care if you are the regional administrator of CPS, I'm the big cheese. You are going to put a guy, or woman, or whatever, you are going to put somebody at this day-reporting center." Because with all these agencies, we all have mutual friends, but nobody wants to work together. (CCO ---)

Another CCO when discussing problems between the sheriff's department and the DOC's use of the county jail indicated that the working relationships at the street level, or with the "grunts," are just fine, but there is need for more consistent communication and collaboration at the administrative level.

> I am not 100% sure, . . . I don't know if it was our administration really trying to work with him [the sheriff]. I think our administration, from what I can tell, here in Spokane, needs to work closer, with the prosecutors, the public defenders, and both our police departments. The grunts are working pretty good with them, but our administration needs to develop a regular meeting with them constantly, so things flow a little easier. (CCO ---)

Other CCOs tended to believe the line-level working relationships were what mattered, regardless of whether administrators attempted to formalize the partnership. For example,

> I think there are unwritten partnerships. I don't know that there's anything official. But you're dealing with all these different agencies and people on a regular basis. I think the network is tight enough that whether there's anything official or not, you can't do your job without these other people being involved. And I think it's reciprocal. They need us, we need them, so everyone tries to work together. (CCO 230)

> I don't view the agency as one big cell. When I find a person in an agency that I work well with, talking on the phone, or I meet them for lunch, or a lot of times if I meet them and we're talking, "Yeah, let's be friends. . . ." Keep their card in the old rolodex and I deal with that one person in that one agency and we make those kinds of contacts and it seems to work really good. That way you are not dealing with an agency, you are dealing with a person. I prefer to deal with it that way. (CCO 234)

Given that CCOs tend to work across systems whether through informal cooperatives between individuals, midlevel coordinated activities at the agency, or a formal collaborative between systems, it is important to consider how those participating in partnerships may be supported and formally recognized as boundary spanners who implement strategies central to achieving the shared goals of agencies within criminal justice and across systems. To acknowledge the work of CCOs and to enhance their role as street-level boundary spanners also means considering the CCO as embedded in a network of people, agencies, and systems. Once the process has been simplified and interagency collaborations sustained over time, individual effectiveness must be considered for those engaged in the partnership. As one CCO puts it, when working to span boundaries and connect offenders to other services, it is not just the offender that needs to be tracked throughout the process

> . . . it's a lot of people to keep track of, and I have to keep notes sometimes...because when you're dealing with one offender, even if you have like 50 people on your caseload, which is I think [is] the optimum number,...because with each offender comes a significant other, possibly an ex-girlfriend or boyfriend, dependents, parents, siblings, attorneys, treatment people, other probation officers, so it really multiplies. So now you're talking instead of 50 offenders you have 50 times 9, 450 people you're dealing with, right . . . ? So that's a lot of people, and then now we're going to add DSHS, and we're going to add whatever, the Guardians, we're going to add all these people, and personally I can't keep track of that many people. (CCO 201)

This CCO's observation complements Armstrong's (2012) contention that the implementation of evidence-based practices, and in this case within coordinated partnerships, places additional burdens on the span of control necessary to supervise offenders effectively. The implementation of EBP tends to increase the time needed to coordinate services and meet with the offender, family members, service providers, and funders (Armstrong, 2012; Skeem, Emke-Francis, & Louden, 2006). Therefore, reentry initiatives should pay as much attention to CCOs as they do offenders when integrating systems of control and care.

CCOs ARE STREET-LEVEL BOUNDARY SPANNERS

A review of the many partnerships developed by CCOs shows CCOs regularly cooperate, coordinate, and, although less often, formally collaborate with other criminal justice agencies, social services, public health agencies, and other community stakeholders. The experiences of CCOs clearly illustrate how important the development of professional relationships across multiple boundaries is to serving the needs of offenders, helping to manage risk, and enhancing the goals of public safety and healthy communities. Professionals from various agencies, both law enforcement and social services, clearly share their coercive power with CCOs to manage risk and provide care. They appear to share information, resources, and expertise to increase their social capital to effect change.

These professional relationships exist because many CCOs are effective boundary spanners. They share many of the core values of other professionals who work with the same clients. They build professional relationships across boundaries to better serve offenders and achieve shared institutional goals. CCOs develop personal relationships across boundaries that result in a common understanding of one another's roles, increased communication, and the exchange of information. They actively translate interdisciplinary expertise from other fields into practical applications within their own. They are able to point out service gaps and work with individuals across agencies to remove barriers, create greater efficiency, and smooth the transition of offenders through multiple systems. Therefore, CCOs are street-level boundary spanners who, with or without support from their respective agencies, create professional pathways for offenders and enable them to receive the services crucial to their successful reintegration.

Through their boundary-spanning activities, CCOs identified issues that tend to sabotage successful collaboration. They expressed concerns about mission distortion by becoming too law enforcement oriented or too social work oriented. They identified the inefficiencies created when systems do not share data and the resulting duplication of services or the unintentional sabotage of the work of others striving to achieve the same goals through different strategies. CCOs saw the potential of great collaborative efforts collapse due to a failure to share resources, restricted budgets, and staff overwhelmed by excessive workloads across all systems.

In spite of these challenges, CCOs quickly identified practical solutions achievable if given priority by system-level administrators. First, reduce caseloads and workloads to support proactive supervision and services versus reactive crisis-driven responses. Professionals across systems appear to acknowledge the need to work together, but finding the time to move past their immediate responsibility within their own agencies to engage the needs of others poses serious challenges. Second, share information across systems so that each professional can see the entirety of what is being provided to an offender. It really is ridiculous that CCOs do not readily know what services are being provided by other agencies and whether the offender is in jail, being supervised by another jurisdiction, or participating in treatment assigned by another agency. Although it is important to keep some information confidential, most data across agencies are benign but crucial to understanding and planning effective case management for offenders across systems. Third, develop interagency agreements at the administrative level that empower midlevel managers and line staff to share resources, information, and professional relationships sustained beyond the transition of the staff that created them.

CCOs, in their everyday work, attempt to make the space for offenders' success. For the most part, they are supportive of and desire coordinated and collaborative relationships with professionals working in other systems. Even when they express frustration, it tends to be related to inaccessibility and a lack of collaboration and not because those systems are considered unnecessary or ineffective. Therefore, community corrections should be central to the creation of seamless systems of care and implementing strategies that enhance continuity in services to achieve safer communities.

NOTES

1. Lehman, 2001, p. 45
2. SRA (Sentencing Reform Act); OAA (Offender Accountability Act); DSHS (Department of Social and Health Services); CPS (Child Protective Services)

WORKS CITED

Alarid, L. F., Sims, B. A., & Ruiz, J. (2011). Juvenile probation and police partnerships as loosely coupled systems: A qualitative analysis. *Youth Violence and Juvenile Justice, 9*(1), 79–95.

Armstrong, G. S. (2012). Factors to consider for optimal span of control in community supervision evidence-based practice environments. *Criminal Justice Policy Review, 23*(4), 427–446.

Bond, B. J., & Gittell, J. H. (2010). Cross-agency coordination of offender reentry: Testing collaboration outcomes. *Journal of Criminal Justice, 38,* 118–129.

Castellano, U. (2011). Courting compliance: Case managers as "double agents" in the mental health court. *Law & Social Inquiry, 36*(2), 484–514.

Clear, T. R. (2007). *Imprisoning communities: How mass incarceration makes disadvantaged neighborhoods worse.* New York: Oxford University Press.

Comfort, M. (2007). Punishment beyond the legal offender. *Annual Review of Law and Social Science, 3*, 271–296.

Drapela, L. A., & Lutze, F. E. (2009). Innovation in community corrections and probabtion officers' fears of being sued: Implementing neighborhood-based supervision in Spokane, Washington. *Journal of Contemporary Criminal Justice, 25*(1), 364–383.

Duwe, G. (2012). Evaluating the Minnesota Comprehensive Offender Reentry Plan (MCORP): Results from a randomized experiment. *Justice Quarterly, 29*(3), 347–383.

Eisenstein, J., & Jacob, H. (1991). *Felony justice: An organizational analysis of criminal courts.* New York: University Press of America.

Fletcher, B. W., Lehman, W. E., Wexler, H. K., Melnick, G., Taxman, F. S., & Young, D. W. (2009). Measuring the collaboration and integration activities in criminal justice and substance abuse treatment agencies. *Drug and Alcohol Dependence, 103S*, S54–S64.

Hamilton, Z. K. (2011). Adapting to bad news: Lessons from the Harlem Parole Reentry Court. *Journal of Offender Rehabilitation, 50*, 385–410.

Hamilton, Z. K., & Campbell, C. (in press). A dark figure in corrections: Failure by way of participation. *Criminal Justice and Behavior.*

Henderson, M. L., & Hanley, D. (2006). Planning for quality: A strategy for reentry initiatives. *Western Criminology Review, 7*(2), 62–78.

Janetta, J., & Lachman, P. (2011). *Promoting partnerships between police and community supervision agencies: How coordination can reduce crime and increase public safety.* Community Oriented Police Services (COPS) Office. Washington, DC: U.S. Department of Justice.

Justice Center: The Council for State Governments. (n.d.). *The National Reentry Resource Center.* Retrieved April 6, 2013, from www.nationalreentry resourcecenter.org/reentry-council

Kim, B., Gerber, J., & Beto, D. R. (2010). Listening to law enforcement officers: The promises and problems of police-adult probation partnerships. *Journal of Criminal Justice, 38*, 625–632.

Lattimore, P. K., Visher, C. A., Winterfield, L., Lindquist, C., & Brumbaugh, S. (2005). Implementation of prisoner reentry programs: Findings from the Serious and Violent Offender Reentry Initiative multi-site evaluation. *Justice Research and Policy, 7*(2), 87–109.

Lehman, J. D. (2001). Reinventing community corrections in Washington State. *Corrections Management Quarterly, 5*(3), 41–45.

Lutze, F. E., & Symons, M. L. (2003). The evolution of domestic violence policy through masculine institutions: From discipline to protection to collaborative empowerment. *Criminology and Public Policy, 2*(2), 319–328.

Lutze, F. E., & van Wormer, J. P. (2007). The nexus between drug and alcohol treatment program integrity and drug court effectiveness: Policy recommendations for pursuing success. *Criminal Justice Policy Review, 18*(3), 226–245.

Lutze, F. E., & van Wormer, J. P. (2008). *Drug court's reliance on interagency collaboration to affect system and offender level change.* A poster presented at the Washington State University Showcase, Pullman, WA, and at the Annual Meetings of the Academy of Criminal Justice Sciences, Baltimore, MD.

Matz, A. K., Wicklund, C., Douglas, J., & May, B. (2012). *Justice-health collaboration: Improving information exchange between corrections and health/human services organizations.* Sacramento, CA: SEARCH Group.

Murphy, D., & Lutze, F. (2009). Police-probation partnerships: Professional identity and the sharing of coercive power. *Journal of Criminal Justice, 37,* 65–76.

Murphy, D., & Worrall, J. L. (2007). The threat of mission distortion in police-probation partnerships. *Policing: An International Journal of Police Strategies and Management, 30*(1), 132–149.

Nissen, L. B. (2010). Boundary spanners revisited: A qualitative inquiry into cross-system reform through the experience of youth service professionals. *Qualitative Social Work, 9*(3), 365–384.

Petersilia, J. (2003). *When prisoners come home: Parole and prisoner reentry.* New York: Oxford University Press.

Pettus, C. A., & Severson, M. (2006). Paving the way for effective reentry practice—The critical role and function of boundary spanner. *The Prison Journal, 86*(2), 206–229.

Roman, C. G., & Travis, J. (2006). Where will I sleep tomorrow? Housing, homelessness, and the returning prisoner. *Housing Policy Debate, 17*(2), 389–418.

Taxman, F. S., Shepardson, E. S., & Byrne, J. M. (2004). *Tools of the trade: A guide to incorporating science into practice.* Washington, DC: National Institute of Corrections.

Skeem, J. L., Emke-Francis, P., & Louden, J. E. (2006). Probation, mental health, and mandated treatment: A national survey. *Criminal Justice and Behavior, 33*(2), 158–184.

Steadman, H. J. (1992). Boundary spanners: A key component for the effective interactions of the justice and mental health systems. *Law and Human Behavior, 16*(1), 75–87.

Taxman, F. S., & Bouffard, J. A. (2000). The importance of systems in improving offender outcomes: New frontiers in treatment integrity. *Justice Research and Policy, 2*(2), 37–58.

Taxman, F. S., Young, D., Byrne, J. M., Holsinger, A., & Anspach, D. (2001). *From prison safety to public safety: Innovations in offender reentry.* Bureau of Governmental Research. College Park: University of Maryland.

Travis, J., Davis, R., & Lawrence, S. (2012). *Exploring the role of the police in prisoner reentry, New Perspectives in Policing Bulletin.* National Institute of Justice. Washington, DC: U.S. Department of Justice.

van Wormer, J. (2010). *The operational dynamics of drug court.* Washington State University, Department of Criminal Justice and Criminology. Pullman: Unpublished dissertation.

Walter, U. M., & Petr, C. G. (2000). A template for family-centered interagency collaboration. *Families in Society, 81*(5), 494–503.

Winterfield, L., Lattimore, P. K., Seffey, D. M., Brumbaugh, S., & Lindquist, C. (2006). The Serious and Violent Reentry Initiative: Measuring the effects on service delivery. *Western Criminology Review, 7*(2), 3–19.

Wolf, R. W. (2011). *Reentry courts looking ahead: A conversation about strategies for offender reintegration.* Center for Court Innovation. Washington, DC: Bureau of Justice Assistance.

Wolff, N., Bjerklie, J. R., & Maschi, T. (2005). Reentry planning for mentally disordered inmates: A social investment perspective. *Journal of Offender Rehabilitation, 42*(2), 21–42.

SEVEN

INVESTING IN COMMUNITY CORRECTIONS OFFICERS AS STREET-LEVEL BOUNDARY SPANNERS

"We can live in fear and make bad policy based on fear or we can have some backbone and make policy based on what really helps our communities." (Patricia L. Caruso, Director, Michigan DOC)[1]

As we engage in a new era of evidence-based practice and collaboration, defining CCOs as street-level boundary spanners provides a framework to guide policymakers toward constructing realistic policies and practices relevant to the future success of community corrections. Without considering the context in which CCOs work and offenders live, it is easy to oversimplify the professional role of CCOs as either law enforcement or social work, focused only on offender-centered interventions and working in isolation from other agencies and systems. When one instead recognizes the complex environment in which CCOs function, it becomes obvious that their role and expertise are central to leading successful reentry initiatives. Of all the criminal justice professionals, CCOs are best positioned to span the boundaries within and between systems in order to address both the risks and needs of offenders to enhance public safety.

Establishing what works in corrections to reduce recidivism and change offenders' behavior is instrumental to understanding the important role of CCOs. The evidence-based practices borne out of theory and research and implemented over the last 25 years illustrate that to effectively intervene with offenders, CCOs must have multiple skills and the ability to work across systems. We now know that effective supervision strategies involve fluid approaches that combine structure, accountability, support, and treatment as needed. Effective treatment must have integrity, address the core issues related to criminogenic behaviors, and include both cognitive and behavioral interventions. The combination of effective supervision strategies with evidence-based treatment interventions has demonstrated that CCOs need the expertise to know when and how to use a combination of coercion, support, and treatment to garner positive responses from offenders and gain the greatest benefit for the community.

The discovery that reductions in recidivism are significantly related to addressing high risk and need should help the field of corrections to become less polarized between advocating punishment or rehabilitation. The importance of addressing offenders' needs in order to reduce risk and enhance public safety helps to inform policymakers that the criminal justice system alone cannot be solely responsible for achieving public safety or long-term reintegration. Although the criminal justice system has tremendous capacity to manage offender risk through formal control mechanisms, it is limited in its ability to provide extensive support to meet the complex needs of offenders and is challenged in finding ways to help strengthen communities to provide informal social controls important to preventing crime and reducing recidivism. A lesson learned from the implementation of evidence-based practices is that to achieve the goals of the criminal justice system, it is necessary to span the boundaries between prisons, law enforcement, social services, public health, education, labor, and the community to achieve successful outcomes. Among all of the professions, however, only community corrections has the power to simultaneously intervene in high-risk criminal behavior and organize the resources necessary to address the needs of offenders.

CCOs are in a strong position to orchestrate the multisystem responses necessary to deal with the entirety of offenders' lives and the risks they pose to the community upon reentry. Recent initiatives responsible for implementing coordinated responses to reentry have also provided a basis to better understand the necessity of defining the role of CCOs as boundary spanners (Lattimore, Visher, Winterfield, Lindquist, & Brumbaugh, 2005). The challenges confronting offenders within the first 90 days of reentry can be overwhelming and require an advocate who can share knowledge and communicate on behalf of offenders and the criminal justice system what needs to be accomplished across agencies and systems. This requires expertise to design individualized case management plans, know what interventions work, interface with experts across systems, and have the ability to navigate complex bureaucracies to obtain resources and services necessary to sustain offenders over time.

Achieving successful outcomes in community corrections is not some abstract idea but is clearly dependent on the professional responsibility of CCOs. How one envisions community corrections and the role of CCOs within it must be expanded and capitalized on to fully exploit the potential of community supervision to enhance public safety through the successful reintegration of offenders. First, it requires an acknowledgment by policymakers that community corrections is more than a service tacked on to the end of the criminal justice system as "something" less than prison and nothing more than an extension of law enforcement in the community. Community corrections and CCOs are uniquely positioned to achieve successful outcomes for the criminal justice system. Second, it requires leaders to structure agencies and institutions to accommodate and support the power of CCOs to effect change by professionally engaging multiple systems of care. Without preparing systems for change, community corrections will continue with "business as usual" and waste the potential of one of the most powerful resources in criminal justice and social services. Third, it must be acknowledged that community corrections is as much about place as it is about people. The power of communities, encompassing all of their strengths and weaknesses, must be emphasized and directly engaged in the work of community corrections to achieve stable outcomes over time. Finally, a failure to invest in community corrections is to directly sabotage the work of CCOs and undermine all of the resources invested in offenders throughout the criminal justice process, whether that is punishment, support, or treatment. Much of the billions of dollars spent on the criminal justice system each year and in prisons specifically is wasted by not providing a high-quality continuum of care from prison to the community that addresses not just the risks and needs of offenders but the professional needs and expertise of CCOs.

INVESTING IN STREET-LEVEL BOUNDARY SPANNERS: PROFESSIONAL RESPECT

Unfortunately, the shift to a more punitive crime control era brought with it a perception of community corrections as nothing more than a necessary evil to accommodate the overflow from prisons. Accompanying this shift was the idea that CCOs are merely "wannabe cops" whose primary role with offenders is to embrace a philosophy of "tag 'em and bag 'em" or "nail 'em and jail 'em" by returning them to prison. It is time to move away from the belief that prisons are the pinnacle of corrections, with community corrections viewed as secondary at best and irrelevant at worst. Although prisons are important institutions and can actively prepare inmates for reentry, offenders in their care are on "hold," where the certainty of their success after release is measured within a confined and safe environment separated from public scrutiny and experience. Once released to community supervision however, the investment made by the public in prisons and the offenders who pass through them is tested "live." Measures of success become real, with failure equating to new victims, harm to the community's well-being, and an ongoing cycle of destruction. Conversely, success means the establishment of prosocial relationships, stronger communities, and outcomes that carry forward benefits to everyone. Thus, it is short-sighted to ignore the importance of community supervision and its relevance to the success of prisons and the criminal justice system (Burke & Tonry, 2006; Matz, Wicklund, Douglas, & May, 2012; Paparozzi & DeMichele, 2008; Petersilia, 2003).

Only recently has it been recognized that community corrections manages a population over 2.5 times greater than the prison population on a significantly smaller budget, with fewer officers, and with a community's safety at stake (Matz et al., 2012). With the majority of resources and prestige directed toward prisons and law enforcement, it is no wonder that CCOs do not generally believe their work is respected by others within the system or the community. This lack of respect, and oftentimes ignorance, allows policymakers and sometimes even corrections leaders to ignore or minimize the correctional burden placed on community corrections without considering the consequences for CCOs, offenders, or the community (Burke & Tonry, 2006). Gaining respect and monetary investment in community corrections can only happen by providing policymakers with a clear vision inclusive of the utility community supervision serves in achieving positive offender outcomes and enhancing public safety (Burke & Tonry, 2006; Paparozzi & DeMichele, 2008). Providing a clear understanding about the utility of community corrections requires presenting CCOs' work in a manner that more accurately reflects what science indicates is effective and the reality of how CCOs engage offenders, other agencies, and the community in their work.

Recommendation: *Educate policymakers about the utility of community corrections and the work of CCOs to enhance public safety above and beyond prisons, law enforcement, and social work.*

CCOs and researchers have also identified systematic barriers to achieving success stemming from major public institutions working in isolation from one another. Administrative leadership from the major public institutions will be important if CCOs are going to be formally recognized and respected as effective boundary spanners. Leaders of state and federal institutions define and set the tone for what constitutes success and how systems may collaborate to provide essential services to achieve shared goals. CCOs across studies expressed frustration about the inability or unwillingness of institutions and agencies to share information, to share resources, to cross-train to achieve interdisciplinary expertise, and to identify how systems may support each other in addressing the needs of a shared service population. Continuing to act as if the criminal justice system has the sole responsibility for public safety is irrational. Understanding the complexity of offenders' needs makes it clear that their success or failure during reentry must be shared across systems.

Although the idea that public safety is the sole responsibility of the criminal justice system has led to incredible levels of investment in police, courts, and prisons, it has created an unrealistic expectation that coercion and control alone can solve individual- and community-level problems related to crime and violence. It is the responsibility of community corrections leaders to educate public officials and to define the vision, mission, and utility of community corrections, not just to the criminal justice system but also to the other systems intertwined with reentry to achieve improved public health and safety. State and local governments must recognize that reentry and public safety are a shared responsibility across systems and that public safety can be achieved through positive investments in support, treatment, and offender accountability (see Justice Center 2013; Justice Policy Institute, 2010).

Recommendation: *Require public investment in the creation and sustainability of intersystem collaborations to achieve desired and realistic outcomes for reentry and public safety.*

In further support of intersystem collaboration and the development of coordinated responses to reentry, it is clear that most CCOs are not solely law enforcers or social workers but instead are fluid combinations of both depending on the risk and needs of offenders and community conditions. To think otherwise unnecessarily narrows the scope of community supervision's potential to effect change. To conceptualize CCOs as an extension of police and nothing more than "get tough" punitive law enforcers deprives them of developing and using strategies to address the underlying causes of offenders' behavior, such as substance abuse, antisocial personalities, and skill deficits that inhibit success. Defining CCOs as nothing more than social workers deprives them of strategies that provide the structure and coercion necessary to respond to potentially harmful behaviors by offenders that place officers and the community in danger. The utility of community corrections and the work of CCOs is the combination of these roles to manage risks, address offender needs, and provide a continuum of care that transitions the gains made in prison to the community and organizes the support necessary from other agencies to achieve long-term success.

Although CCOs willingly cooperate and coordinate across agencies and systems, some challenges can only be solved at the highest levels of government and by planned interagency collaborations at the upper levels of administration. Highlighting the utility of CCOs' work as boundary-spanning agents of change capable of implementing EBP and leading coordinated responses to reentry gives the necessary rationale for state and federal policymakers to invest in community supervision in general and CCOs specifically.

> Recommendation: *Reframe the role of CCOs to reflect their relevance as boundary spanners capable of orchestrating the control, support, and treatment necessary to enhance the success of community-wide, coordinated reentry initiatives.*

The need to respect the power of community corrections to achieve positive outcomes through the coordination of reentry initiatives across systems is also relevant to managing how the criminal justice system responds to public concerns about crime. Community supervision is often hampered by laws and policies created by state legislatures or administrators far removed from understanding the work of CCOs, the challenges confronting offenders, or the communities affected (see Paparozzi & DeMichele, 2008). This lack of understanding is often evident in the belief that public safety can best be achieved by investing in the police and prisons and not more holistic approaches inclusive of the helping professions. Oversimplification has resulted in narrow responses to crime, especially in media-driven sensational cases, which nearly always result in laws and policies emphasizing harsher punishments and increased restrictions on behavior (Mele & Miller, 2005). Laws created in reaction to extreme and sensational events oftentimes conflict with evidence of what works in supervising and managing the vast majority of offenders. Although these events should not be ignored, they should be understood in the specific context in which they happen, with an effort to determine whether the failure was an outlier due to an individual offender's psychological and behavioral condition, an individual professional's error, or if it truly was the result of a more systemic failure of the agency or institutions involved.

Many of the policies developed out of sensational cases or a general hysteria about a particular type of crime may have tremendous popular support, and the emotionally charged climate that inspires political action to create new laws is understandable, but the results oftentimes generate additional problems contrary to what is known to work (Griffen & Stitt, 2010). Possibly the best community supervision examples are the civil penalties implemented in response to the crack cocaine epidemic and the war on drugs during the 1980s that banned drug offenders for life from accessing public housing, state-licensed professions, educational opportunities, and welfare support. Many of these penalties remain 30 years later, even though these types of support are essential to reducing recidivism, supporting long-term reintegration, and enhancing public safety (Justice Center, 2013; Justice Policy Institute, 2010; Petersilia, 2003). Reactionary policies also tend to result in outcomes that negatively affect poor and minority communities more than others (Clear, 2007; Petersilia, 2003). New methods need to be designed to inform policymakers how to respond to sensational cases in accordance with what works and is most likely to result in real change and enhanced public safety (Lutze, Johnson, Clear, Latessa, & Slate., 2012; Paparozzi & DeMichele, 2008).

Recommendation: *Review all potential legislation in relation to how it achieves its intended goals. Evaluate its potential to result in unintended consequences for vulnerable populations and determine how it enhances or fits within existing evidence-based practice.*

State-level leaders should set the tone to take full advantage of community corrections and then prepare systems to receive the innovations necessary to implement evidence-based practices that span boundaries between systems. Unless the mission, goals, and utility of community supervision are clearly communicated to policymakers, policymakers will continue to fill the void with ineffective and counterproductive public policy (Paparozzi & DeMichele, 2008). Without a clear vision, the convenience of requiring community corrections to do more with less will continue and innovation will be stifled. The record for implementing innovative new strategies within corrections has shown that the best ideas are often crushed under the weight of existing institutional practices and conditions slow to change (McCorkle & Crank, 1996; Rothman, 1980). The danger of promoting community corrections and CCOs as street-level boundary spanners capable of achieving significant change is that CCOs will be promoted as yet another panacea to achieve public safety, without the necessary support and investment to be effective. Once public- and system-level leaders are convinced of community corrections' potential and utility to achieve public safety, systems must be prepared to implement an evidence-based response to successful reentry.

PREPARING FOR INNOVATION: PRACTICAL
IMPLICATIONS OF SUPPORTING CCOs AS
BOUNDARY SPANNERS

The criminal justice system, especially corrections, has a habit of overlaying new approaches or strategies onto existing systems and unrealistically expecting different results. New approaches are borrowed from other jurisdictions without conducting preliminary evaluations to determine whether the innovation is compatible with existing systems and whether the new strategies will actually work to achieve the intended outcomes within the state's political, economic, or social context (Henderson & Hanley, 2006). Stacking new practices onto the old or embedding them into existing dysfunction merely sets the stage for policy manuals to grow thicker and more complicated, administrative tasks to supplant time spent with offenders, and time spent with offenders lacking the integrity necessary to make a difference. In addition, new strategies are often offender focused, giving consideration to how offenders' lives will be affected, without much consideration given to the professional needs of the CCOs responsible for implementing the new strategy or intervention. Within this context it should not be surprising that the effectiveness of innovative new approaches is seriously diminished by failing to adequately plan for implementation.

A failure of systems and agencies to plan for innovation oftentimes leaves CCOs in the awkward position of wanting to embrace new practices but being bound by existing structure and traditions that do not easily accommodate change. Listening to CCOs, one clearly hears an ongoing desire to reduce recidivism and enhance public safety embedded within the dilemma of having to choose between the administrative needs of the agency and meeting the needs of the offender. To meet the needs of offenders, CCOs often grapple with structural barriers systemic to community corrections, such as excessively large caseloads or workloads, time-consuming administrative tasks, a lack of sharing between systems to help inform decisions, an absence of resources necessary to manage both offenders' risk and needs, concerns about professional safety and security, and the ability to participate in decisions relevant to their work. These are clear indicators of how community corrections will need to improve and prepare to support CCOs as effective boundary spanners responsible for implementing innovative evidence-based practices.

In implementing new strategies and interventions, CCOs do not need to be convinced that the goals of community corrections—public safety and reintegration—are worthy and important to the well-being of all involved. In addition, most CCOs still believe rehabilitation is just as important as surveillance to improving the chances of offenders' success (Payne & DeMichele, 2011). What CCOs are skeptical about, however, is whether they will receive the political and organizational support necessary to achieve the goals of the organization and meet the expectations of the community. Capitalizing on the capacity of CCOs' work as street-level boundary spanners requires creating the space within and between systems for them to engage their work efficiently and effectively.

Recommendation: *Prepare systems, agencies, and CCOs for change before implementing a new strategy or evidence-based practice.*

Preparing systems for change requires leaders to clearly define the goals of community supervision, what equals success, and how success will be measured. The goal of "enhancing public safety" is rather broad and can be achieved in multiple ways within and across systems through a combination of offender accountability, support, and treatment. Yet achieving public safety is often translated into strategies that rely primarily on narrowly defined punitive approaches that can be easily tracked and used to defend the agency against external criticism (e.g., counting field contacts, office visits, urine analyses, sanctions) instead of the strategies staff use to achieve positive outcomes (e.g., EBP, quality contacts with offenders, support, treatment, incentives, sanctions, surveillance). The consequence of focusing on administrative tasks as the measure of success is that staff achievement is as easily based on offenders' failures (e.g., number of revocations, arrests, and readmissions to prison) as on offenders' success (e.g., successful termination of supervision, treatment completion, maintaining employment) (Burke & Tonry, 2006). This has had serious consequences for corrections and the community, resulting in increased and costly prison populations, destabilized communities and coerced mobility, and the failure to achieve long-term reintegration of offenders as prosocial, law-abiding members of society (Burke, Gelb, & Horowitz, 2007; Clear, 2007). This is not to say that revocation, arrest, and readmission to prison are unnecessary or do not achieve public safety when addressing dangerous and violent offenders. It instead reasons that when these methods are overrelied on without the option of alternative interventions, there is no incentive for staff to pursue strategies proven to be effective in achieving long-term success and reducing harm to offenders, their families, and the community (Burke et al., 2007).

Recognizing that the goal of enhancing public safety can be achieved through a broad array of strategies sets the tone for community supervision to prepare systems and agencies to accommodate innovation. It signals to staff that EBP, in multiple forms, has utility and that community corrections is not just about law enforcement or social work but about both in combination. All actors need to embrace community corrections as a means to achieve successful reentry through balanced approaches to supervision.

Recommendation: *Develop a clear mission and set of goals to guide community corrections. Communicate that the successful completion of supervision is the ultimate goal in achieving public safety. Provide an array of evidence-based strategies and practices to achieve the stated mission and goals.*

Although clarifying goals and expanding the philosophy of community corrections as inclusive of a fluid approach to practicing supervision is important, several practical barriers need to be removed in order to achieve successful implementation. When preparing community corrections for CCOs to act as boundary spanners, agencies need the appropriate number of expert and experienced staff, the technology to support their work, evidence-based programs to support offenders, and interagency agreements and protocols to support collaboration. Midlevel managers and CCOs also need to be included in the planning process and consideration given to their observations regarding practical applications and processes relevant to informing best practices. CCOs' practical experience and professional expertise are relevant to informing decisions about policies that directly affect their work, not to obstruct change but to inform its practical implementation and establish its utility to achieve intended goals.

New strategies and programs will only be effective if founded on the expertise of qualified staff that can assure program integrity. Before implementation of innovative strategies, staff members need to be selected that have the qualifications and skills essential to implementing and sustaining the new intervention. Relying on existing staff may not be enough to implement new strategies in an era of coordinating supervision and services founded on evidence-based practice. Interagency collaboration requires CCOs with a fluid supervision approach who have the skills necessary to be effective boundary spanners willing to work across disciplines to create innovative solutions mutually beneficial to all. This may require hiring CCOs from a variety of disciplines with the expertise to supervise offenders who pose unique risks (e.g., gang members, sex offenders) or have specialized needs (e.g., histories of trauma, mental illness, substance abuse). CCOs with the expertise to understand and implement EBPs and the ability to engage other experts across systems are essential to achieving successful outcomes.

A significant barrier to the implementation of innovative approaches to community corrections is the burden of administrative tasks requiring extensive documentation to justify and track everything CCOs do to monitor, support, and treat offenders. Aside from providing a chronological record of case management, many administrative tasks and data entry requirements are simply irrelevant. Administrators and managers need to streamline data collection by identifying which data have utility in supporting administrative needs and are directly relevant to the work of CCOs. Too often data are collected only to disappear within the administrative ranks, without reemerging to inform the daily practices and needs of CCOs to assist with supervision decisions. If data collection does not have utility, then it becomes just another wasted task that takes time away from quality supervision. Data must be analyzed and the results shared through a feedback loop that informs administrators, midlevel managers, and CCOs that the process and interventions are working to achieve outcomes.

To implement EBP, information needs to be exchanged between systems. It is discouraging that so far into the technological and information age, state-level systems and agencies within the same jurisdiction cannot integrate data and share information about mutual clients. Common excuses justifying the lack of information sharing across systems are technological incompatibility of data management systems, professional distrust of other agencies, and the protection of sensitive data and professional turf (Matz et al., 2012). Frequently cost is blamed for the incompatibility of management information systems without any consideration given to the expenses associated with the duplication of services or interagency sabotage due to one system not knowing about the work of another. The development of interagency agreements will go a long way to increase trust by reducing barriers to sharing generally benign information and to building protocols to guide how and when to share sensitive data relevant to informing a unified response across systems to meet offender needs. Sharing data across systems should result in improvement in the continuum of care, physical and behavioral health outcomes, public safety, the implementation of EBP, cost reductions, and policy and practices related to what works (Matz et al., 2012).

A lack of trust between professionals also hampers the potential to develop effective cross-system relationships. Distrust often emerges out of a lack of familiarity, knowledge, and understanding about what others do as professionals and how their expertise may enhance, not replace, that of another. Intersystem and interagency agreements do not mean professionals lose their autonomy or professional identity. Professionals in each system serve a significant population that does not overlap with other systems, and these populations need to remain independent. For instance, not all offenders need the support of social services or public health agencies, just as a large proportion of the social services population is not accountable to criminal justice agencies. At times, professionals may need to rely on the expertise of another system regarding how offenders are treated. At other times, however, professionals may need to act according to, and within, the powers of their own systems (see Matz et al., 2012; Murphy & Lutze, 2009). There will be occasions when a CCO may want an offender to remain in treatment, but the treatment provider cannot justify retaining the offender because of bad behavior and a failure to comply with treatment protocols. Similarly, CCOs may not be able to accommodate police by taking a purely law enforcement approach because they must work with offenders over time in multiple capacities and in different contexts than the police. Therefore, collaborations must be based on professional equality and not the power of one distorting the mission of the other (see Murphy & Lutze, 2009).

CCOs responsible for implementing EBP need a network of providers already in place in order to be effective boundary spanners. Offenders often need safe and affordable housing, education, employment, and providers capable of offering specialized treatment to meet their needs. Immediate access to support and treatment is crucial to success. Long delays in accessing services or treatment can mean almost certain failure, especially for those who are homeless or have mental health or substance abuse problems. When programs are not available in the community, community corrections professionals will have to develop services within community corrections or work with local providers to develop additional resources to meet the needs of offenders. Community corrections leaders need to be assured that the treatment providers they and offenders rely on implement EBT and are capable of achieving positive outcomes with integrity. Community corrections agencies must use their power to contract only with providers implementing rigorous, evidence-based treatment (see Lutze & van Wormer, 2007).

Finally, an important part of preparing systems for change is providing CCOs the opportunity to participate in the creation and implementation of innovative programs. CCOs have valuable insight about what is working, what is not, and how systems may be improved to smooth the implementation of new supervision strategies. CCOs empowered to inform the decisions influencing their work have a greater likelihood of remaining engaged, experiencing increased job satisfaction, feeling less stress, and remaining with the profession longer. The benefit of a more positive work environment is to retain the valuable expertise that comes with experience and continuity in the implementation of EBP over time.

Recommendation: *Structure agencies to support CCOs as boundary spanners by developing a network of reliable EBT providers, reducing administrative tasks, enhancing information sharing, and implementing participatory management.*

Preparing systems for change and implementing evidence-based practice often means changing how administrators, managers, and frontline staff are evaluated. Distinguishing CCOs as street-level boundary spanners who use multiple resources and approaches to effect offender change requires a shift from exclusively counting whether specific tasks have been completed to valuing a broad array of strategies and their potential to achieve positive outcomes. It is no longer acceptable to ignore successful outcomes of supervision as a coincidence or as merely representing an invisible absence of failure. Achieving termination from supervision based on positive outcomes, such as treatment completion, sustaining employment, reintegration with family, and participation in prosocial activities deserves recognition by being included in performance evaluations. The successful completion of supervision should be prominent and failure questioned against a backdrop of whether the agency and CCOs are effectively implementing evidence-based practices and whether the offender is actively engaged in the process of change. Balance must be achieved within evaluations to determine how well CCOs, professional collaborators, and offenders are working toward achieving successful outcomes.

Recommendation: *Implement a process for professional evaluation that includes measures emphasizing the prosocial completion of supervision. Expand measures of success to include accomplishments that lead to reductions in recidivism, revocations, and readmissions to prison.*

Preparing systems for change also has to take into account the concerns expressed by CCOs about sensational cases and fears of being held professionally liable for an offender's actions. Systems need to be prepared to defend the implementation of evidence-based practice, not as a perfect science or solution but as the best opportunity to reduce recidivism and increase community safety. Realistic acknowledgment must be given to the fact that when working with high-risk and -need offenders, there is an inherent risk of catastrophic failure that cannot be completely avoided whether relying on control or treatment. Risk can only be minimized, not completely eliminated.

An organizational foundation has to be built that gives EBP standing equal to or better than coercion and control strategies alone.

Until CCOs are confident in the integrity and utility of EBP, and especially the value of risk- and need-assessment tools to inform their practice in meaningful ways, fear of liability will drive decision making toward a narrow set of interventions that feel politically and professionally safe, such as surveillance, sanctions, revocation, and arrest. Although these strategies when used alone are known to be less effective than when balanced with EBP, punitive interventions are seen as less likely to be legally questioned than the use of treatment strategies where the results are not immediate and viewed as less tangible and therefore less defensible. Reducing the threat of liability is important because it is not realistic to think CCOs or the agencies they work for will take the risk associated with treating substance abuse, mental illness, and antisocial personalities if they believe they will be held responsible for every potential tragic event.

Recommendation: *Actively manage risk through evidence-based practice and increase protections against professional liability.*

A major stressor and contributor to fears of being sued is related to the responsibility of managing large caseloads. Preparing systems for innovations in corrections and the implementation of EBP requires bringing caseloads to a manageable size. Workload measures have traditionally focused on the number of high-risk offenders supervised on a given caseload and have less often been related to offenders' need. Offender-centered supervision strategies only account for the time necessary to track the offender within the criminal justice system and not necessarily the time needed as a boundary spanner to develop relationships with offenders, offenders' families, treatment providers, support services, and a multitude of key community stakeholders.

Excessive caseloads stifle innovation and prevent the possibility of meaningful professional relationships with offenders that inform whether a sanction, support, or treatment is most likely to create a positive way forward. Having and sustaining the expertise to implement evidence-based supervision and the ability to know offenders well enough to connect them to reliable forms of evidence-based treatment is time consuming. CCOs need time to learn new skills through continuing education; become familiar with new practices; and implement EBP through office visits, field contacts, and collaborating with others involved in an offender's life. Evidence-based supervision practices and treatment require ongoing interaction with everyone involved in the offender's process of change. This broadens supervision to be proactive and prevention oriented in managing offenders' risk and need and not solely process and reaction oriented in response to crises. Large caseloads and their associated administrative tasks decrease CCOs' ability to become familiar with offenders or with key community stakeholders critical to diminishing risk and preventing crises.

> Recommendation: *Reduce caseloads and craft workload measures inclusive of boundary-spanning activities and the time demands inherent in evidence-based practice.*

Preparing systems for change is essential to the successful implementation of programs with the structural and practical integrity to achieve positive outcomes. Although many CCOs already participate in boundary-spanning activities, formalizing their role means providing them with the resources necessary to assure their success. Creating professional space for CCOs to fully engage offenders, other agencies, and the community as boundary spanners means reconsidering not just how CCOs and offenders interact with systems but also how they interact with, and function within, the community.

INVESTING IN STREET-LEVEL BOUNDARY SPANNERS: ACHIEVING CORRECTIONS OF PLACE

The overall health of communities is crucial to the success of community corrections. Disadvantaged communities and concentrated incarceration pose serious challenges to community supervision and the potential of CCOs to guide offenders toward long-term reintegration. In communities where social capital and collective efficacy are weak, the prospects for social support and informal social control to guide offenders toward legitimate opportunities are extremely limited (Clear, 1996, 2005, 2007). Without help from the community, the likelihood of CCOs and offenders achieving success is dismal. These challenges posed by community conditions justify the importance of reframing the identity of community corrections to reflect the significance of both *community* and *corrections*. It is only as boundary spanners that CCOs can engage offenders as integrated *members* of society and not as isolated *individuals* who are the sole responsibility of corrections. Identifying the power of CCOs to work with offenders and the community provides a vision for how to create opportunities by investing in, and protecting the integrity of, all communities to support reentry initiatives.

Poverty, and the lack of social capital and collective efficacy to escape it, leaves many communities struggling to provide the most basic of human needs, such as adequate nutrition, safe housing, routine health care, functional literacy, and personal safety at home and in public (Rank, 2004). The failure to acquire the basics is often presented as a result of individual shortcomings instead of structural inequality that traps entire families and communities in poverty. Abandoning entire communities to poverty and violence is a human rights violation, and CCOs are unrealistically expected to reintegrate offenders into communities that often provide less than that afforded to offenders in prison, such as stable housing, adequate nutrition, health care, treatment, and education (Lutze et al., 2012).

The extreme disadvantage experienced by many communities rarely seems to pose the ethical dilemma it should when discussing the criminal justice system except when it is argued that prisoners should not receive more than our poorest citizens, and therefore we should make prisons harsher places to live instead of making our communities better places to live. Yet CCOs have to reintegrate offenders into communities experiencing "concentrated" disadvantage on a daily basis. There is no legitimate way for CCOs to maintain integrity in the "corrections" side of their work when policymakers fail to invest in the "community" side. Although these conditions are beyond the scope of what community corrections alone can solve, it is possible for community corrections to partner with other institutions to invest in high-risk, disadvantaged communities to build the social, political, and economic capital necessary to enhance public safety and stop recycling poor people through the criminal justice system, especially prisons, and back into poor communities.

> Recommendation: *Recognize reentry as a human rights issue within disadvantaged communities. Empower community corrections to partner with community stakeholders to address the challenges posed by offender reentry and to assist in sustaining or building social capital and collective efficacy.*

Most research shows that healthy and safe communities contain essential public services, good jobs, affordable and safe housing, access to health care, good public schools, and strong civic and social organizations—mostly things the criminal justice system cannot provide but can support. CCOs clearly understand the role the criminal justice system can play in achieving healthy communities. Effectively dealing with crime and disorder gives formal and informal social systems an opportunity to thrive. CCOs also recognized that the criminal justice system alone cannot fully create the conditions necessary to prevent and fully respond to all the social ills that high-crime communities experience, but they did identify the need for strong local governments, and the provision of social services, public health, education, justice, and civic organizations to enhance public safety. Importantly, when given the opportunity, CCOs expressed a willingness to span boundaries to assist in organizing more accessible public services, garner the support of community- and faith-based organizations, engage employers and landlords to provide opportunities to offenders, and generally work to integrate offenders into the community and help to empower community members to invest in their neighborhoods and in offenders.

It is only possible to capture the power of the community to support offender change if CCOs know the neighborhoods in which their offenders live (Drapela & Lutze, 2009; Murphy & Lutze, 2009; Petersilia, 2003). When CCOs' time is dominated by completing administrative tasks, interpreting policy, and managing excessive caseloads, little time is left to get to know the primary stakeholders in the community, making contact with citizens who engage the offenders on their caseloads, or attend public forums to educate the community on the importance of a shared partnership to collaboratively help manage the risk and needs of offenders. When CCOs primarily partner with other criminal justice professionals such as the police, they are more likely to engage the community only when offenders on their caseloads are experiencing crisis, resulting in responses skewed toward removing offenders and returning them to prison (see Drapela & Lutze, 2009; Murphy & Lutze, 2009). Expanding CCOs' partnerships to include community stakeholders enhances their ability to engage the community around positive responses to offenders that allows CCOs a more realistic vision of how offenders may be controlled and supported within the community versus through their removal (Petersilia, 2003). When CCOs have a greater understanding of the community's strengths as well as its weaknesses, it strengthens relationships with the community and prioritizes prevention and proactive problem solving.

Recommendation: *Enhance formal community corrections partnerships with community organizations and stakeholders, social services, and police that focus on problem-solving issues important to supporting the development of healthy communities characterized by achieving public safety.*

Investing in communities can at times appear overwhelming and present an impossible challenge to community corrections or other social services. Some scholars and policymakers have begun to argue that the social and economic health of the community could be significantly enhanced and justice outcomes improved if the money saved by reducing mass incarceration and closing prisons was reinvested in the communities most affected by concentrated disadvantage (see Clear, 2007, 2011). Through "justice reinvestment" the devastating effects of poverty could be eased and the social, political, and economic capital built could empower communities to absorb offenders, provide the opportunity necessary to achieve long-term reintegration, and stop the devastating trajectory, especially for young men, from poverty to prison (Clear, 2007, 2011).

Public money to address social problems is often locked within state-level bureaucracies, such as prisons or human service agencies, with the bulk of the money spent on employees and programs located outside of the communities most in need (Clear, 2011). What money does siphon down to those living in disadvantaged neighborhoods also tends to be spent outside of the local community. For example, citizens often pay rent to absentee landlords and purchase other essential services from businesses located outside of the community, such as grocery stores, shopping malls, and health care providers. Legitimate employment also tends to be located in more advantaged communities, requiring time and resources to travel to and from work. Thus, what wealth exists in poor neighborhoods is transferred out of the community instead of circulating within the local economy where it can multiply and create the economic base to provide opportunity for offenders within the community.

As many states have attempted to close prisons as cost-saving measures during the recession, communities home to prisons have pushed back and successfully argued for states to keep prisons open because of the perceived economic benefit of saving corrections jobs and supporting businesses in the community. Ironically, this is an example of how more advantaged communities with greater levels of social capital and collective efficacy are able to capitalize on the hardships of other citizens, in this case inmates and those living in poor communities, to sustain their own well-being. The failure to close prisons to sustain the economic security of one community by doing harm to another is unethical, and state-level leaders and policymakers have to directly address this issue. Reinvesting the money saved through reductions in mass incarceration is a complicated and challenging endeavor but one worthy of exploring.

Recommendation: *Further explore justice reinvestment and the role community corrections may serve in transitioning disadvantaged communities from high rates of concentrated incarceration to becoming self-sustaining and relevant to supporting successful reentry initiatives.*

Helping prepare communities to offer opportunity to those ready for change is crucial to the likelihood of success for community corrections. CCOs, to be successful, need healthy communities to balance their work between formal institutional control and informal social control in the community to achieve reintegration. Engaging offenders as integral to the community's health and well-being requires adequate attention be given to assuring a continuum of care and essential services are coordinated in a way that protects the investment made in offenders throughout multiple systems and especially on their arrival back into the community following prison.

SUPPORTING OUR JUSTICE INVESTMENT THROUGH CCOs AS BOUNDARY SPANNERS

There is a justifiable expectation that the billions invested in the criminal justice system, and specifically corrections, should have direct purpose and utility in reducing crime and enhancing public safety (Cullen & Jonson, 2012). Billions are invested in corrections alone with the belief that prisons should not only punish but also change behavior. Although investment in prison programs has diminished in recent decades and oftentimes falls far short of meeting the needs of those who could benefit, serious efforts are still made within prisons to influence future behavior by providing education, vocational training, work opportunities within prison industries, life skills development, substance abuse treatment, and mental health counseling and treatment. Most prisons, in addition to depriving offenders of their liberty as punishment, invest in interventions and prison environments with the intention that offenders will either be deterred from committing crime or will no longer want to due to prosocial change (Cullen & Jonson, 2012). Ironically, after spending billions to both punish and treat, inmates are then released into a community corrections environment challenged to follow up on the progress made in prisons due to excessive caseloads, lack of resources to provide evidence-based treatment, disadvantaged communities with few resources to provide adequate support, and a climate of distrust that anything other than a punitive response to noncompliance may result in harsh public reactions.

Although research shows that aftercare is important to sustaining the success achieved in individual treatment programs, community corrections is not always framed as aftercare[2] essential to reinforcing offenders' progress and as a necessary means to protect an investment in order to capitalize on the long-term gains of successful reintegration. Through several recent reentry initiatives (see Burke & Tonry, 2006; Justice Center, 2013), the need is clear to plan in advance for an inmate's release from prison into the community and reduce fragmentation of interventions by coordinating resources to address both the risk and needs of offenders on reentry (Burke & Tonry, 2006). In spite of these major initiatives focusing on system-level change, the important role of CCOs in guiding the success of reentry initiatives is still often narrowly conceptualized or ignored (for exceptions see Lattimore et al., 2005; Nissen, 2010; Pettus & Severson, 2006; Taxman, Shepardson, & Byrne, 2004). CCOs are the much needed boundary spanners capable of providing aftercare to produce positive outcomes at both the individual and system levels of reentry. They are ideally positioned at the nexus between prison and the community, with the power and expertise to deal with offenders' risk, the ability to garner the resources necessary to address needs, and the knowledge to communicate across systems to improve outcomes.

Recommendation: *Recognize CCOs as providing the aftercare essential to protecting our investment in the criminal justice system.*

CCOs must be viewed as the keystone to developing an aftercare plan for offenders. Corrections, in collaboration with other social services and public health systems, needs to be organized to provide for a continuum of care beginning on the first day of incarceration, flowing into community supervision, and solidifying in the community long term (see Lattimore et al., 2005; Matz et al., 2012; Taxman, 2002; Taxman, Young, Byrne, Holsinger, & Anspach, 2001). Ad hoc and isolated interventions sporadically applied to offenders as they pass through the system are likely to be less effective than what may be achieved through planned change over time. An organized response across systems that parallels the processing of offenders through the criminal justice system allows for planning that minimizes the opportunity for the system to sabotage itself by making sure staff can implement, and offenders can complete, interventions before being transferred to another institution or forward into the criminal justice process (Taxman, 2002). Data sharing of relevant information from one entity to the next along the continuum is crucial to increasing efficiency, reducing error, and sustaining the integrity of the process (Matz et al., 2012).

Recommendation: *Implement a continuum of care that encompasses offenders' entire process of change from beginning to end. Synchronize systems and interventions to be responsive to, and coordinated with, how offenders' cases actually flow through the criminal justice system.*

Through science and practice comes a much clearer understanding about what works to enhance community supervision and reduce recidivism. It is no longer acceptable to invest in policies and practices that result in nearly 65% of offenders leaving prison only to fail within 3 years due primarily to technical violations and less so to new crimes (Burke & Tonry, 2006). This rate of failure can no longer be viewed as solely the fault of offenders but must be attributed to a failure across systems, and as a failure of the criminal justice system specifically, to give up traditional practices that do not work. Community supervision has the potential to provide the aftercare necessary to complete the continuum of care vital to success. Community corrections is the critical link to assuring the success of a long criminal justice process and is responsible for protecting our investment in the multiple systems engaged in reentry (Burke & Tonry, 2006).

CONCLUSION

Community corrections is critical to the success of the criminal justice system. Conceptualizing and respecting the work of CCOs as street-level boundary spanners creates a context to inform policymakers and administrators about why they need to invest in community corrections. Community corrections represents the culmination of the criminal justice process and demonstrates a utility to serve justice and enhance public safety. CCOs serve as experts at the crucial nexus where prisons and the community meet and where success or failure in working with offenders is measured in real terms related to public safety and reintegration. Investing in community supervision and recognizing CCOs as proactive agents of change presents an opportunity to achieve real success in the criminal justice system resulting in meaningful outcomes instead of symbolic, and oftentimes empty, promises to enhance public safety.

Oftentimes the problems facing offenders, their families, and the community appear to be so overwhelming that it is easy to start from a position of defeat dedicated to managing individual crises instead of proactively solving problems and preventing harm. Remaining positive about guiding offenders through the process of reintegration is especially daunting when the potential for change and innovation is locked within very large bureaucracies with long-held traditions and hard-fought turf to protect. Yet change can occur—and relatively quickly. This is evident in the swiftness of the shift from rehabilitation to retribution in the late 1970s and its solidification during the 1980s. Thus, change is possible by being prepared when the opportunity arises. The current economic crises combined with scientific support for EBP and its cost effectiveness may very well provide the social, economic, and political context for change to rapidly occur. Conceptualizing CCOs as boundary spanners provides a framework to respond to change and to launch innovation within community corrections and between systems. If CCOs continue to be thought of as working with offenders in isolation from their families, communities, and other systems, then responses to community supervision will be similarly narrow and remain stagnant. By conceptualizing CCOs as boundary spanners engaging in a broad array of work involving offenders embedded within families, communities, and multiple systems, it is easy to imagine adapting current systems to embrace innovation and recognize the key role of CCOs.

Most of the discussion about reentry and community corrections reform has focused on the experiences of offenders, the attributes of successful interventions, and the complexity of the criminal justice process, without a holistic consideration of the professionals responsible for implementing change and working directly with offenders and the community. What is learned by focusing on the "invisible side of reentry," by reviewing the research on CCOs and listening to their experiences within the complex world of community corrections, is that it is possible to achieve effective supervision that enhances community safety through long-term reintegration. CCOs lend valuable insight about their comprehensive professional role in managing offenders' risks to the community and addressing offenders' extensive needs that if unattended sabotage their opportunities for success and create a burden for the systems and communities responsible for their care.

Too often the criminal justice system, symbolized by police, courts, and prisons, is presented by politicians as the panacea most likely to bring about safer communities. This image often conveys coercion and force as the best or only responses capable of easing the fears of law-abiding citizens. Often absent from public debate is a vision of how communities are made stronger through social support, building social capital, enhancing collective efficacy, and improving the conditions of citizens' lives by easing the pains of poverty. CCOs recognize that entire communities are hurting from concentrated incarceration and disadvantage. Without a broad array of support, offenders will continue to rejoin communities incapable of providing the informal social controls so important to reducing recidivism and preventing crime. Due to CCOs' intimate familiarity with offenders' lives within the communities, during both good times and bad, they clearly understand the need to work across systems. It is time to move CCOs out from behind the cloak of invisibility and highlight their importance to the success of the criminal justice system through the implementation of comprehensive reentry initiatives.

Considering reentry from the perspective of CCOs offers the reminder that community supervision is a human business concerned with the success and depth of interpersonal relationships. CCOs appear ready for policymakers, corrections leaders, and the community to understand the complexity of their role and the professional need to be respected for the important work they do with offenders and their contributions to enhancing public safety. Understanding the reality of working with offenders, who to CCOs are not just abstract statistics to be managed but complex individuals who also experience the joy of success and the agony of defeat, brings one closer to realizing that CCOs need the time and space to fully engage offenders to effect meaningful change. The complexity of their professional relationships with colleagues and the diversity in beliefs on how to supervise offenders illustrates that CCOs' work cannot be easily categorized but instead exists on a continuum. CCOs' decisions are influenced by the quality of the human relationships in which they engage and whether they trust the potential effectiveness of providing support, treatment, sanctions, or some combination of the three. The importance of understanding community corrections as a human profession based in relationships is to enhance the ability to make sure CCOs have multiple trustworthy options at their disposal to manage both risk and need so that their work is not unnecessarily biased toward one philosophy or another. Their professional expertise must empower them to have the discretion necessary to use coercion, support, or treatment based on the circumstances.

Focusing on CCOs instead of offenders adds an important dimension to be considered when implementing innovative new strategies and interventions within community corrections. Offender-focused research on reentry has highlighted the need to immediately address offenders' risks and needs to achieve successful outcomes and the importance of implementing evidence-based practices and treatment. Often absent from the discussion and the research, however, is whether CCOs have the support, tools, education, time, incentives, and opportunity to implement EBP. Without understanding, recognizing, and accommodating the professional needs of CCOs to successfully implement best practices, innovation and change will be seriously challenged. Just as during the Progressive Era, the era responsible for sweeping in correctional rehabilitation and a belief that offenders could be successfully treated and reintegrated into the community (much like today's move to implement EBP), if policymakers do not adequately prepare systems for change by relying on the convenience of existing staff and dysfunctional systems, the conscience behind the implementation of EBP will not be realized (Rothman, 1980). CCOs made it clear that without reducing caseloads and administrative tasks and expanding their time to be effective boundary spanners, there is little potential to implement change and to conduct their job with integrity. In other words, as in the past, convenience, or business as usual, will supersede conscience and the implementation of best practices because the system is currently structured to accommodate failure through an overreliance on coercion and punitive practices. The lessons learned from research conducted on CCOs and their work are how to avoid the mistakes of the past and implement EBP with integrity. All that's needed is the political and professional will to do so.

The good news is that community corrections now has the expertise, informed by theory, science, and practice, to achieve successful outcomes. It has become clear that ideologically driven policies do not work and political ignorance about community corrections is no longer acceptable. The foundation necessary to build an effective community corrections response to offender reentry and supervision is in place. CCOs are well positioned and motivated to implement effective reentry initiatives. It is time for CCOs to reclaim their profession from the depths of political ignorance and ineffective leadership. To achieve the respect and public investment necessary to be effective, they must communicate their utility to policymakers in terms that clearly demonstrate their worth to the criminal justice system beyond police, courts, and prisons and their ability to coordinate the power and expertise of other public institutions to enhance public safety. Community corrections officers are powerful and effective street-level boundary spanners critical to the success of the criminal justice system and achieving public safety. Community corrections officers deserve our collective investment as they work to make the world a better and safer place for everyone.

NOTES

1. Justice Policy Institute, 2010, p. 8
2. The idea of framing community corrections as "aftercare" for the prison system similar to aftercare provided to treatment participants to sustain the effects of treatment over time was presented to me by Dr. Laurie Drapela, Washington State University, during a telephone conversation about reentry on February 21, 2013.

WORKS CITED

Burke, P., Gelb, A., & Horowitz, J. (2007). *When offenders break the rules: Smart responses to parole and probation violations.* Washington, DC: The PEW Center on the States.

Burke, P., & Tonry, M. (2006). *Successful transition and reentry for safer communities: A call to action for parole.* Silver Spring, MD: JEHT Foundation.

Clear, T. R. (1996, August). Toward a corrections of "place": The challenge of "community" in corrections. *National Institute of Justice Journal, 231,* 52–56.

Clear, T. R. (2005). Places not cases?: Re-thinking the probation focus. *The Howard Journal, 44*(2), 172–184.

Clear, T. R. (2007). *Imprisoning communities: How mass incarceration makes disadvantaged neighborhoods worse.* New York: Oxford University Press.

Clear, T. R. (2011). A private-sector, incentives-based model for justice reinvestment. *Criminology & Public Policy, 10*(3), 585–608.

Cullen, F., & Jonson, C. (2011). *Correctional theory: Context and consequences.* Thousand Oaks, CA: Sage.

Drapela, L. A., & Lutze, F. E. (2009). Innovation in community corrections and probabtion officers' fears of being sued: Implementing neighborhood-based supervision in Spokane, Washington. *Journal of Contemporary Criminal Justice, 25*(1), 364–383.

Griffen, T., & Stitt, B. G. (2010). Random activities theory: The case for "Black Swan" criminology. *Critical Criminology, 18,* 57–72.

Henderson, M. L., & Hanley, D. (2006). Planning for quality: A strategy for reentry initiatives. *Western Criminology Review, 7*(2), 62–78.

Justice Center. (2013). *The National Reentry Resource Center.* Retrieved February 2013, from www.nationalreentryresourcecenter.org/reentry-council

Justice Policy Institute. (2010). *How to safely reduce prison populations and support people returning to their communities.* Washington, DC: Justice Policy Institute.

Lattimore, P. K., Visher, C. A., Winterfield, L., Lindquist, C., & Brumbaugh, S. (2005). Implementation of prisoner reentry programs: Findings from the Serious and Violent Offender Reentry Initiative multi-site evaluation. *Justice Research and Policy, 7*(2), 87–109.

Lutze, F. E., Johnson, W., Clear, T., Latessa, E., & Slate, R. (2012). The future of community corrections is now: Stop dreaming and take action. *Journal of Contemporary Criminal Justice, 28*(1), 42–49.

Lutze, F. E., & van Wormer, J. (2007). The nexus between drug and alcohol treatment program integrity and drug court effectiveness: Policy recommendations for pursuing success. *Criminal Justice Policy Review, 18*(3), 226–245.

Matz, A. K., Wicklund, C., Douglas, J., & May, B. (2012). *Justice-health collaboration: Improving information exchange between corrections and health/human services organizations.* SEARCH Group.

McCorkle, R., & Crank, J. P. (1996). Meet the new boss: Institutional change and loose coupling in parole and probation. *American Journal of Criminal Justice, 21,* 1–25.

Mele, C., & Miller, T. A. (2005). *Civil penalties, social consequences.* (Eds.) New York: Routledge.

Murphy, D., & Lutze, F. (2009). Police-probation partnerships: Professional identity and the sharing of coercive power. *Journal of Criminal Justice, 37*, 65–76.

Nissen, L. B. (2010). Boundary spanners revisited: A qualitative inquiry into cross-system reform through the experience of youth service professionals. *Qualitative Social Work, 9*(3), 365–384.

Paparozzi, M., & DeMichele, M. (2008). Probation and parole: Overworked, misunderstood, and under-appreciated: But why? *The Howard Journal, 47*(3), 275–296.

Payne, B. K., & DeMichele, M. (2011). Probation philosophies and workload considerations. *American Journal of Criminal Justice, 36*, 29–43.

Petersilia, J. (2003). *When prisoners come home: Parole and prisoner reentry.* New York: Oxford University Press.

Pettus, C. A., & Severson, M. (2006). Paving the way for effective reentry practice—The critical role and function of boundary spanner. *The Prison Journal, 86*(2), 206–229.

Rank, M. R. (2004). *One nation, underprivileged: Why American poverty affects us all.* New York: Oxford University Press.

Rothman, D. (1980). *Conscience and convenience: The asylum and its alternatives in progressive America.* Boston: Little, Brown and Company.

Taxman, F. S. (2002). Supervision: Exploring the dimensions of effectiveness. *Federal Probation, 66*(2), 14–27.

Taxman, F. S., Shepardson, E. S., & Byrne, J. M. (2004). *Tools of the trade: A guide to incorporating science into practice.* Washington, DC: National Institute of Corrections.

Taxman, F. S., Young, D., Byrne, J. M., Holsinger, A., & Anspach, D. (2001). *From prison safety to public safety: Innovations in offender reentry.* Bureau of Governmental Research. College Park: University of Maryland.

INDEX

Notes and figures are indicated by n and f respectively, after the page number.

ABOUT THE AUTHOR

Faith E. Lutze, PhD, is an associate professor in the Department of Criminal Justice and Criminology at Washington State University. She received her MA in criminal justice from the University of Cincinnati in 1988 and her PhD in the administration of justice from the Pennsylvania State University in 1996. Her current research interests include drug courts, the professional role of community corrections officers, offender adjustment to community corrections supervision, violence against women, and gender and justice with an emphasis on masculinity in prisons. She currently teaches criminal justice courses related to corrections, violence toward women, ethics, and gender and justice. Dr. Lutze has published her research related to boot camp prisons, masculine prison environments, community corrections officers, and drug courts in various journals, including *Justice Quarterly*, *Crime & Delinquency*, *Criminology and Public Policy*, and *The Journal of Criminal Justice*. She is also the recipient of the Coremae Richey Mann Leadership Award (2010), presented by the Minorities and Women Section of ACJS, and the recipient of the ACJS Corrections Section Award (2010) for scholarship and service in corrections.

ⓈSAGE research**methods**

The essential online tool for researchers from the world's leading methods publisher

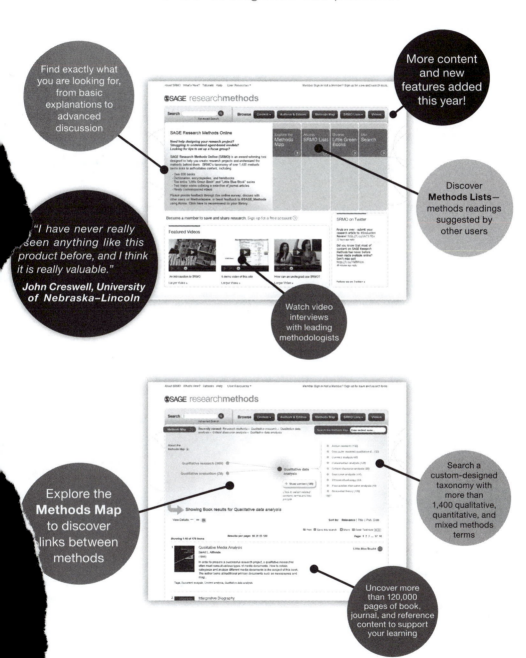

Find exactly what you are looking for, from basic explanations to advanced discussion

More content and new features added this year!

Discover **Methods Lists**— methods readings suggested by other users

"I have never really seen anything like this product before, and I think it is really valuable."
John Creswell, University of Nebraska–Lincoln

Watch video interviews with leading methodologists

Explore the **Methods Map** to discover links between methods

Search a custom-designed taxonomy with more than 1,400 qualitative, quantitative, and mixed methods terms

Uncover more than 120,000 pages of book, journal, and reference content to support your learning

d out more at
w.sageresearchmethods.com